I0483458

NEW YORK CITY

After sandy & before the end of the World

Photographs

by

NADIA RUSS

NeoPopRealismPRESS

First time published in 2012 by NeoPopRealism PRESS

PO BOX 366
New York, NY 10013
NeoPopRealismPRESS@mail.com

New York City: After Sandy & Before the End of the World
by NeoPopRealism PRESS

2012 © NeoPopRealism PRESS
Photographs Copyrighted by Nadia Russ

Front cover image: Anastasia Ilinykh, Lower Eastside
Back cover image: St. Thomas Church, Fifth Avenue

All rights reserved. Apart from any fair dealing for the purpose
of the criticism and review, no part of this book may be
reproduced, stored in a retrieval system, or transmitted in any
form or by any means, electronic or mechanical, including
photocopy, without the prior written permission of the
copyright owner.

ISBN-13: 978-0615734637
ISBN-10: 0615734634

12 13 14 15 16 10 9 8 7 6 5 4 3 2 1

Published in the United States of America
Language: English

This book is the black & white edition. It offers a collection of
photographs taken by Nadia Russ in New York City between
November 4 -13, 2012..

www.neopoprealism.org

$\mathcal{I}$NTRODUCTION

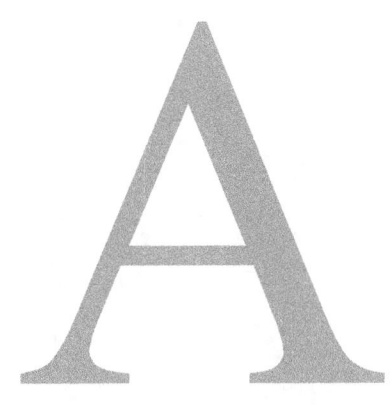n idea about making a photography book *"New York City"* was not knew. I was

thinking about it before. However, now this seemed very relevant, it was a few days after the super-hurricane Sandy. Even I am not sure if Apocalypse is coming, after this hurricane I know how it would look. Sandy went out of control and made a lot of damage, ruining people's homes and lives, some people are even dead...

But this book is not about drama. New York is the fascinating, high energy city. For many years it is the international center of culture. Today, the U.S. is in transition... Many people do not know where we are going. I hope this unique city will not lose its charm, beauty and power, which attract, energize and stimulate the most talented people from all over the globe. Photographs featured in this book were taken between November 4 - 13, 2012. In the New York state of mind...

Nadia Russ

$\mathcal{U}$nion Square is an important and historic intersection in Manhattan in New York City. Union

Square Park is bounded by 14th Street on the south, Union Square West on the west side, 17th Street on the north, and on the east Union Square East. It links together Broadway and Park Avenue South to Fourth Avenue and the continuation of Broadway. Union Square is famous for its impressive equestrian statue of U.S. President George Washington, created by Henry Kirke Brown and unveiled in 1856, the first public sculpture erected in New York City since the equestrian statue of George III in 1770, and the first American equestrian sculpture cast in bronze. Other statues in the park include the Marquis de Lafayette, sculpted by Frédéric-Auguste Bartholdi and dedicated at the Centennial, July 4, 1876, Abraham Lincoln, sculpted by Henry Kirke Brown (1870), and the James Fountain (1881), a Temperance fountain with the figure of Charity who empties her jug of water, aided by a child, sculpted by Adolf Donndorf. A statue of Mahatma Gandhi in the southwest corner of the park was installed in 1986.

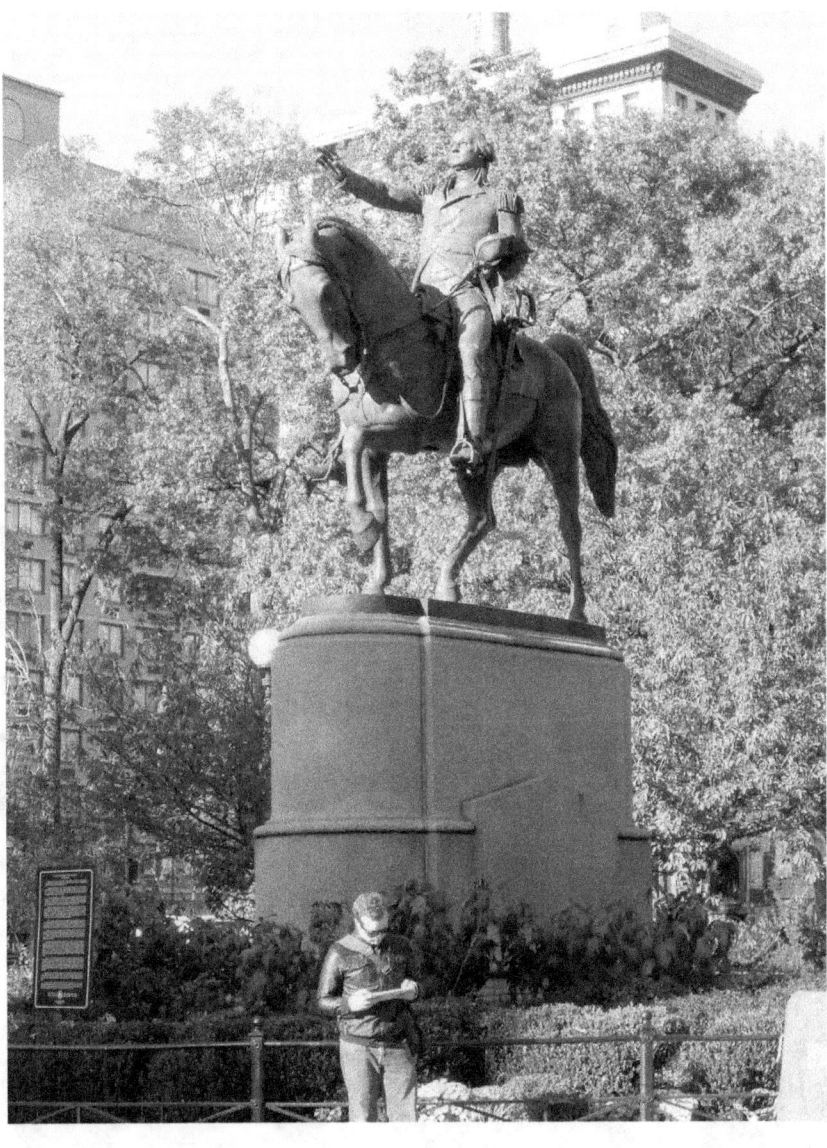

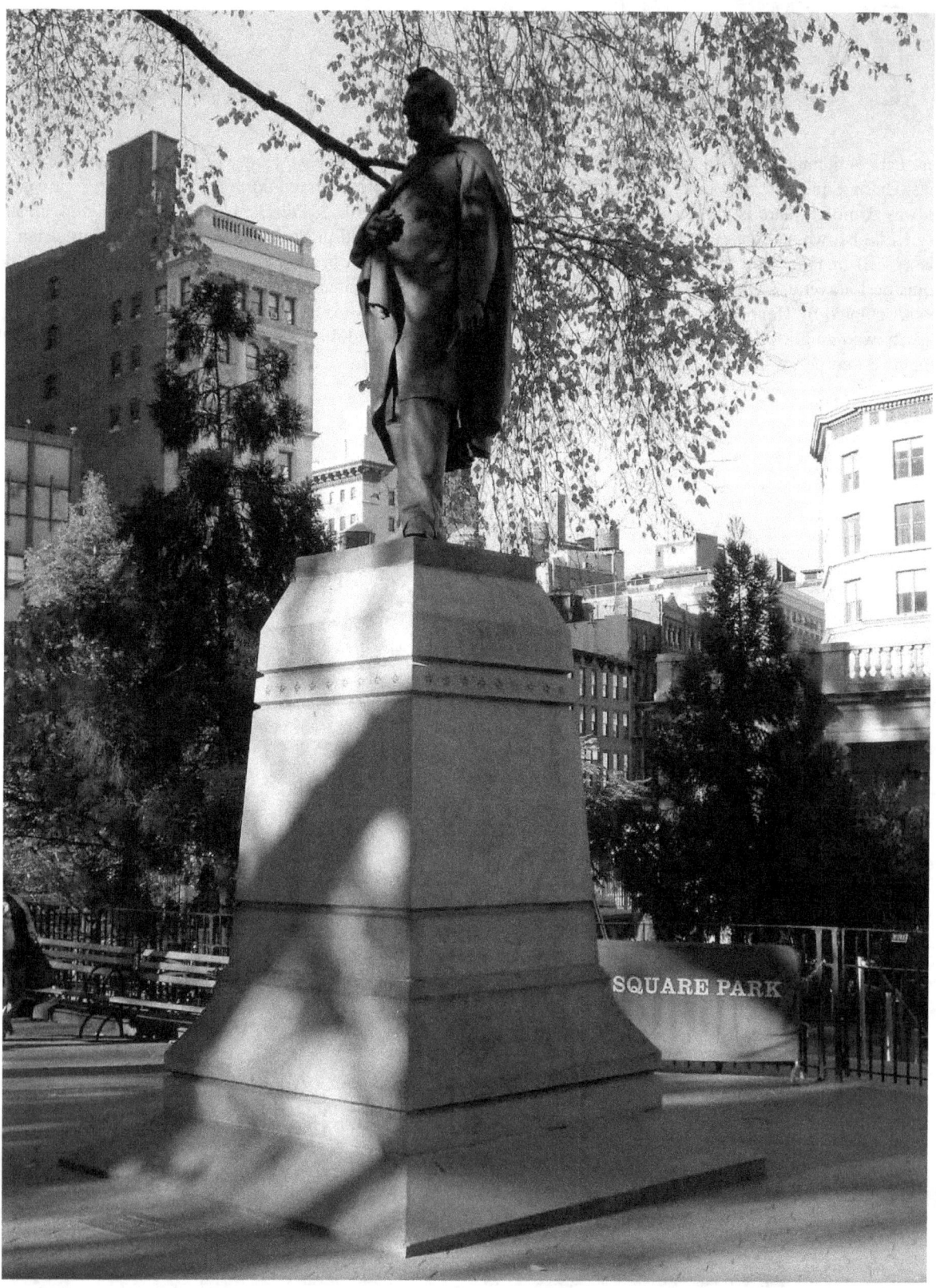

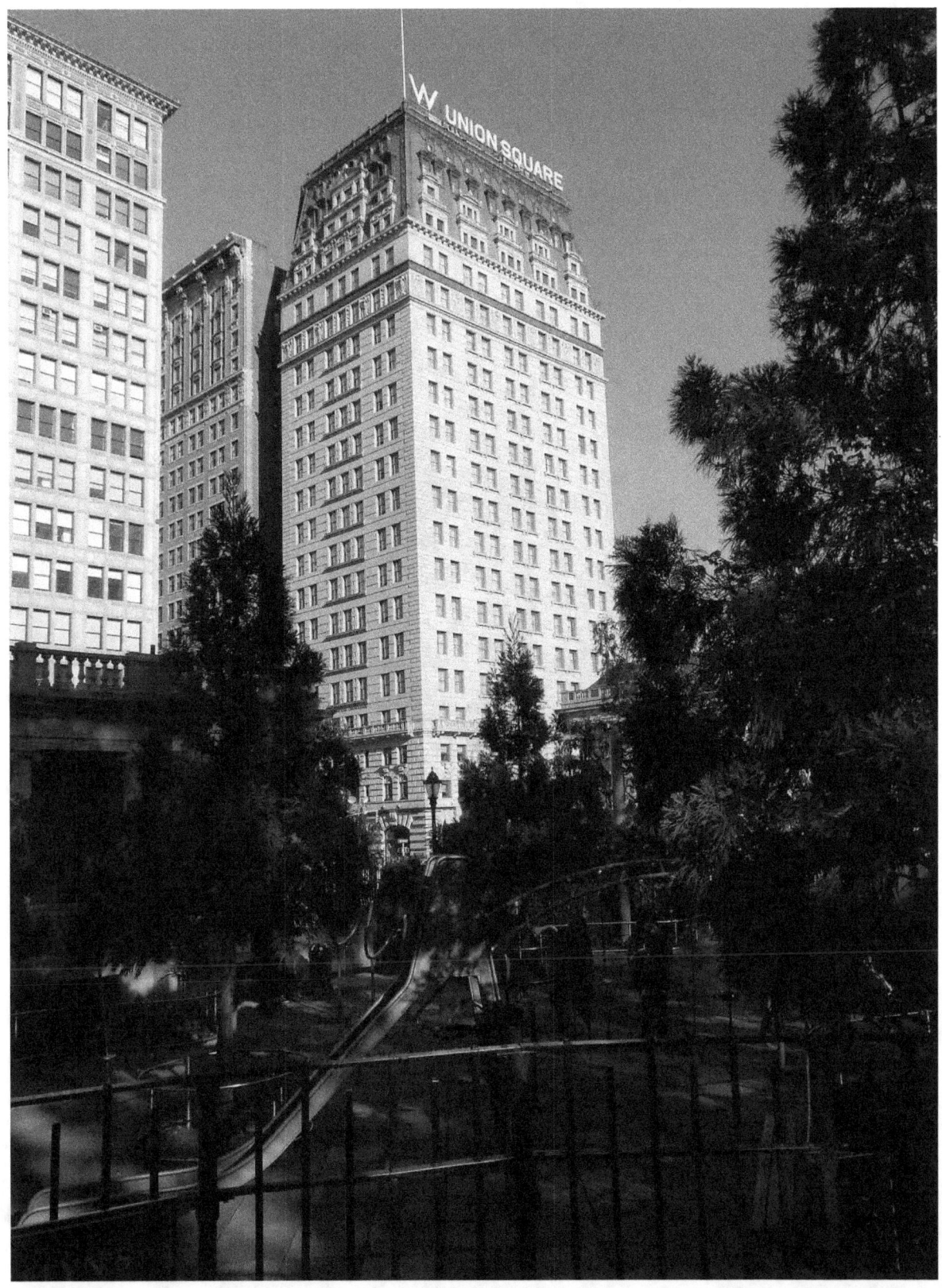

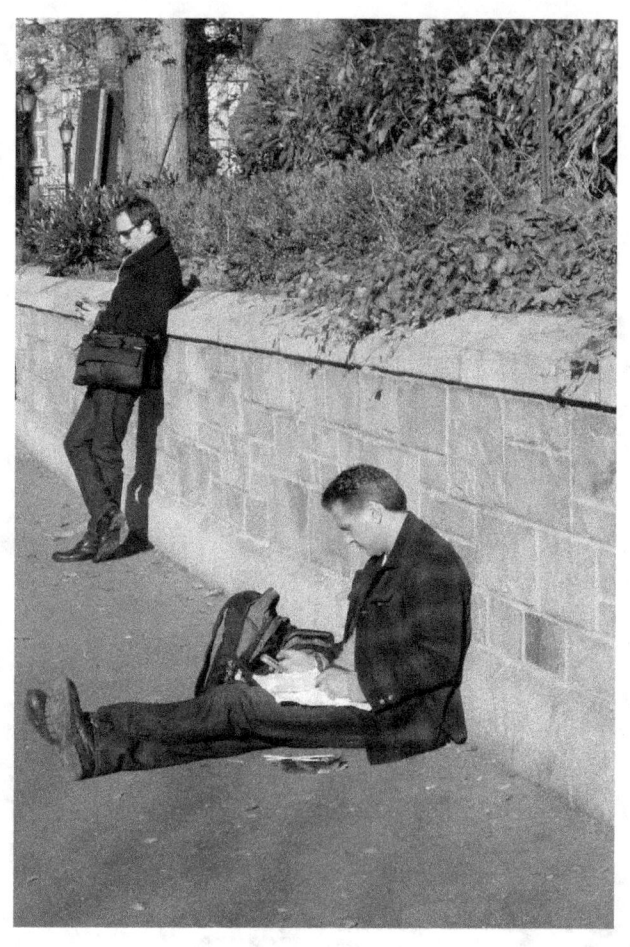

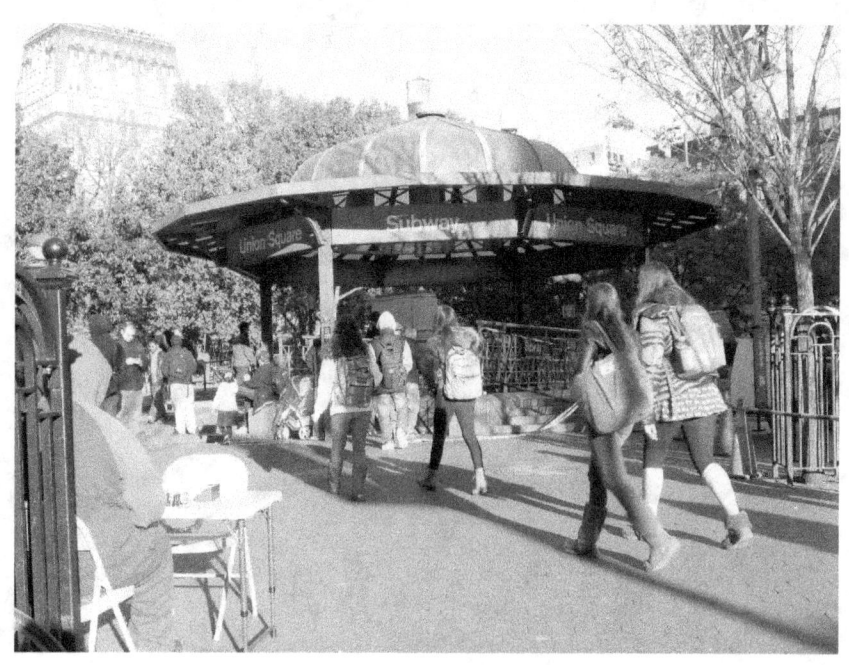

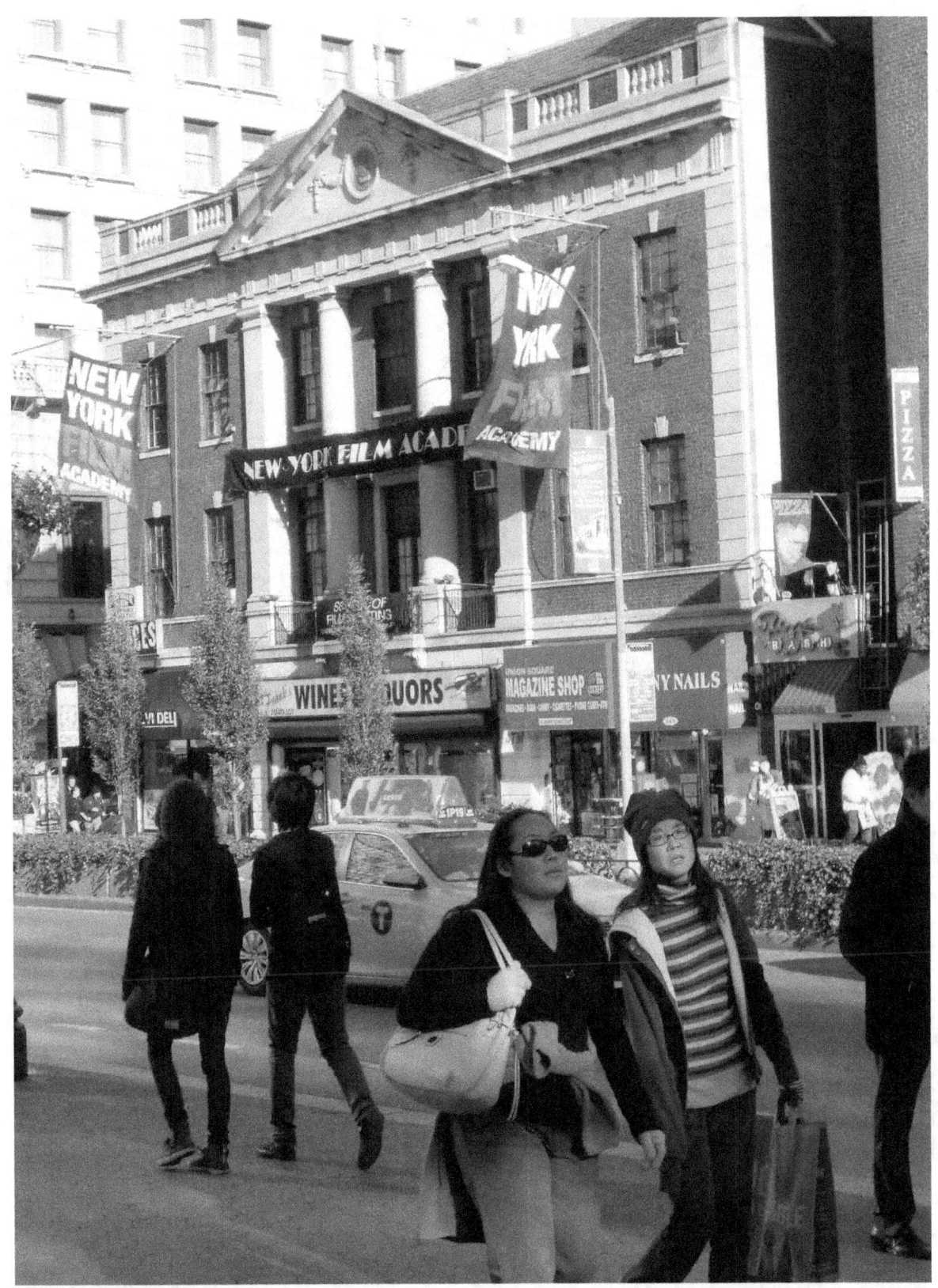

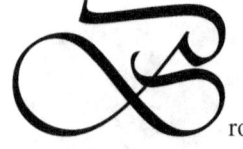roadway runs in New York City through the borough of Manhattan. It runs 15 miles through

Manhattan and The Bronx, exiting north from the city to run an additional 18 miles through the municipalities of Yonkers, Hastings-On-Hudson, Dobbs Ferry, Irvington, Tarrytown and terminating north of Sleepy Hollow in Westchester County. It is the oldest north–south main thoroughfare, dating to the first New Amsterdam settlement. The name Broadway is the English literal translation of the Dutch name, Breede weg. Broadway is known worldwide as the heart of the American theatre industry.

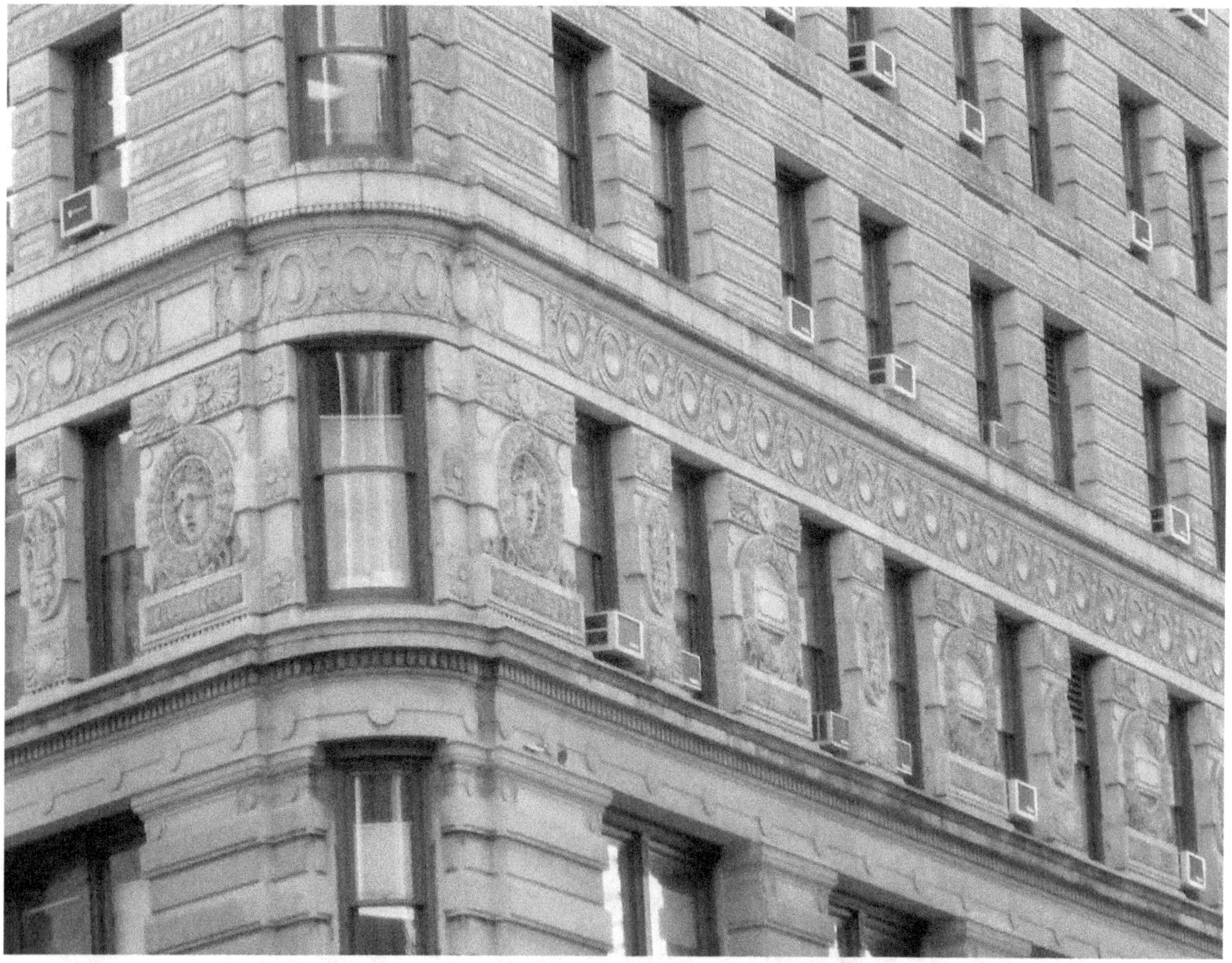

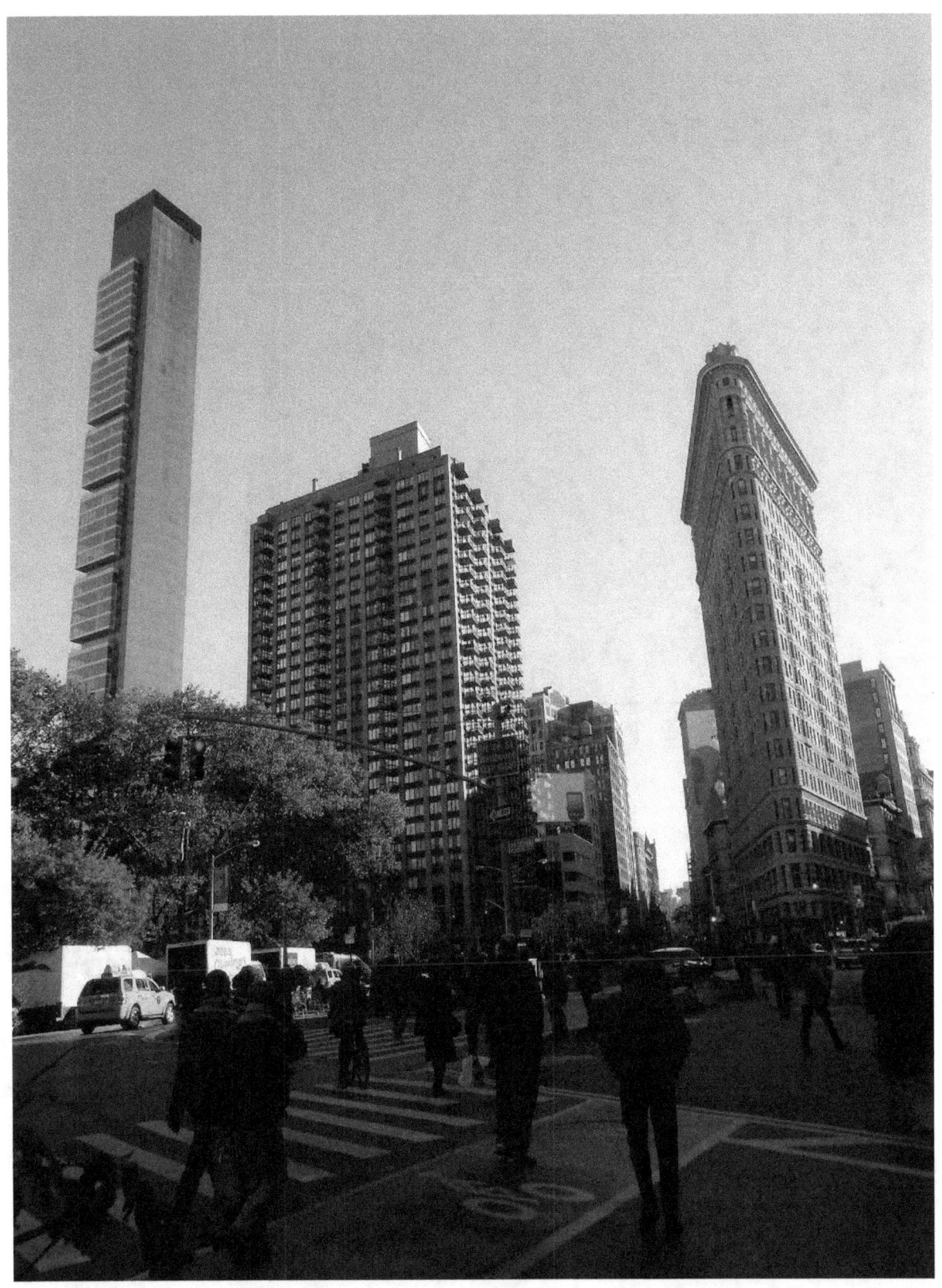

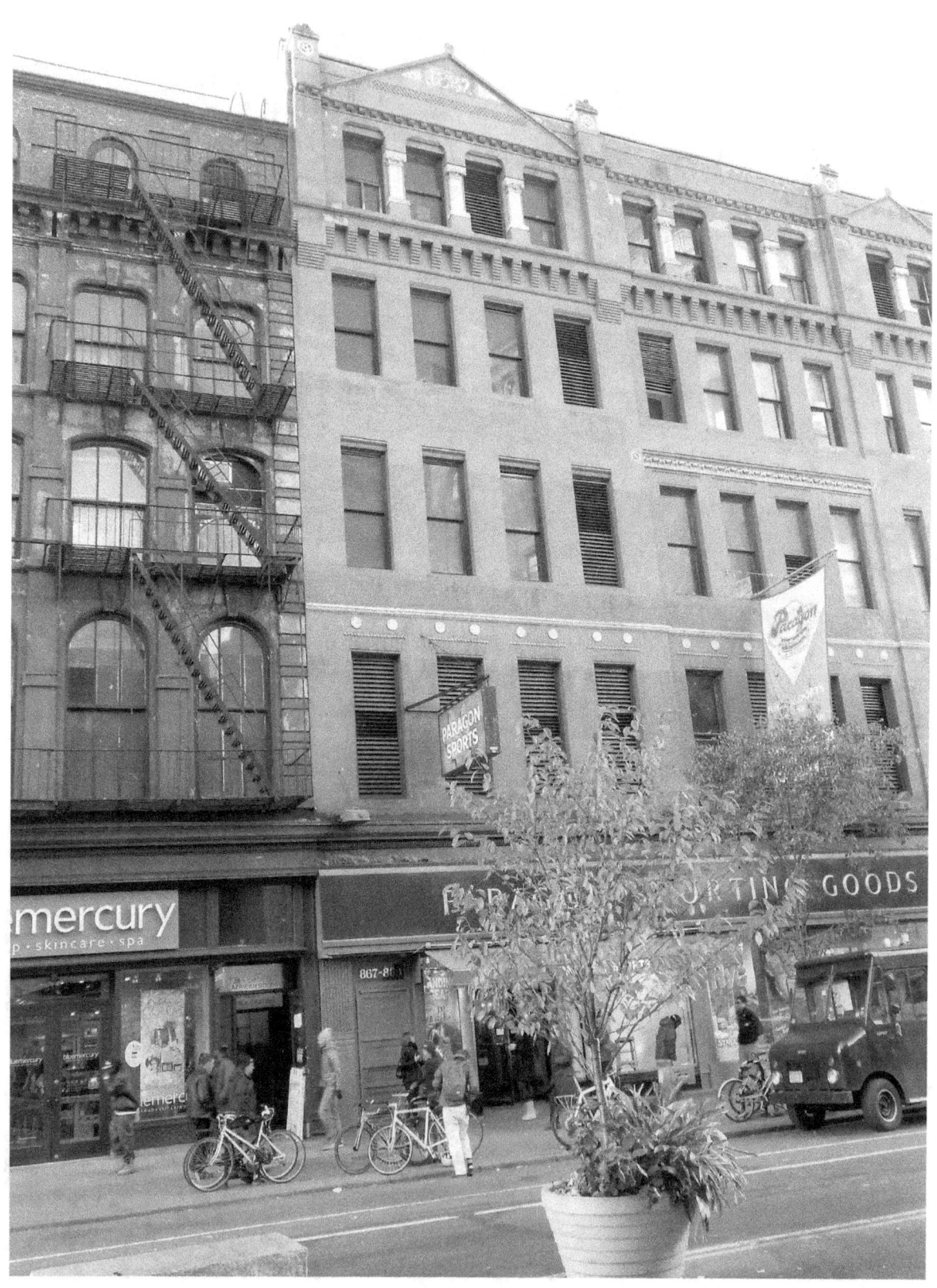

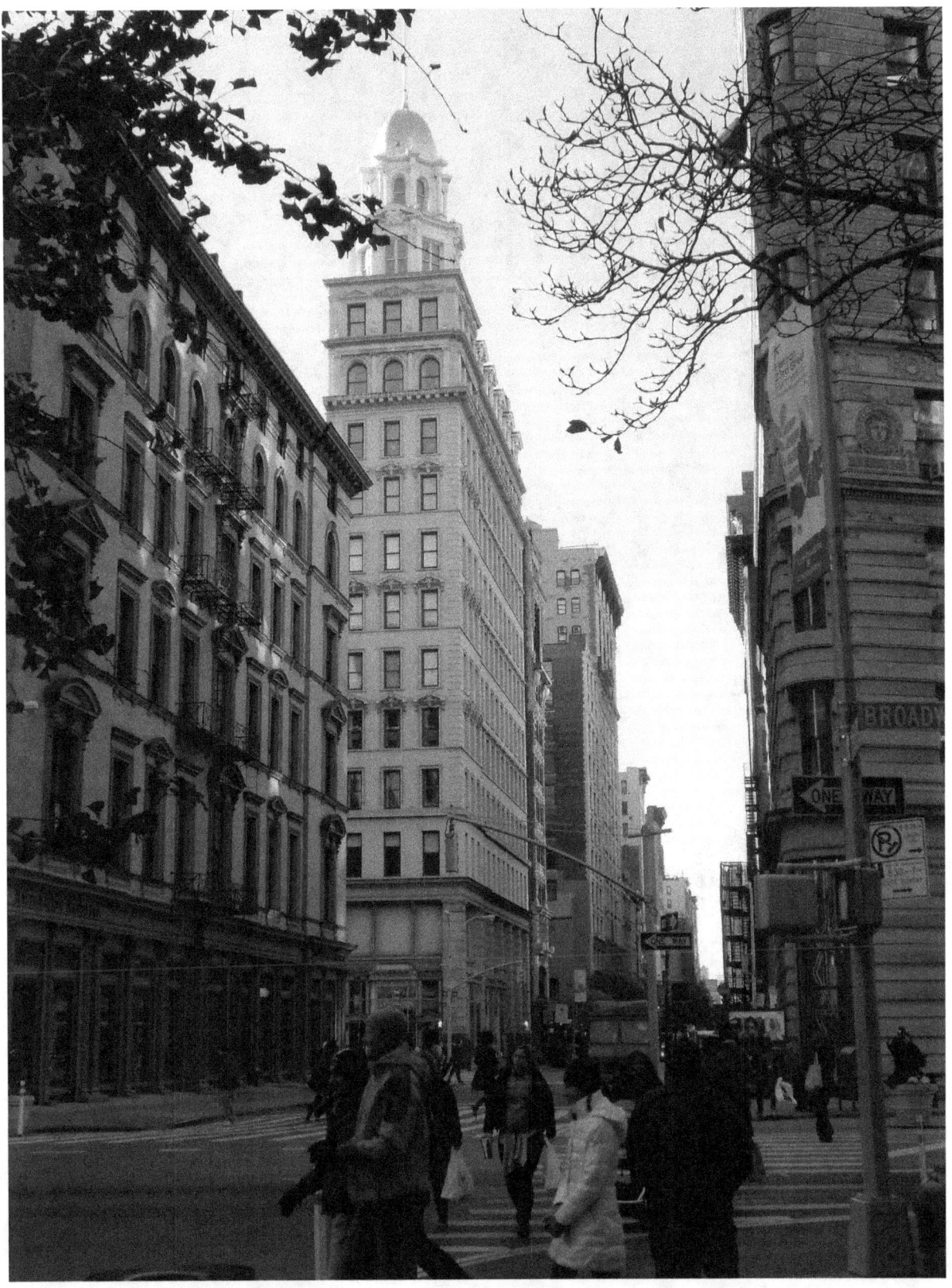

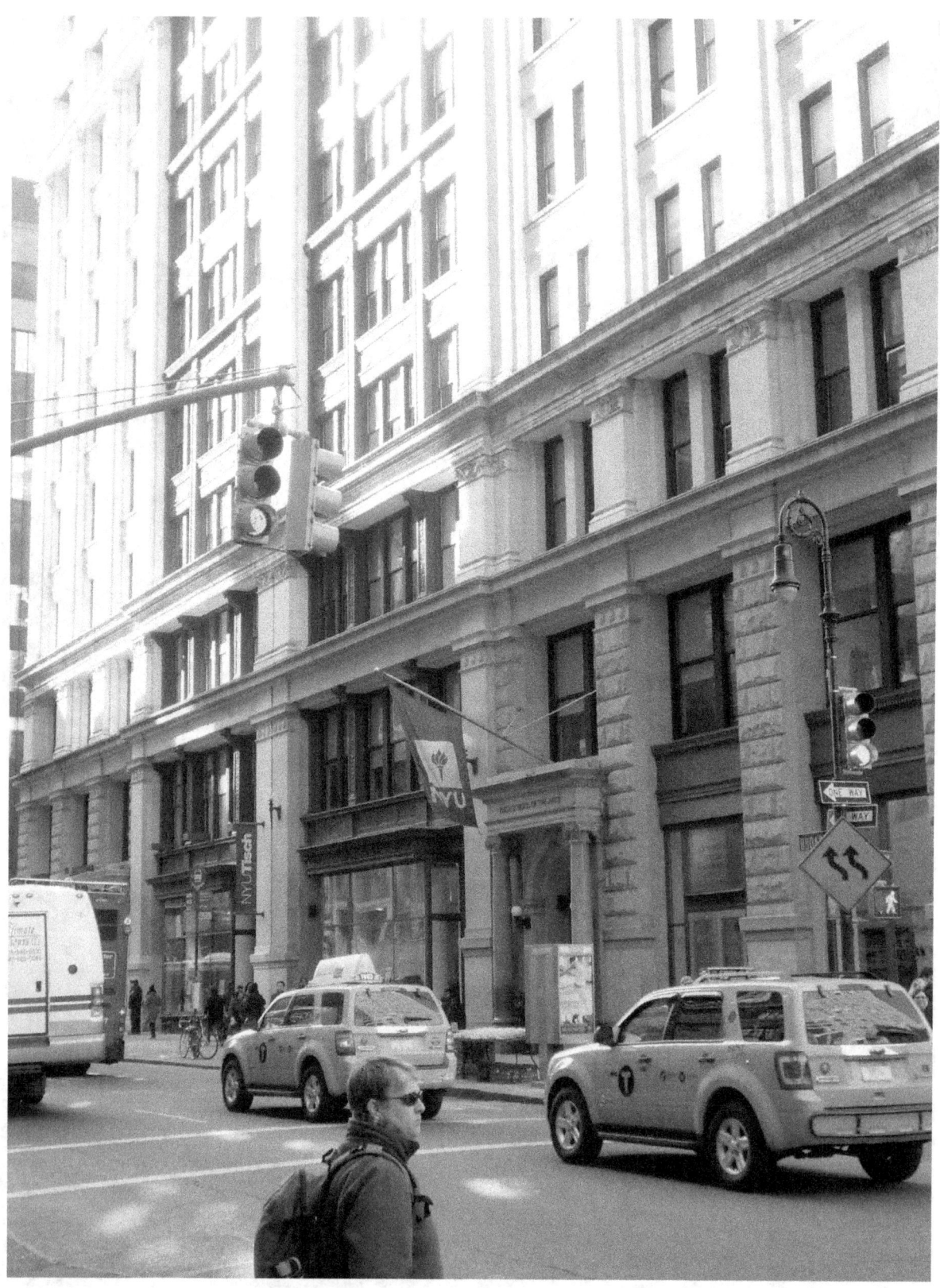

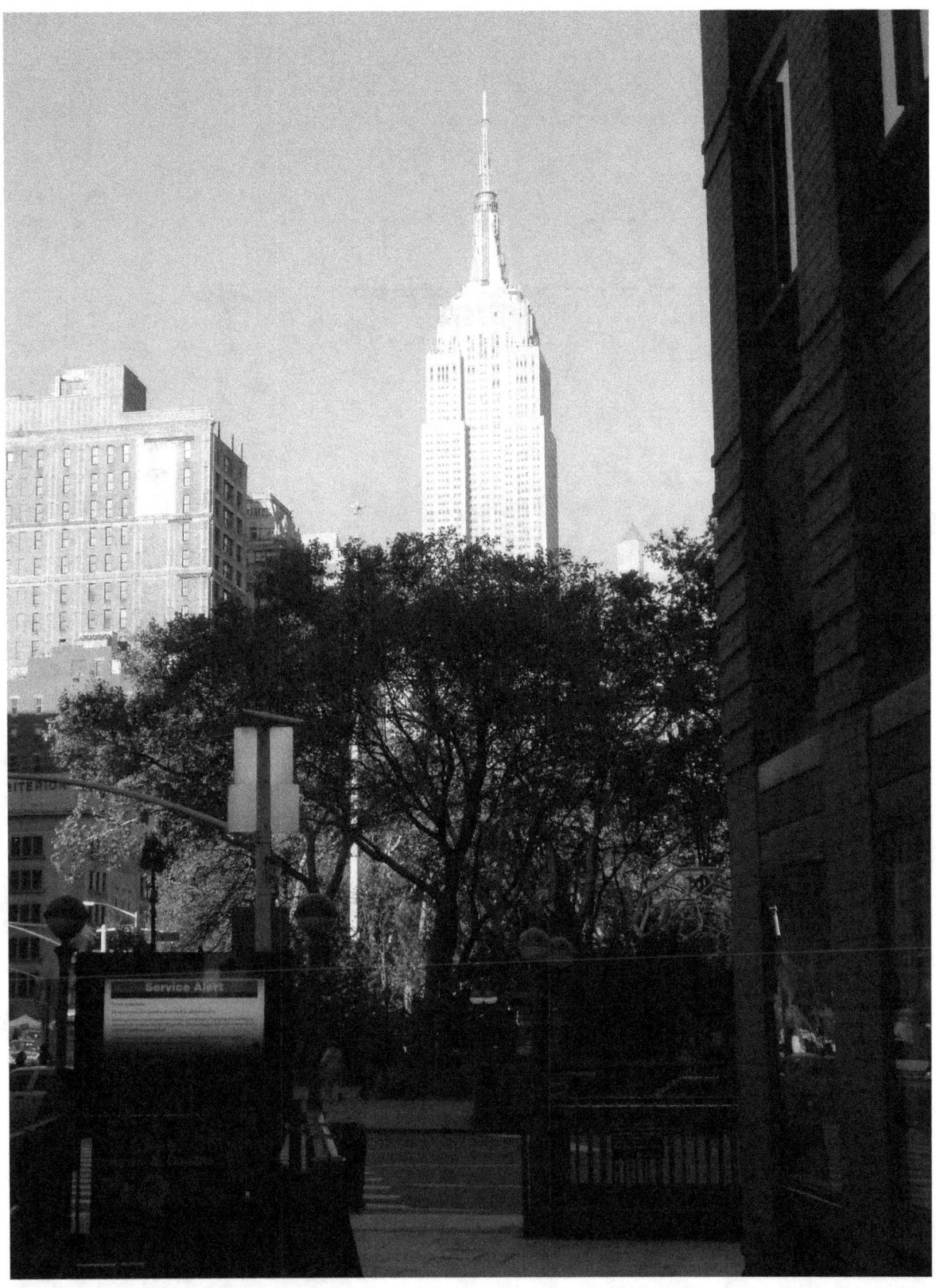

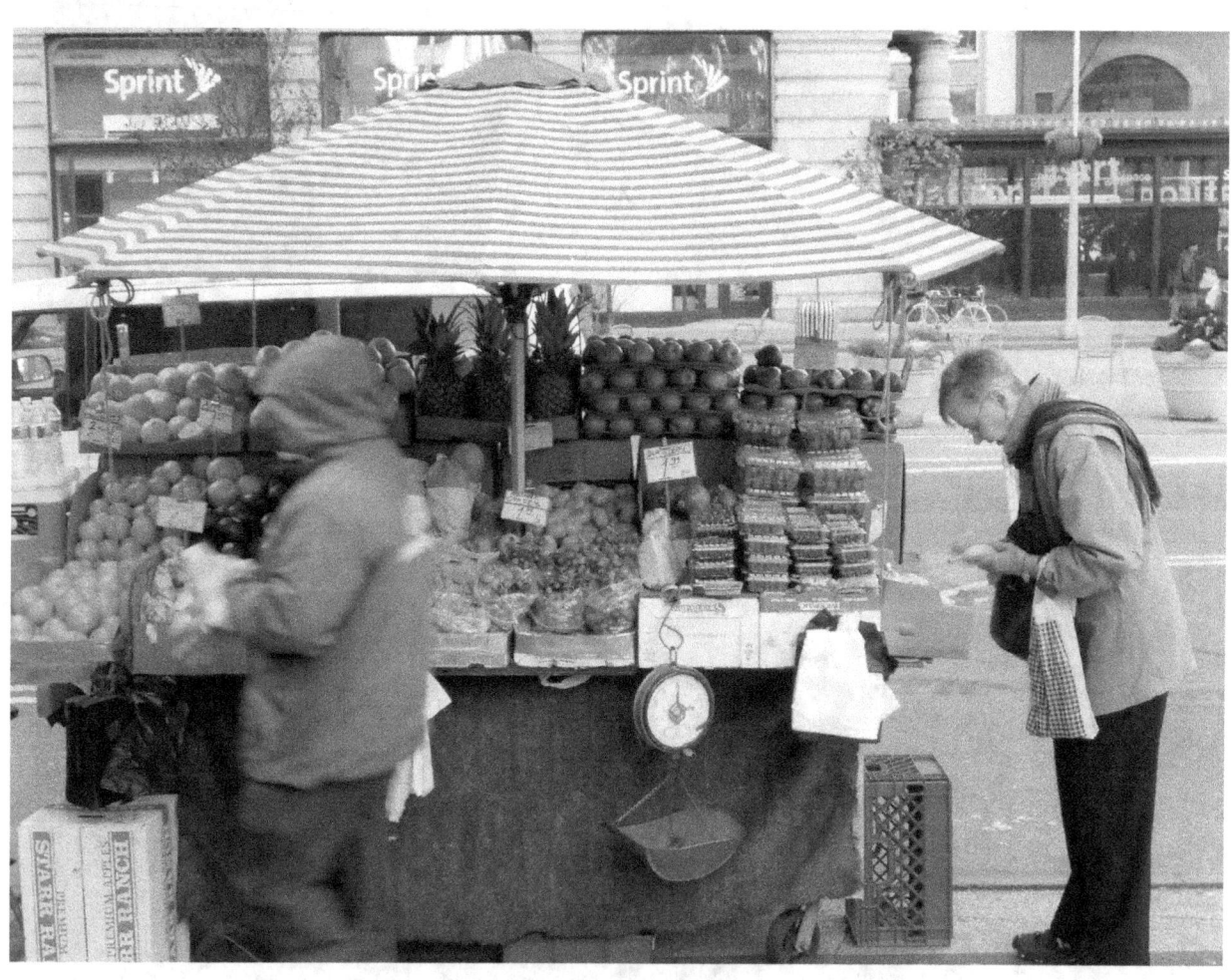

*M*adison Square is formed by the intersection of Fifth Avenue and Broadway at 23rd Street. The square was named for James Madison, fourth President of the United States and the principal author of the United States Constitution. The focus of the square is Madison Square Park, a 6.2 acre public park, which is bounded on the east by Madison Avenue, which starts at the park's southeast corner at 23rd Street; on the south by 23rd Street; on the north by 26th Street; and on the west by Fifth Avenue and Broadway as they cross.

The bronze statue of William H. Seward (1801–1872) was created by Randolph Rogers. William Henry Seward was the 12th Governor of New York, United States Senator and the United States Secretary of State under Abraham Lincoln and Andrew Johnson. A determined opponent of the spread of slavery in the years leading up to the American Civil War, he was a dominant figure in the Republican Party in its formative years, and was widely regarded as the leading contender for the party's presidential nomination in 1860. Denied the nomination, he became a loyal member of Lincoln's wartime cabinet. Seward is the first New Yorker to be honored with a monument in the city.

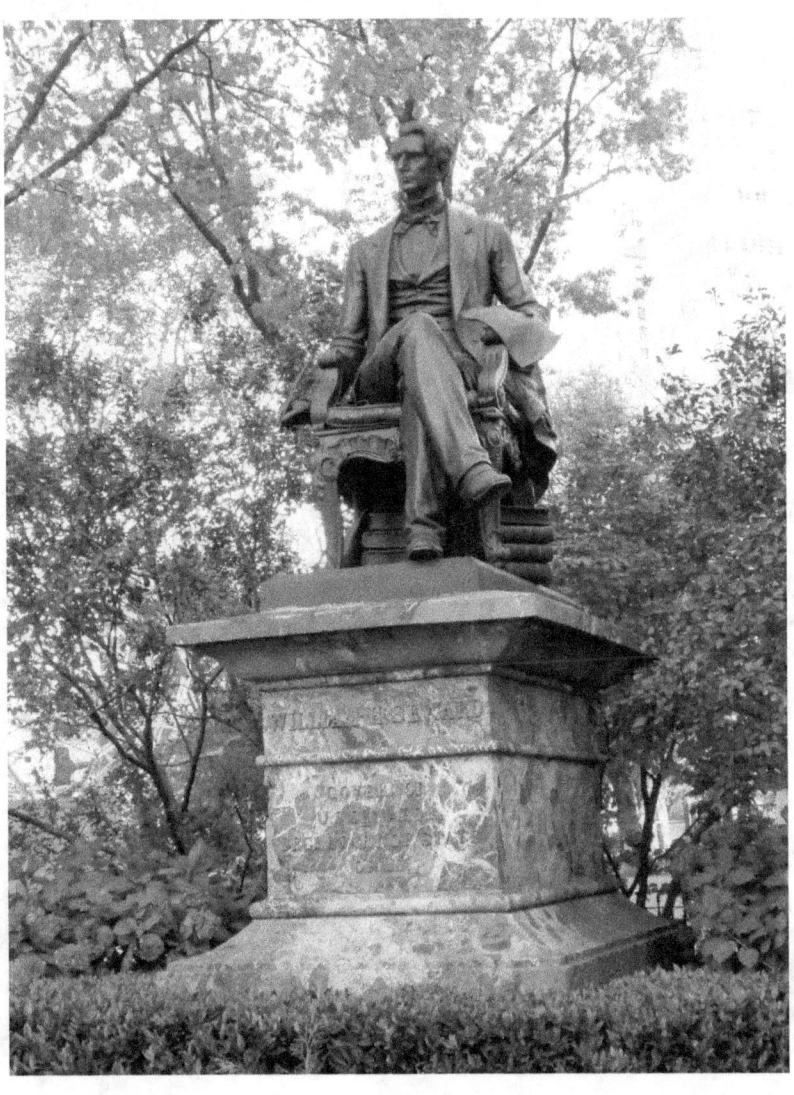

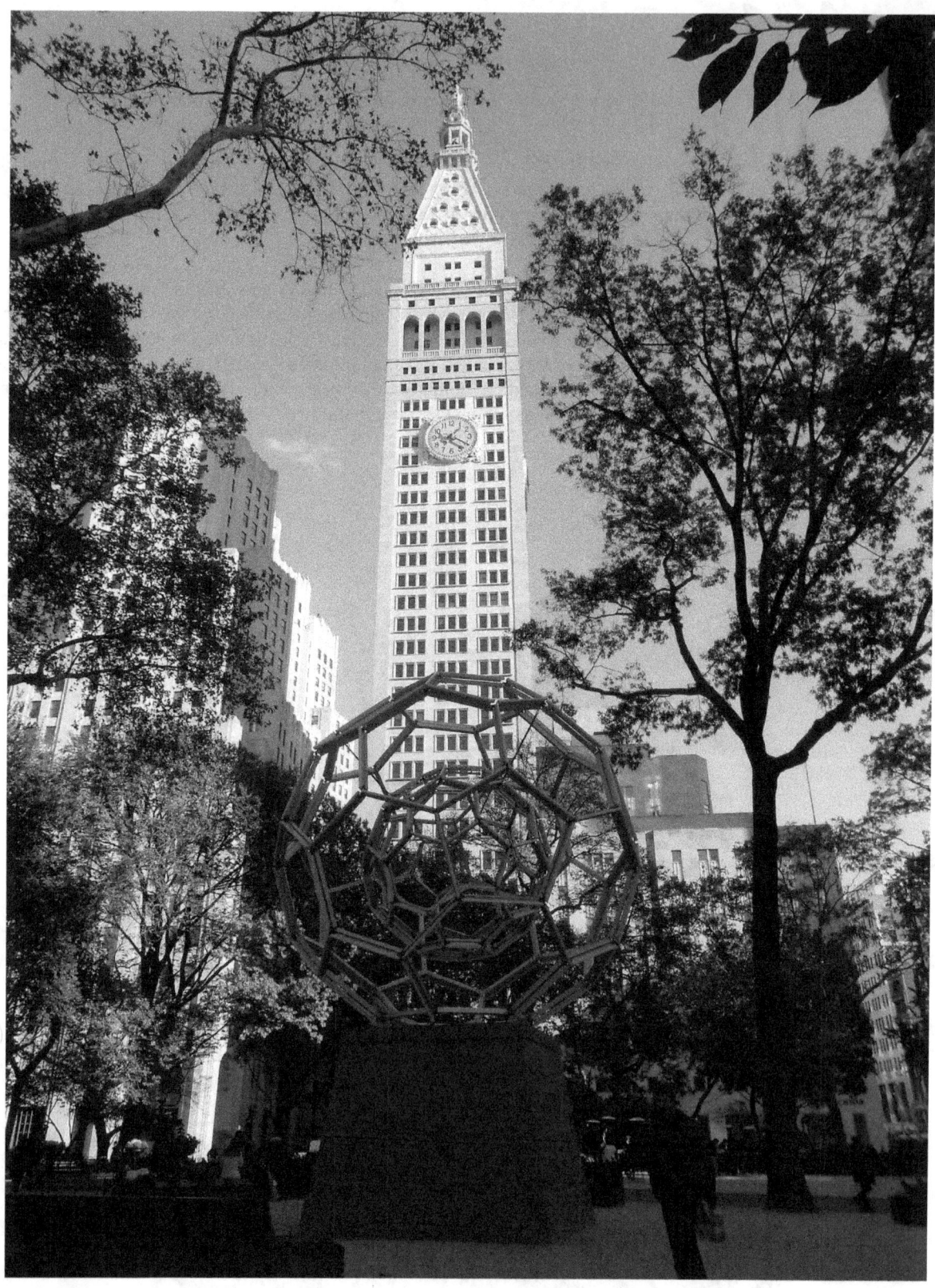

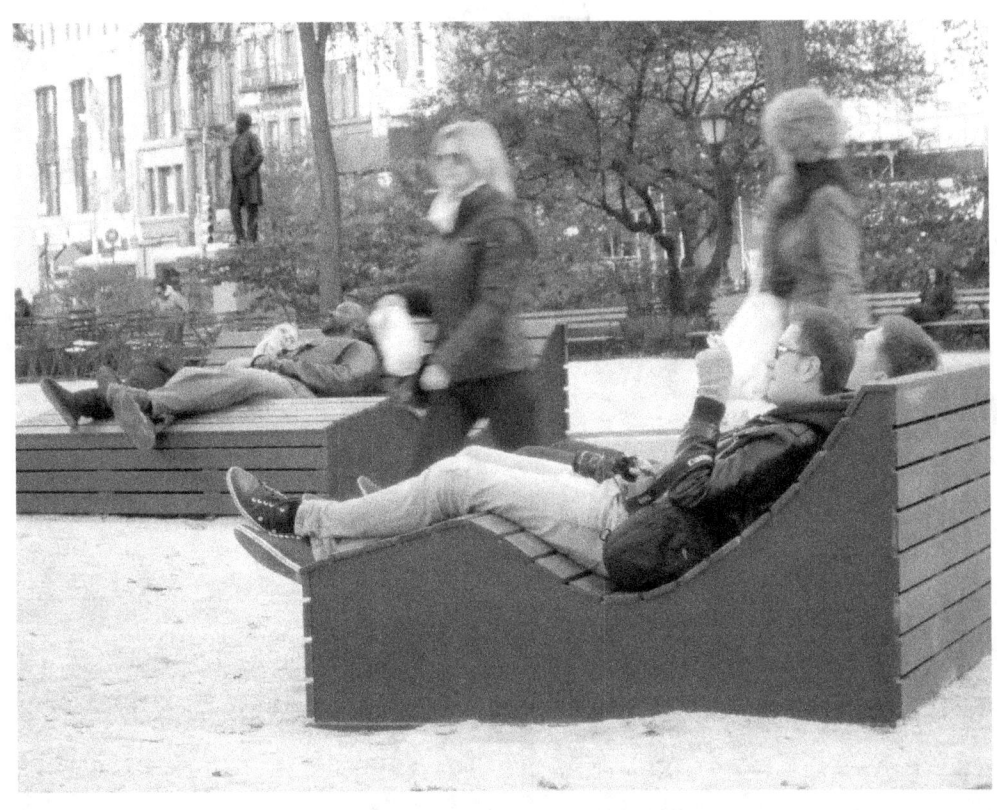

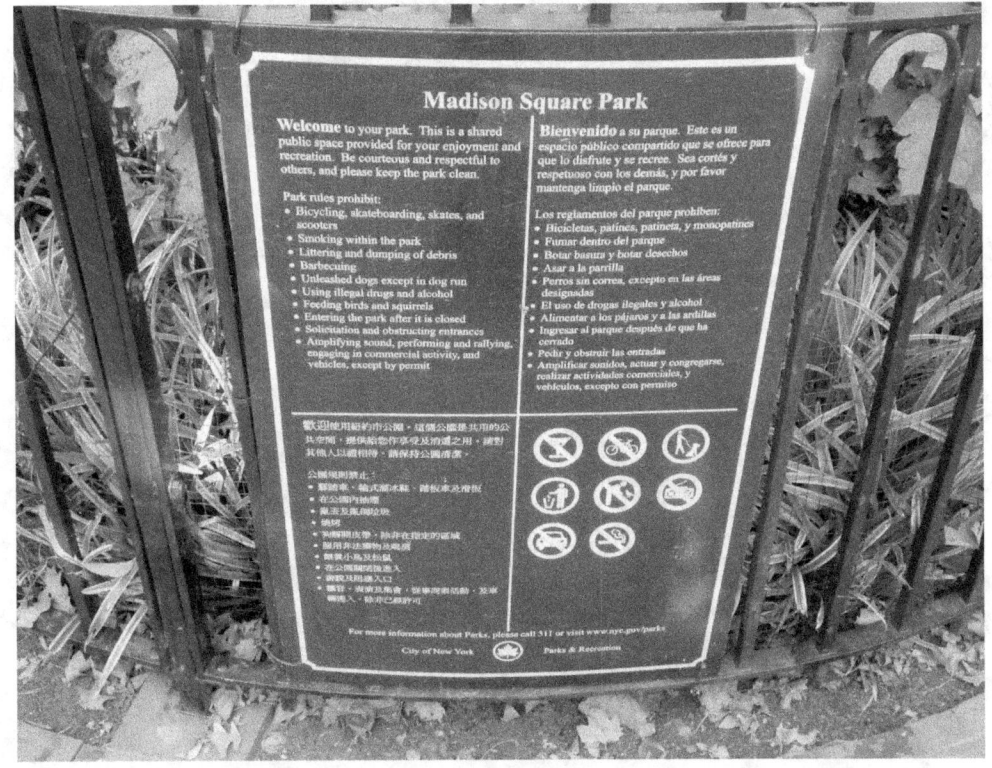

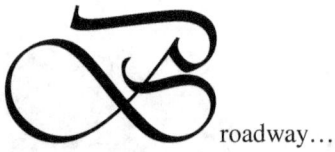

roadway…

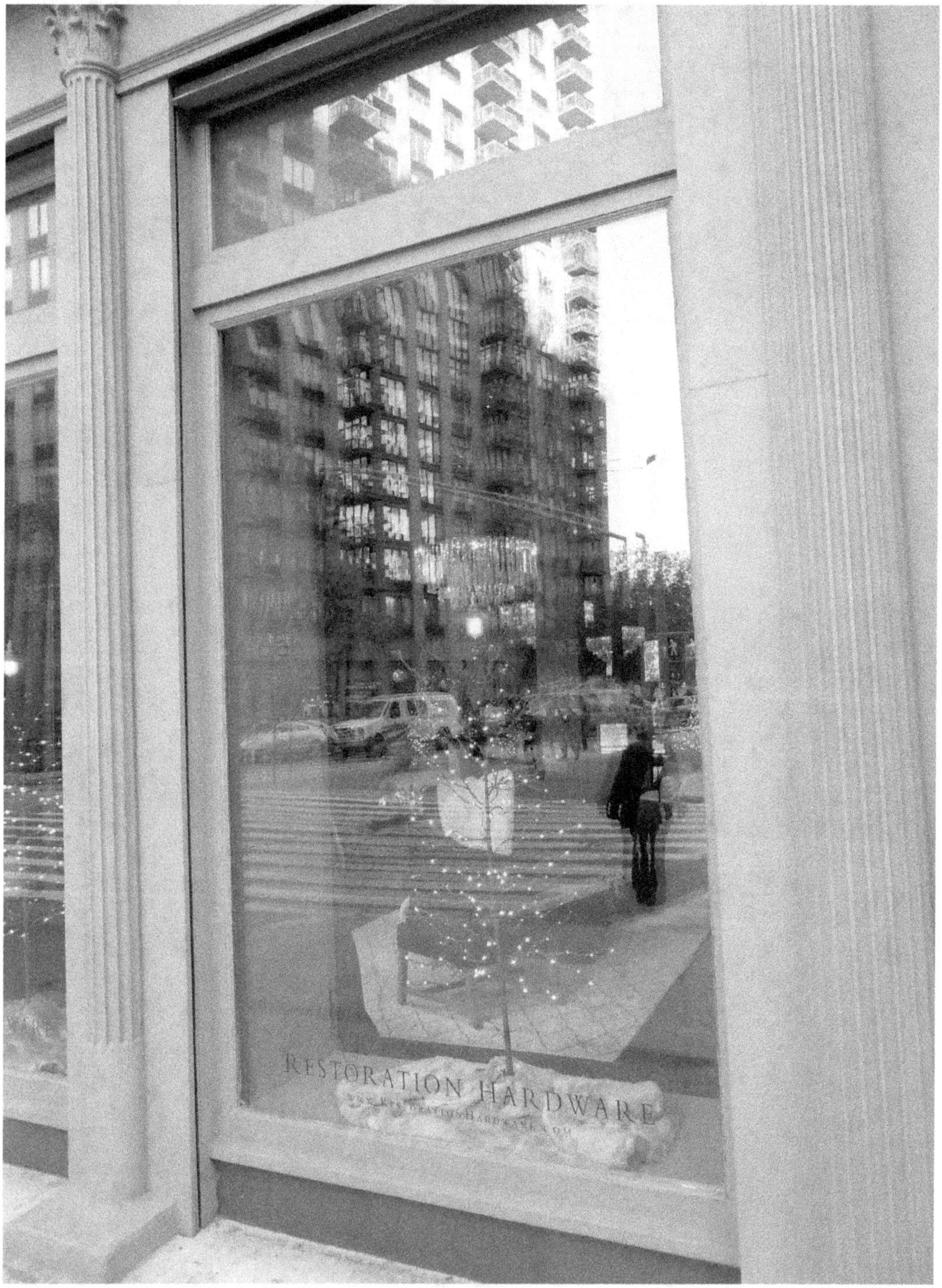

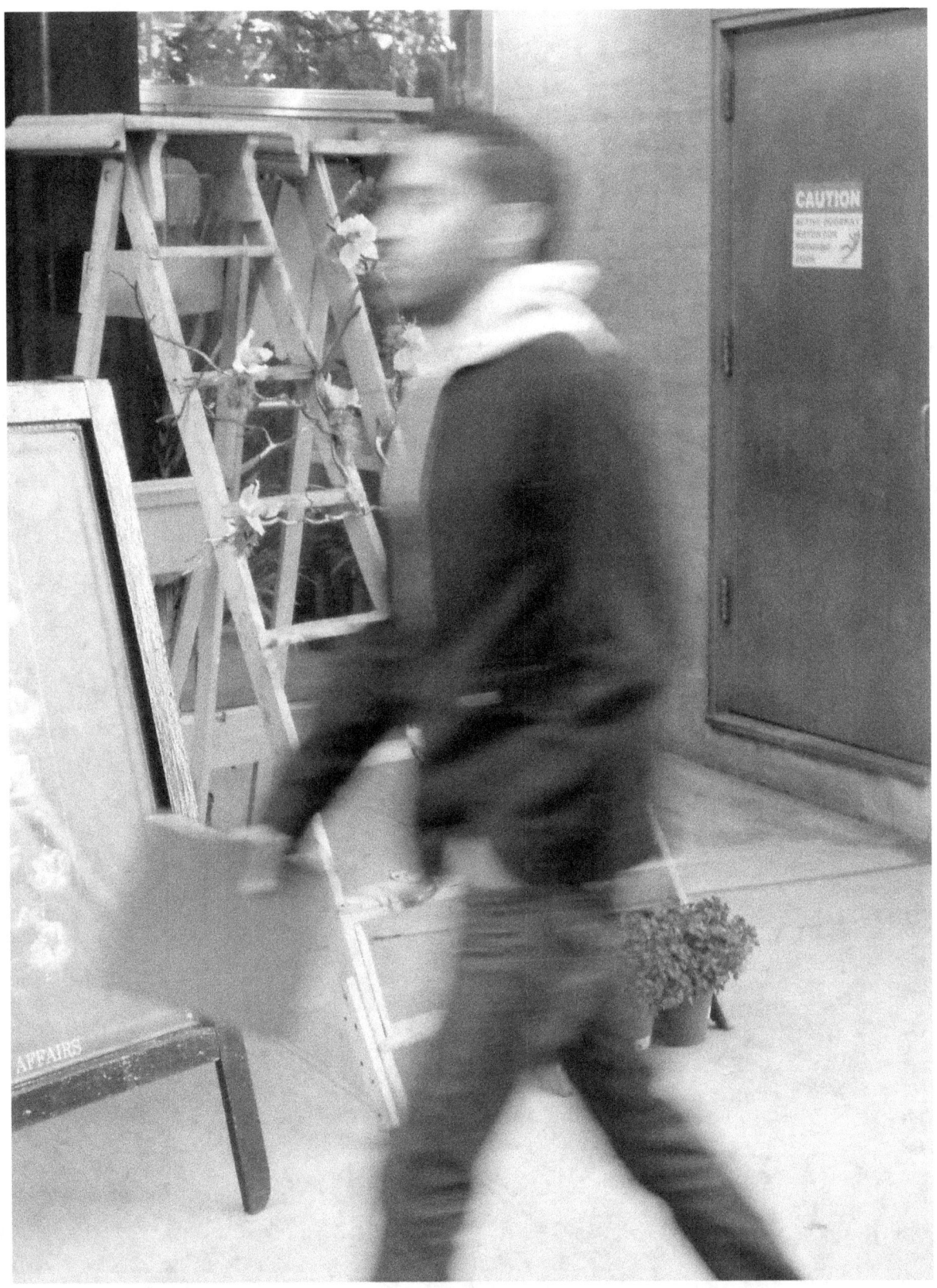

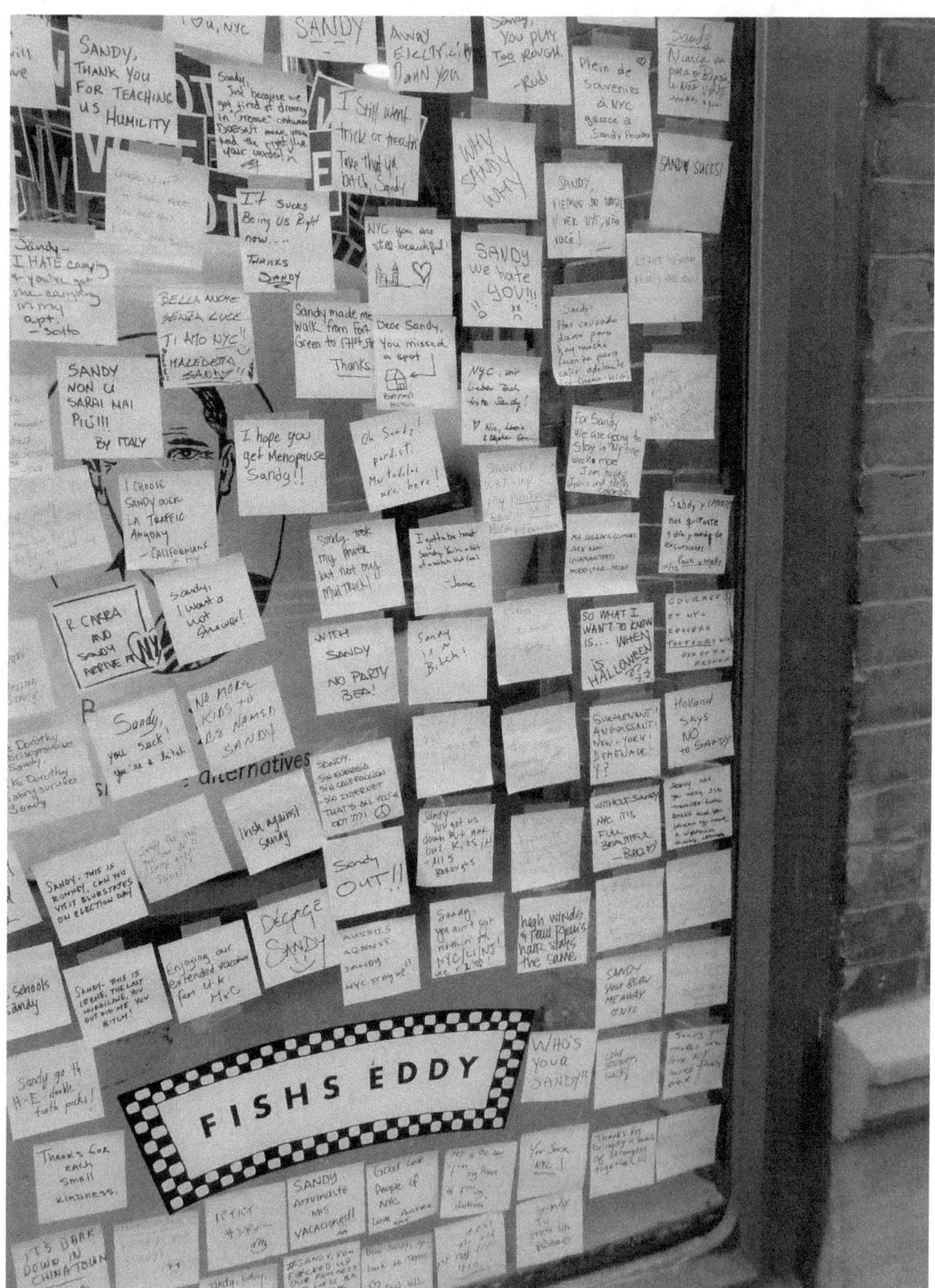

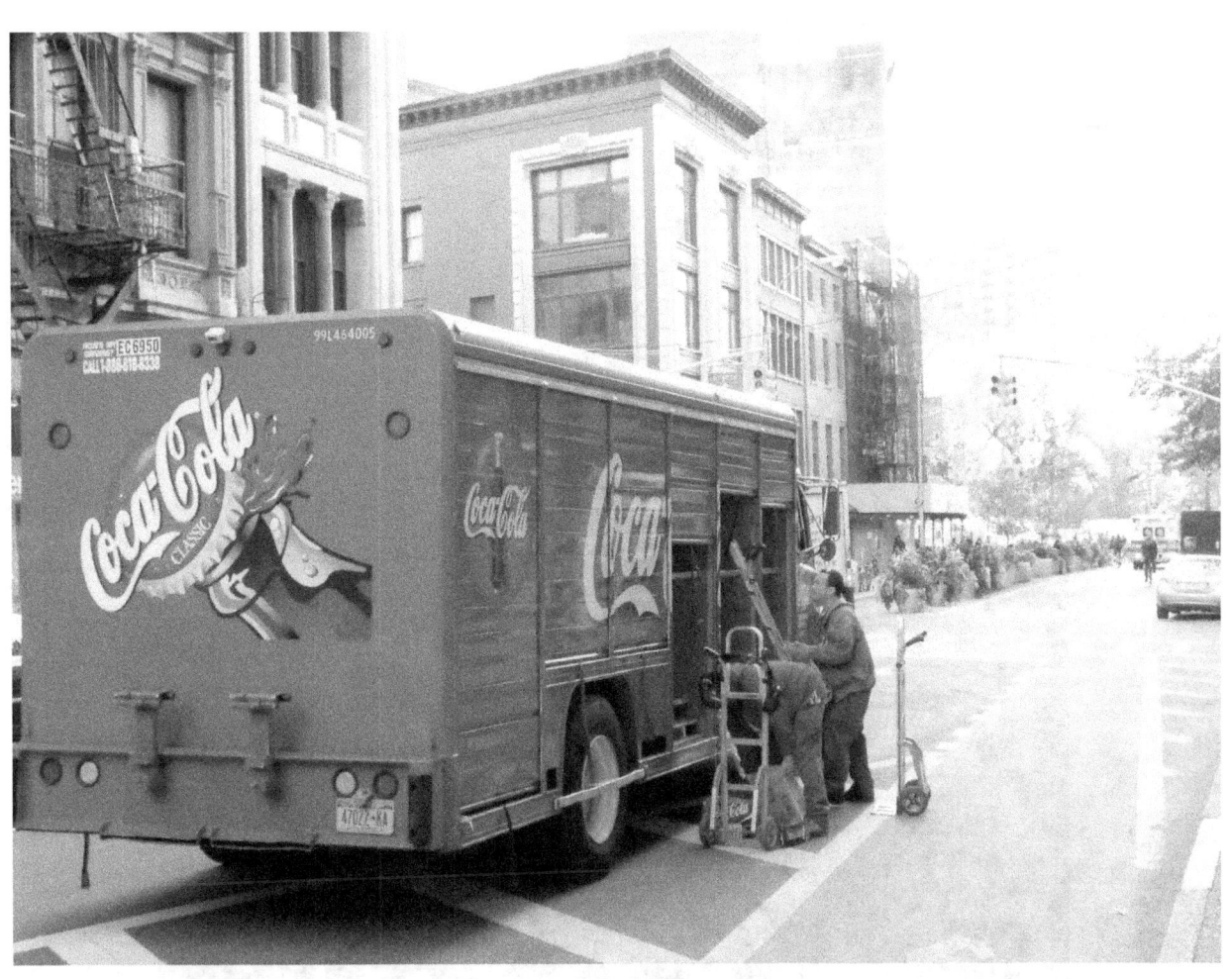

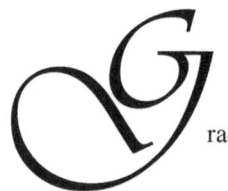race Church is a historic parish church in the Episcopal Diocese of New York. It is located at 800 and

804 Broadway at the corner of East 10th Street, where Broadway bends to the north, with Grace Church School and the church houses – which are now used by the school – behind it at 86-98 Fourth Avenue between East 10th and 12th Streets. It is a French Gothic Revival masterpiece designed by James Renwick, Jr., his first major commission. The church is one of the New York City's greatest treasures.

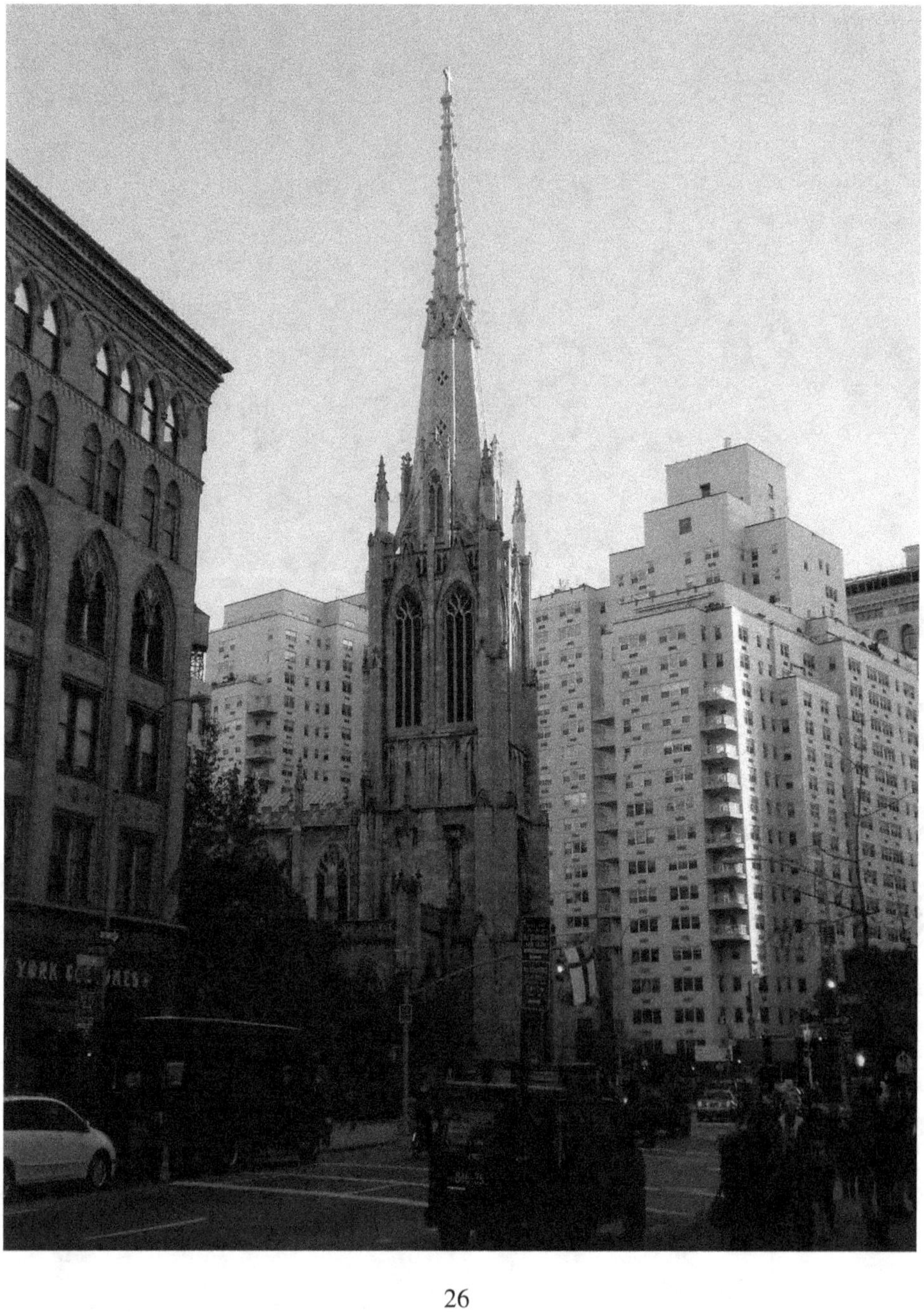

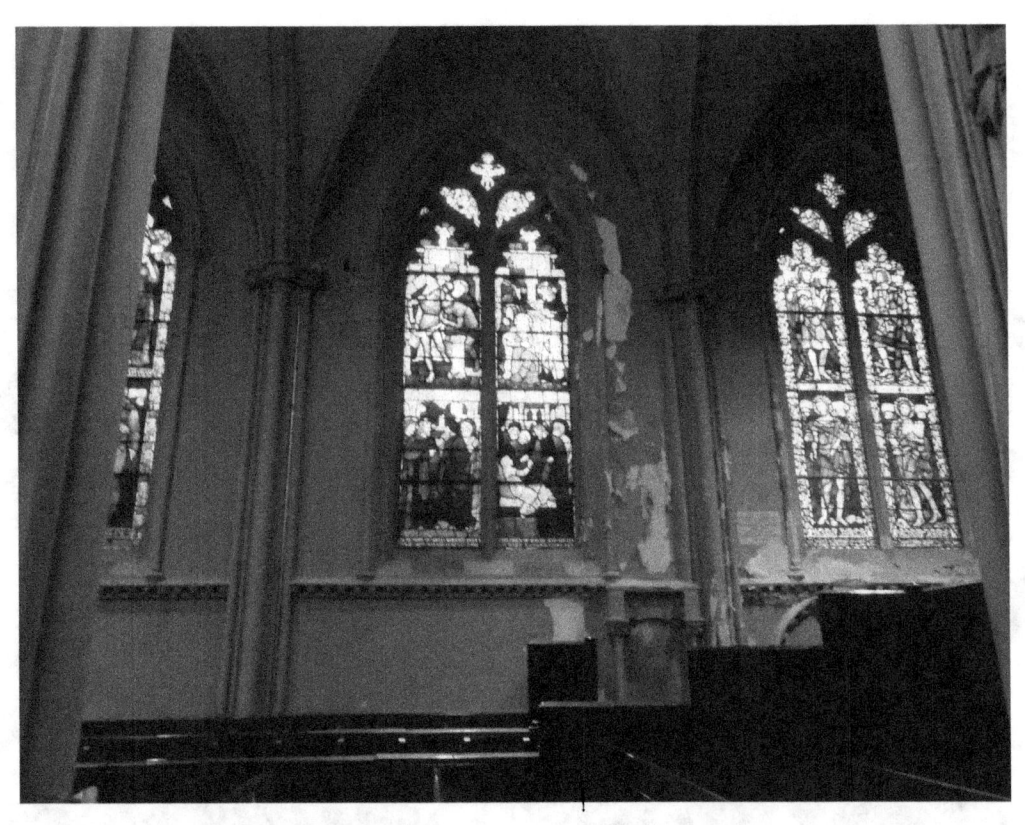

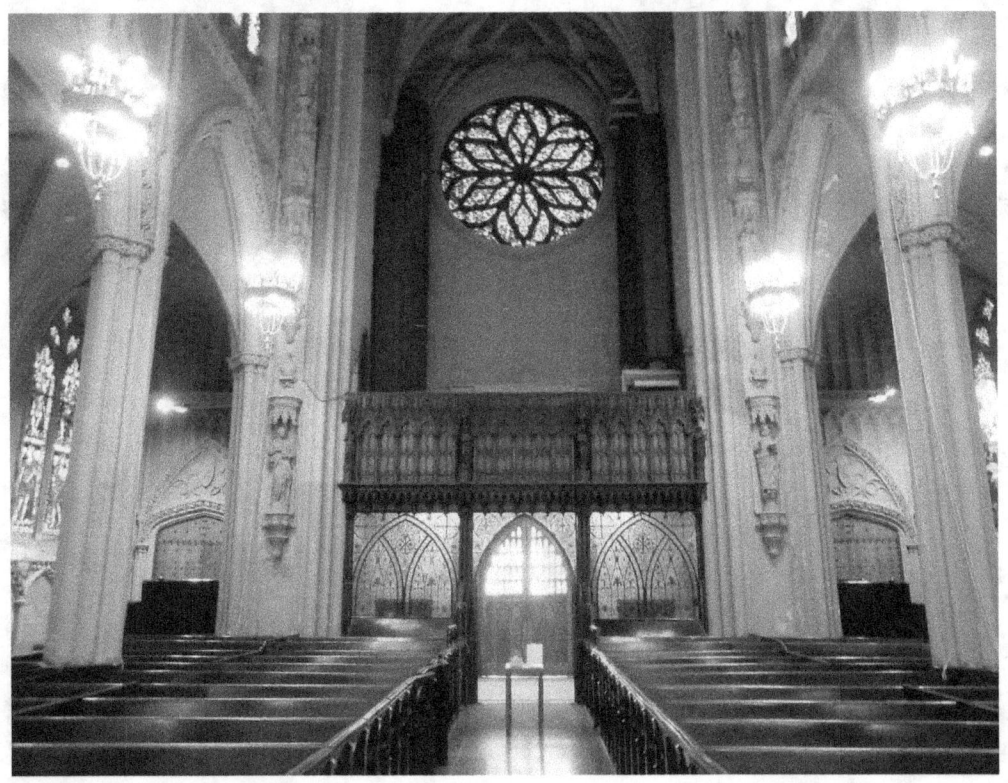

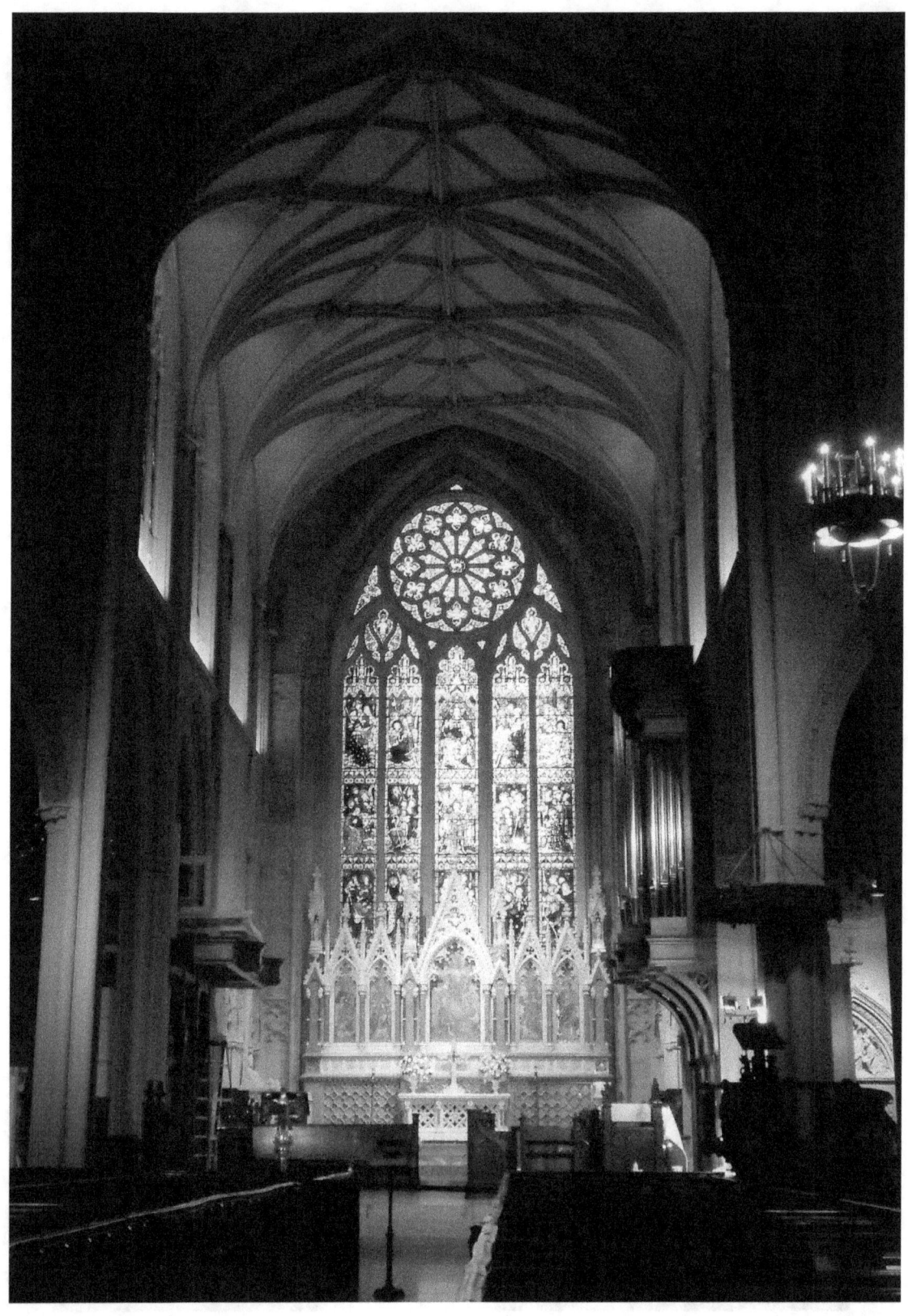

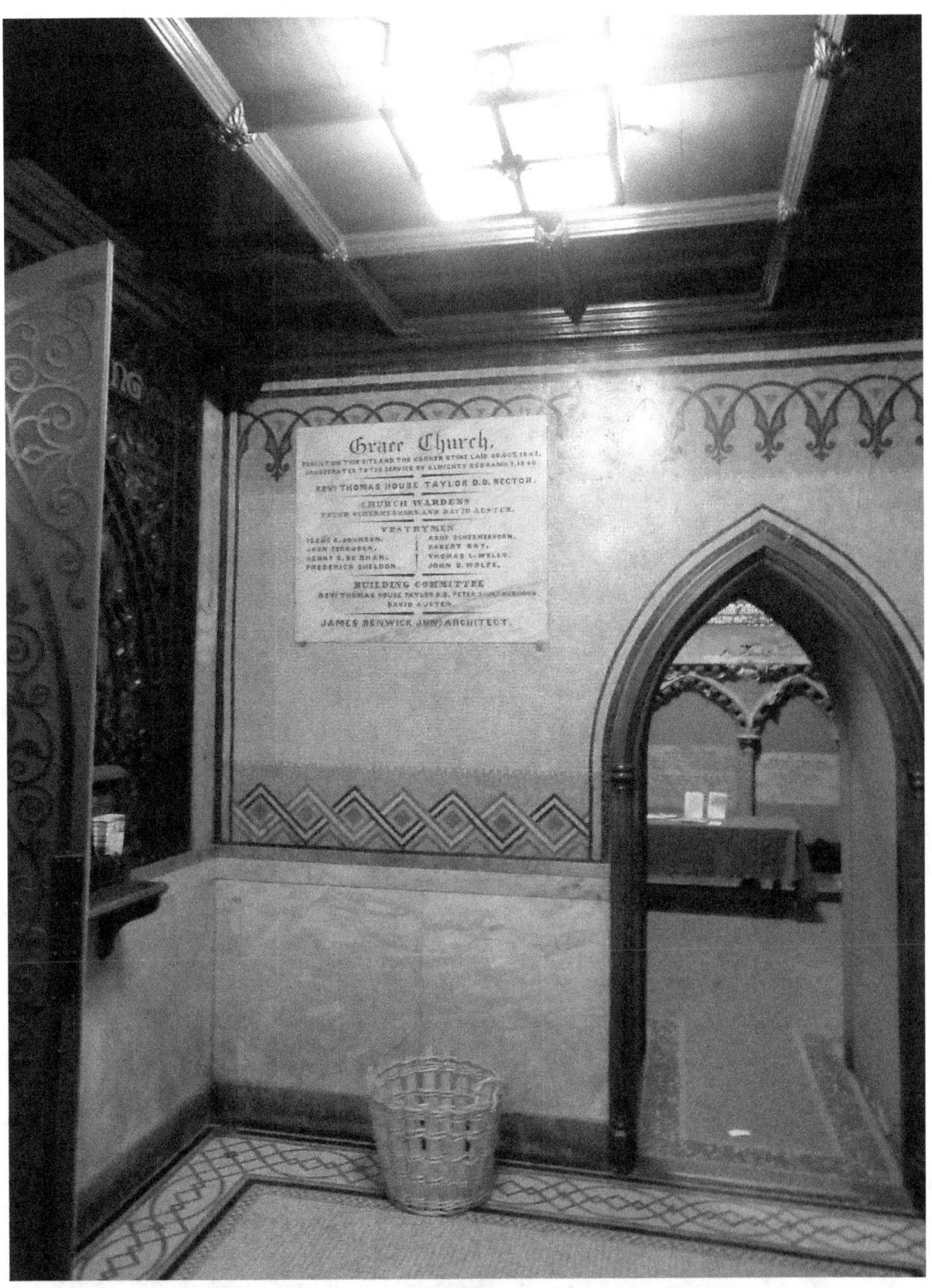

29

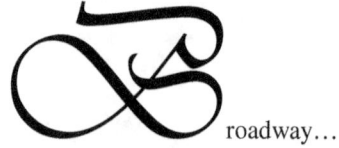roadway…

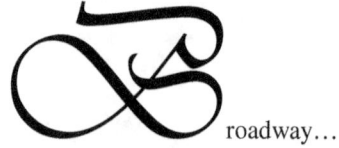

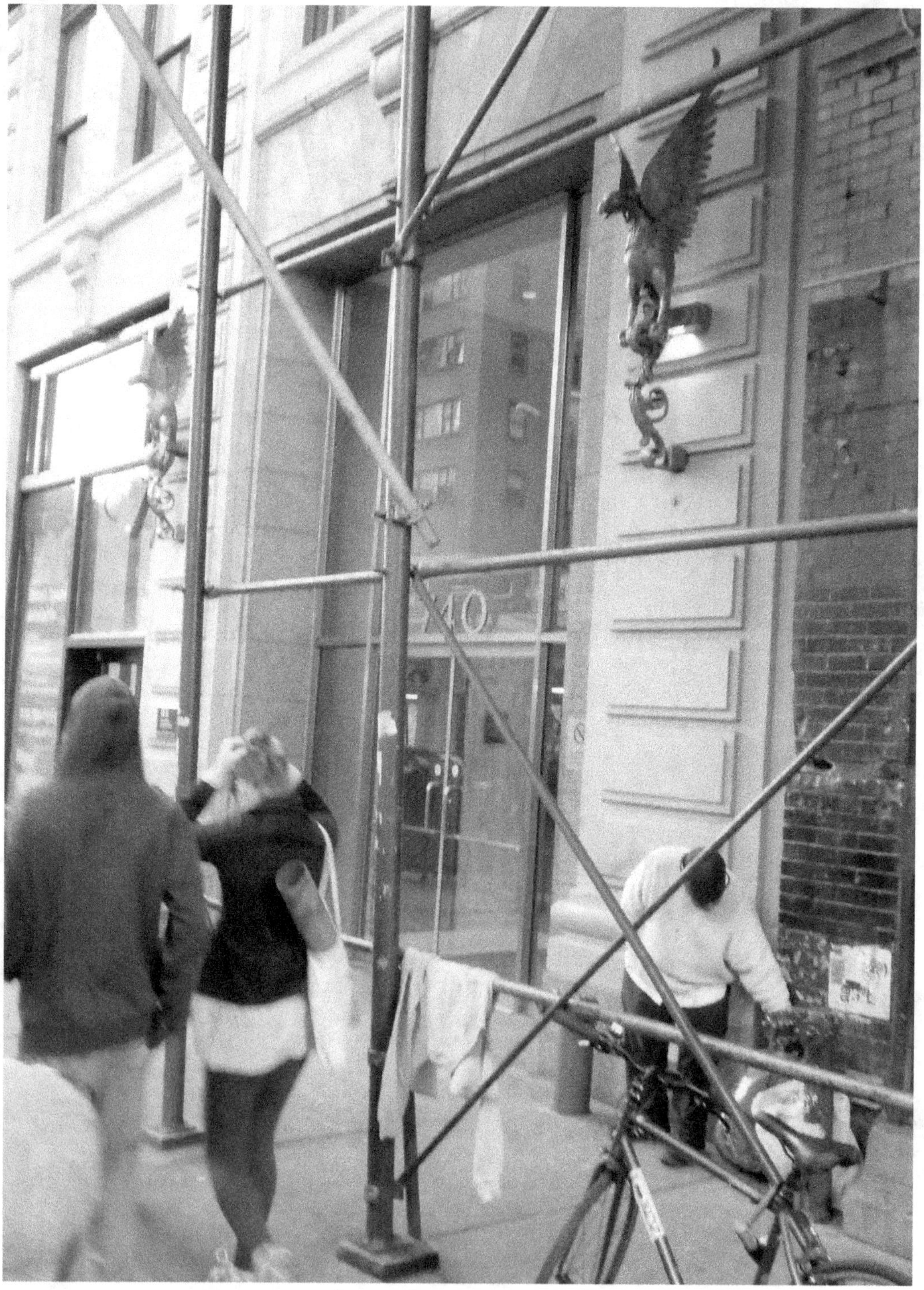

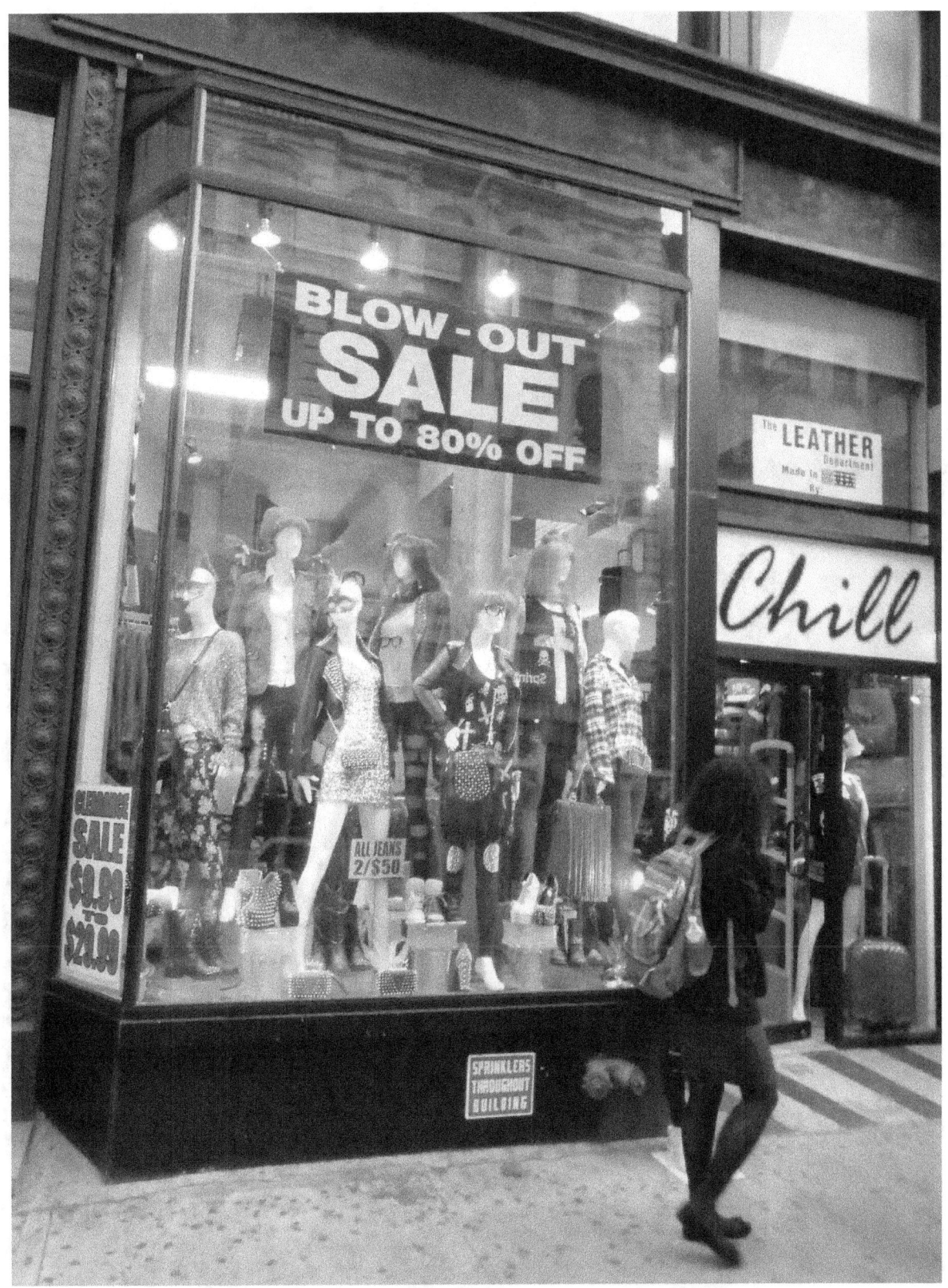

31

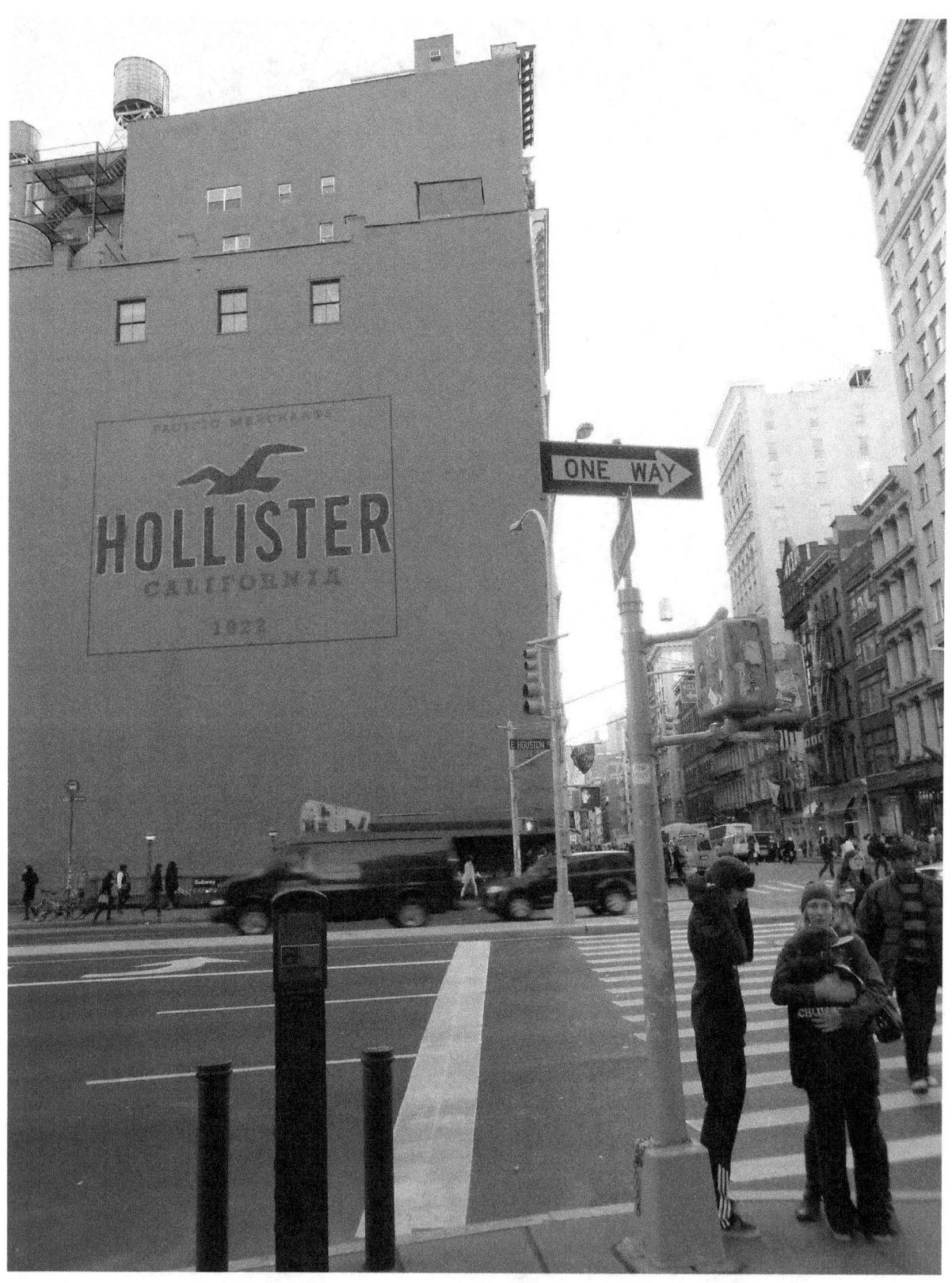

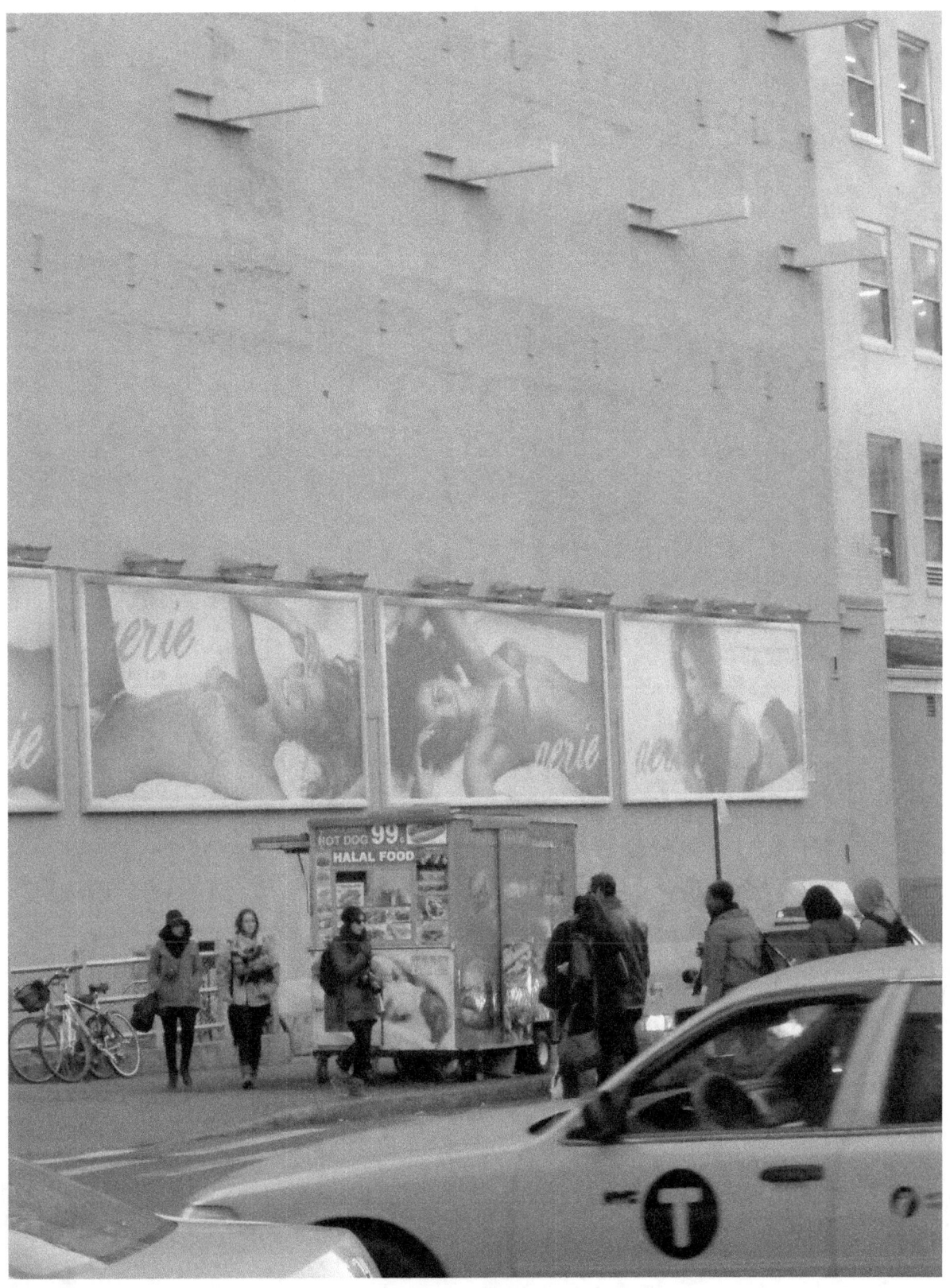

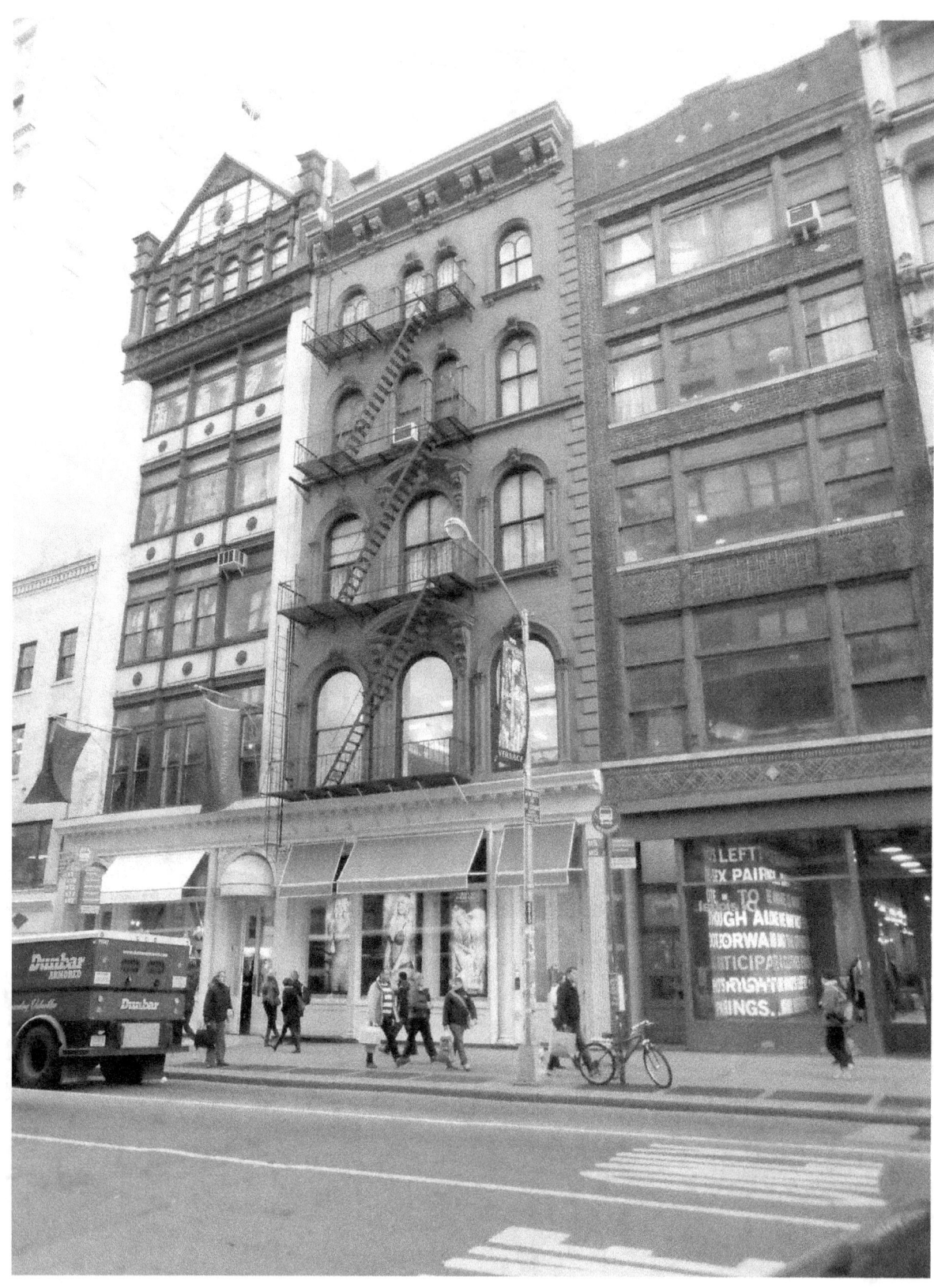

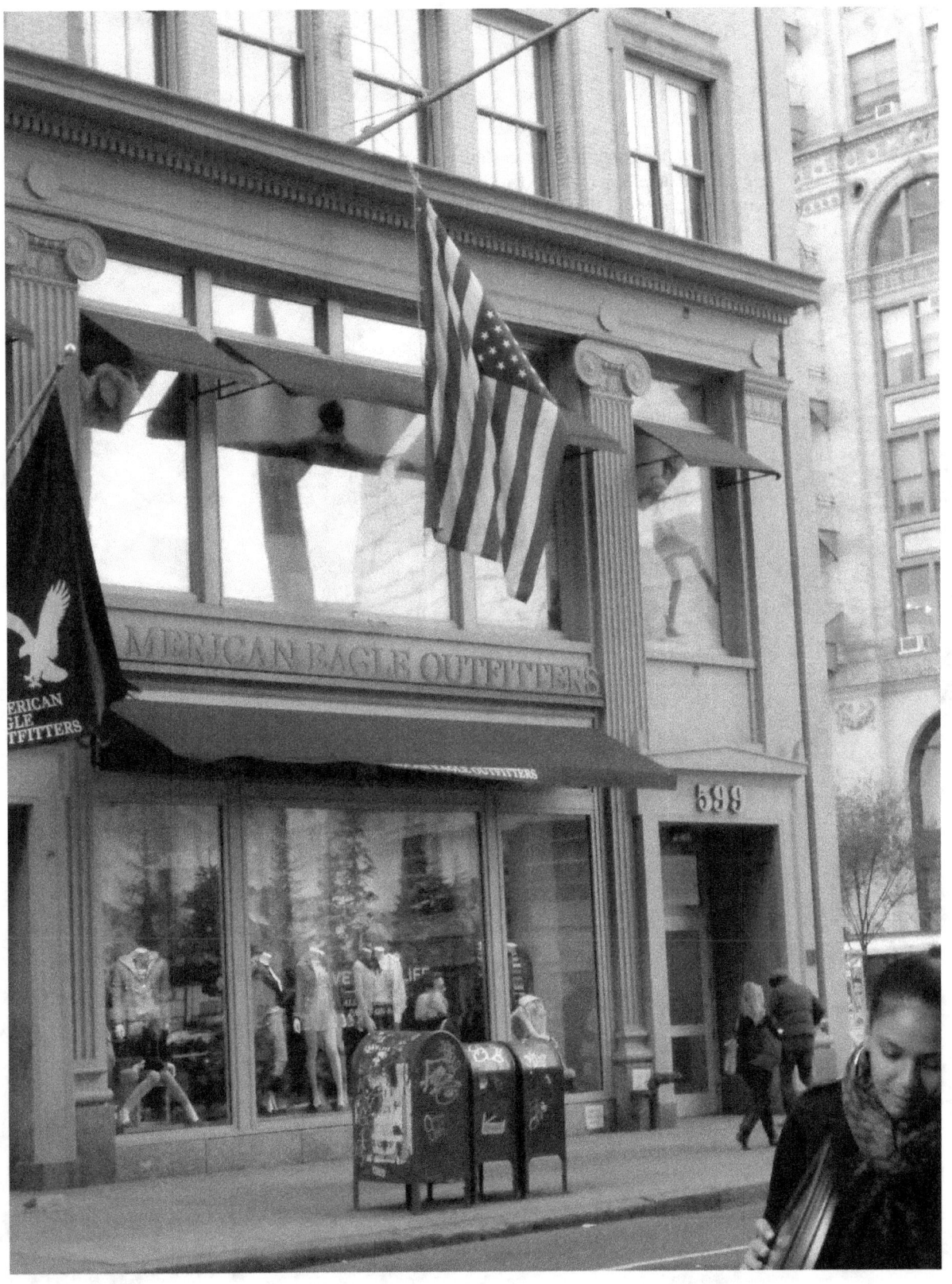

𝒯he Manhattan Bridge is the suspension bridge, it crosses the East River connecting Lower Manhattan at Canal Street with Brooklyn at Flatbush Avenue Extension. The bridge was designed by Leon Moisseiff, who later designed the infamous original Tacoma Narrows Bridge that opened and collapsed in 1940. The Manhattan Bridge was opened to traffic on December 31, 1909. It has four vehicle lanes on the upper level, split between two roadways. The lower level has three lanes, four subway tracks, a bikeway and a walkway. The upper level has two lanes in each direction, and the lower level is one-way and has three lanes in peak direction.

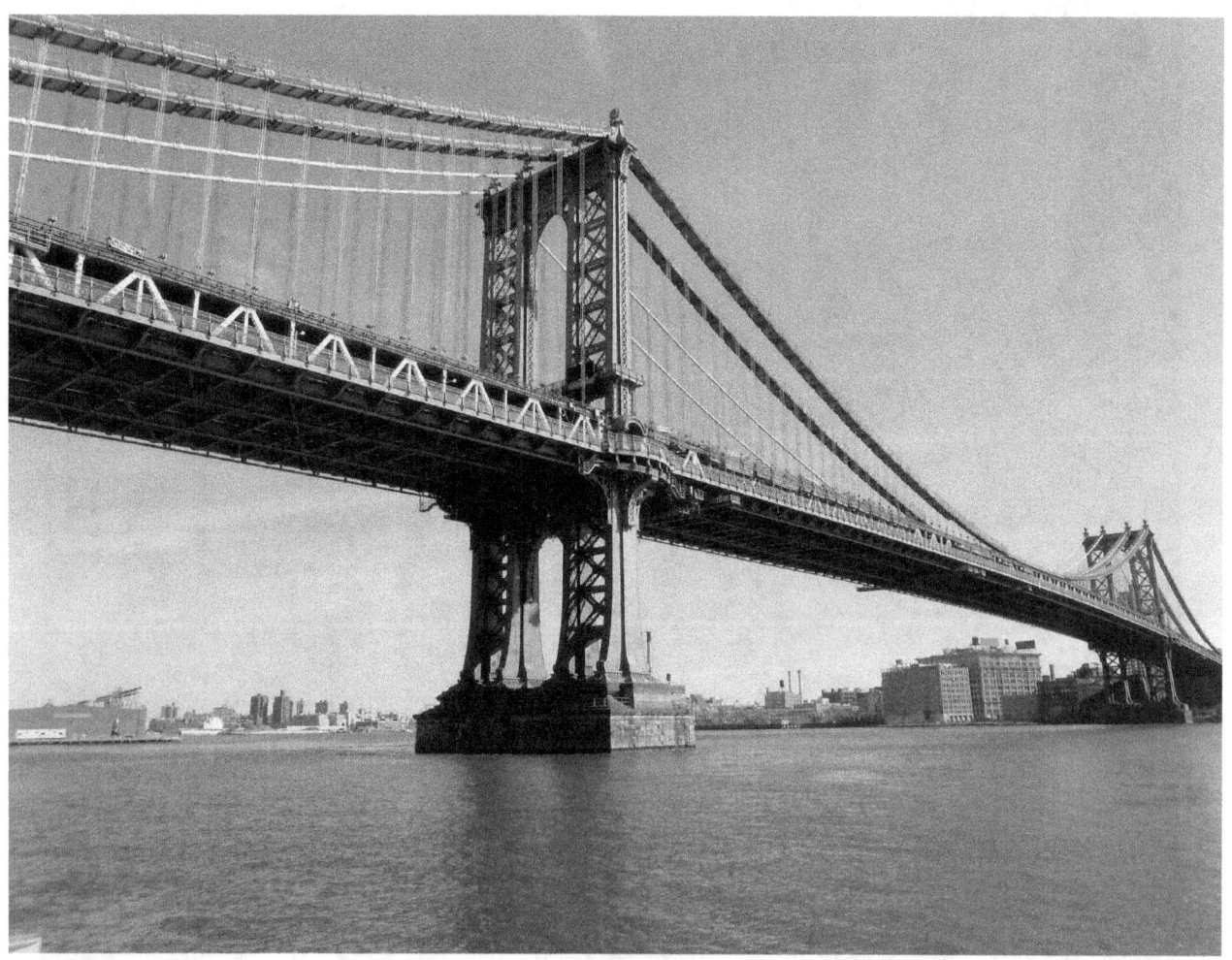

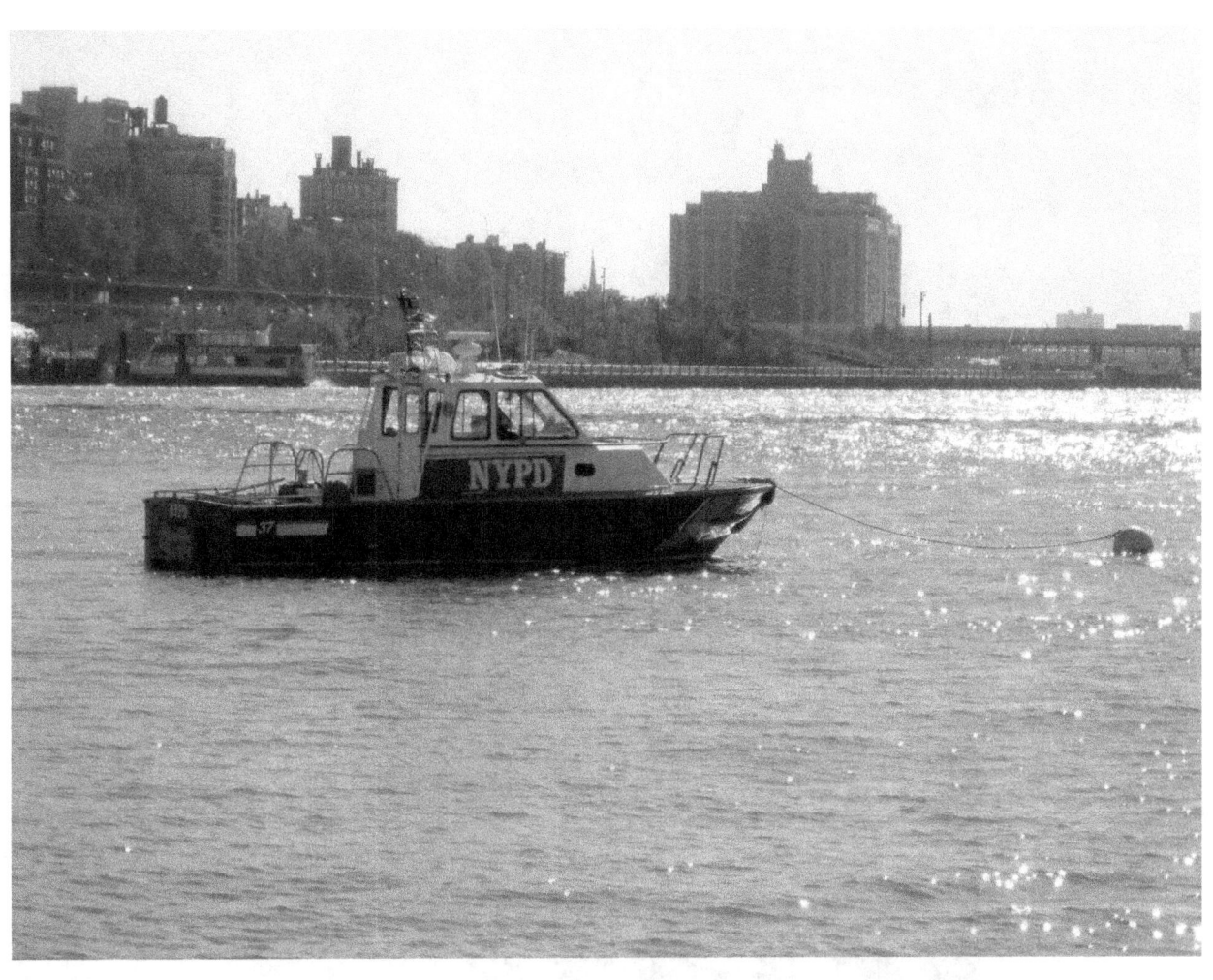

$\mathcal{T}$he Brooklyn Bridge is one of the oldest suspension bridges in the United States. Completed in 1883, it connects the boroughs of Manhattan and Brooklyn by spanning the East River. It was the first steel-wire suspension bridge and the longest suspension bridge in the world until 1903. Since its opening, it has become an icon of New York City, and was designated a National Historic Landmark in 1964 and a National Historic Civil Engineering Landmark in 1972.

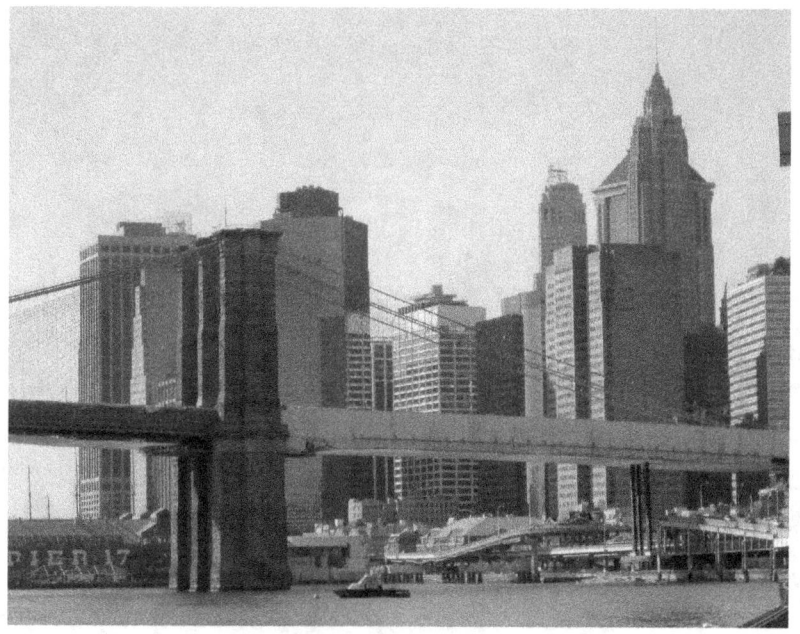

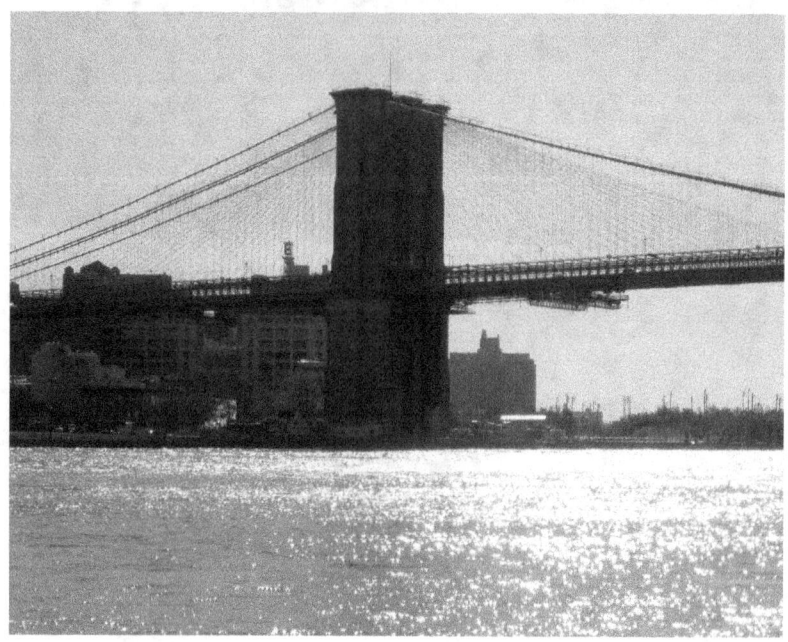

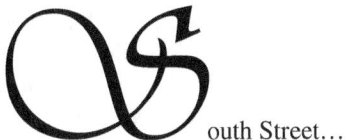

outh Street…

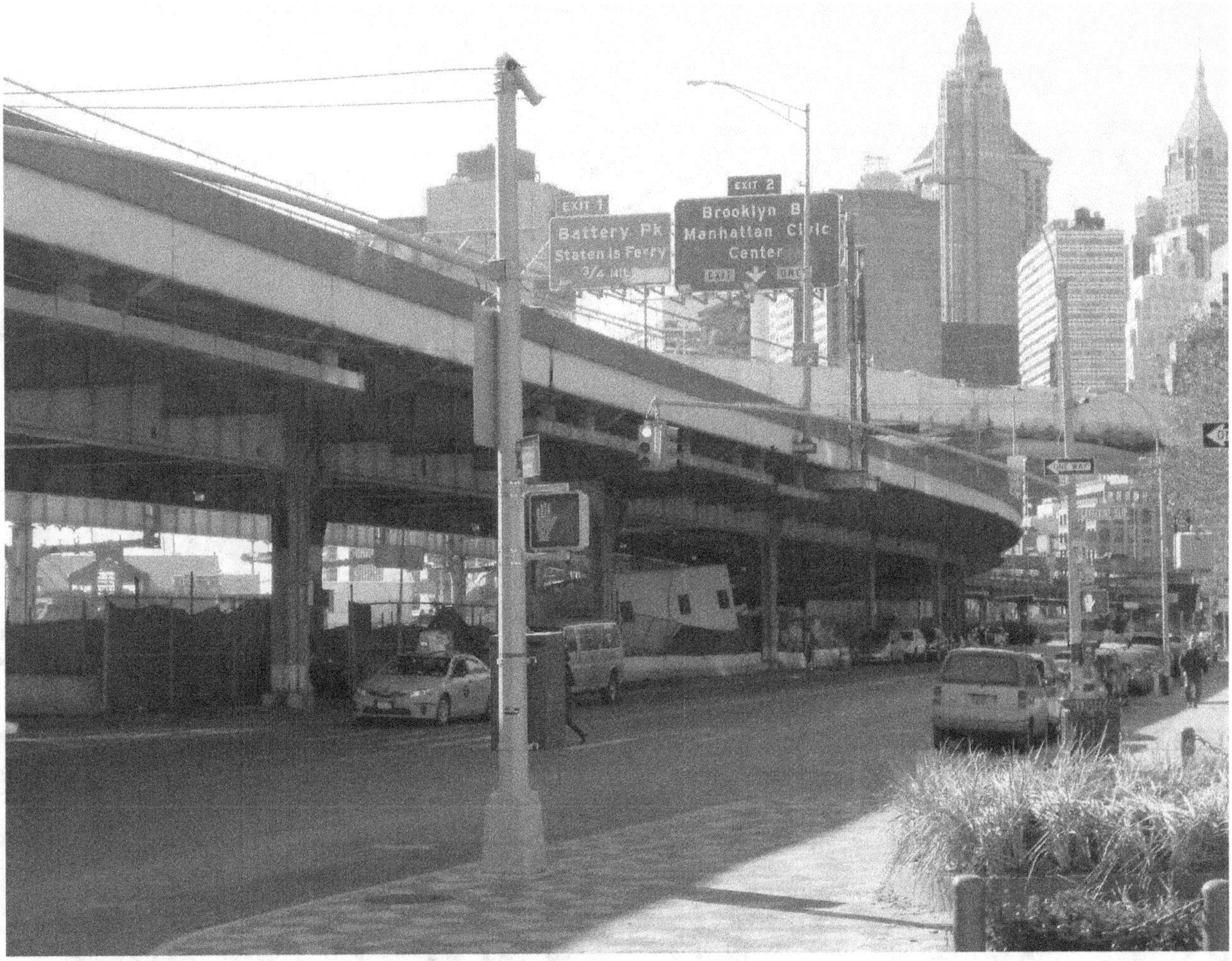

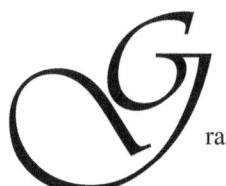rand Street, Chinatown… Grand Street runs east-west parallel to and south of Delancey Street, from

SoHo through Chinatown, Little Italy, the Lower East Side to the East River. With an estimated population of 90,000 to 100,000 people, Manhattan's Chinatown is one of the oldest ethnic Chinese enclaves outside of Asia, with many of its residents Cantonese-speaking and originating from various regions in China, mainly from Guangdong and Fujian provinces, and Hong Kong. It is one of three Chinatown neighborhoods in New York City. Two others located in the boroughs of Queens and Brooklyn.

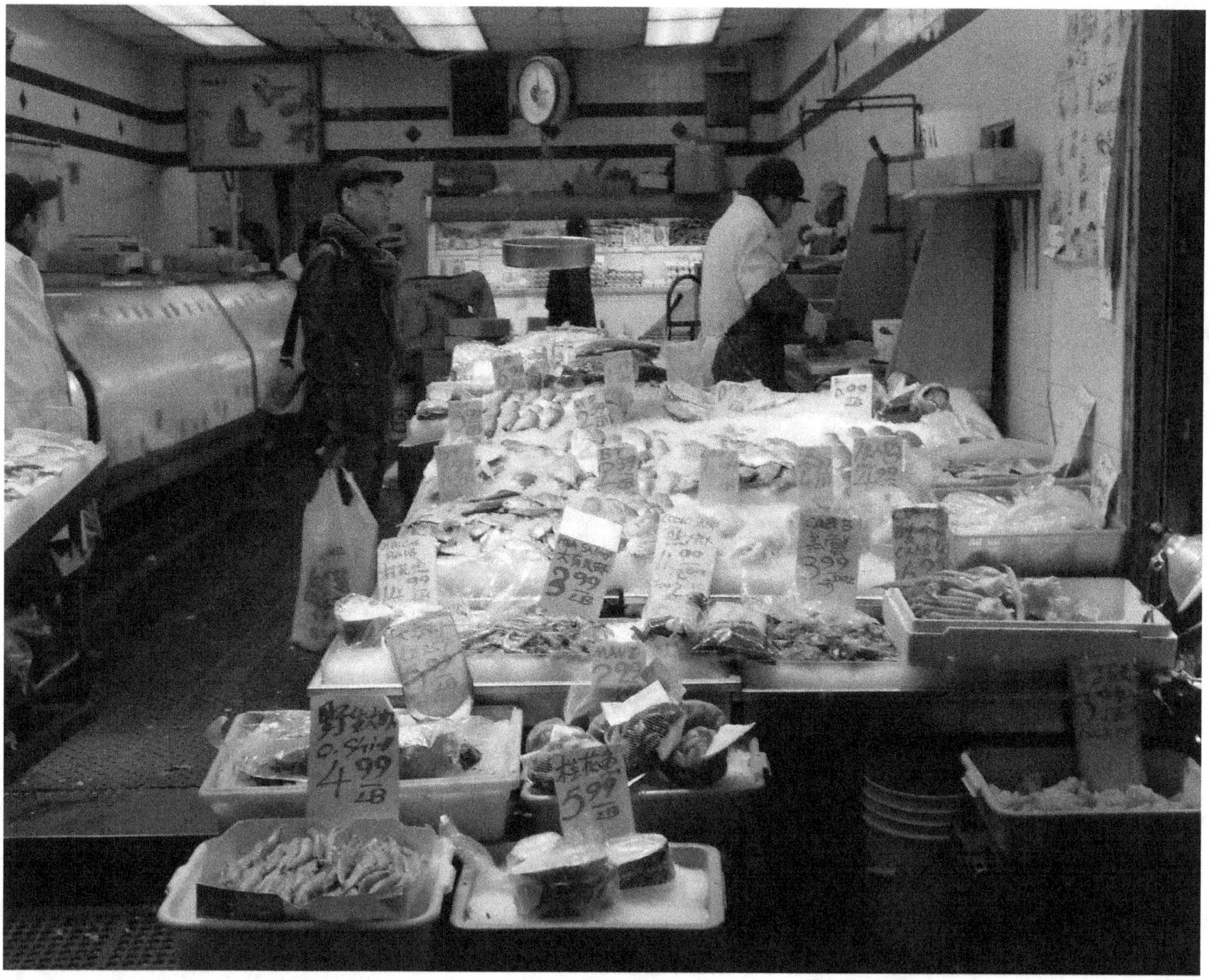

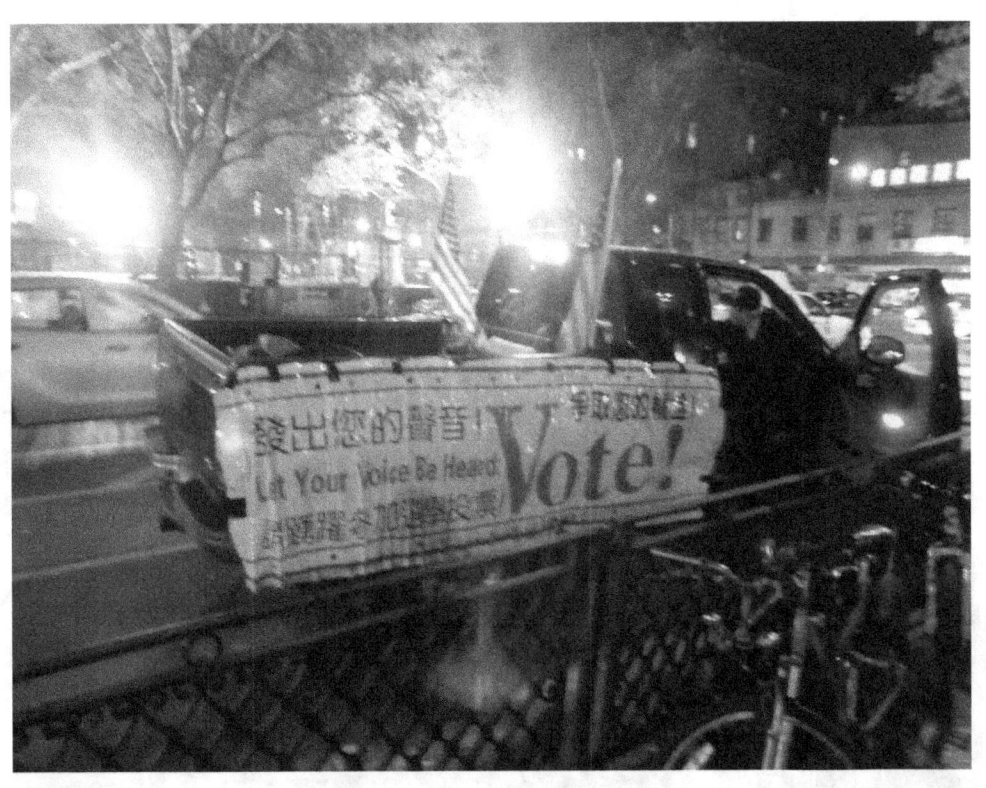

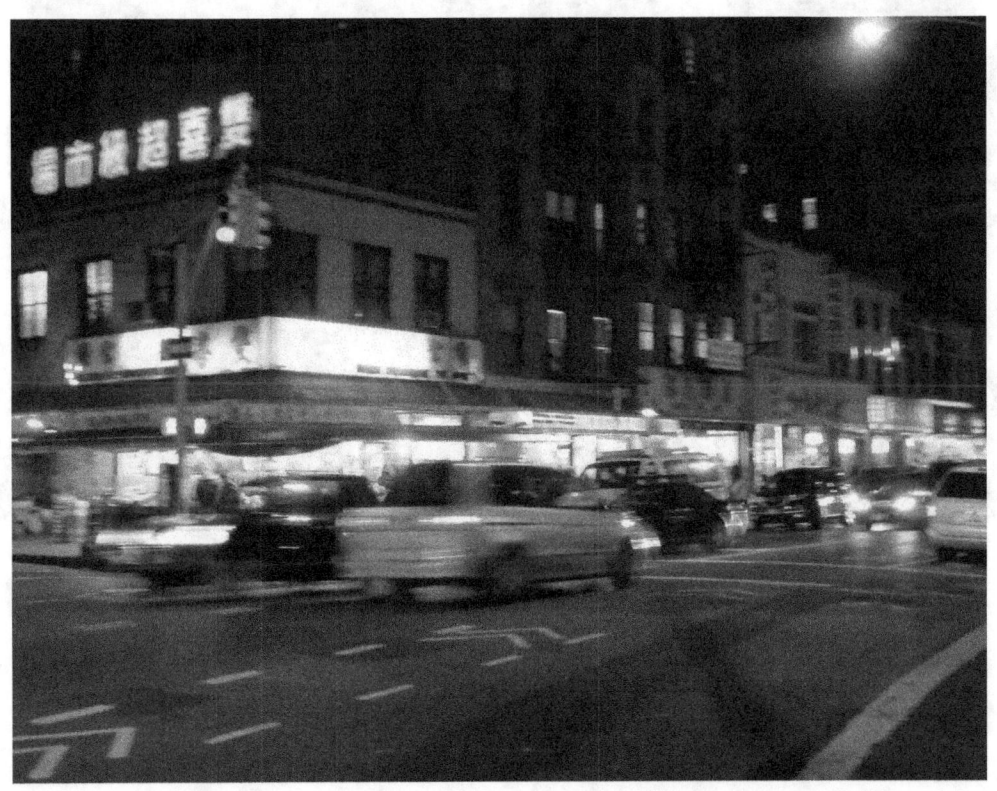

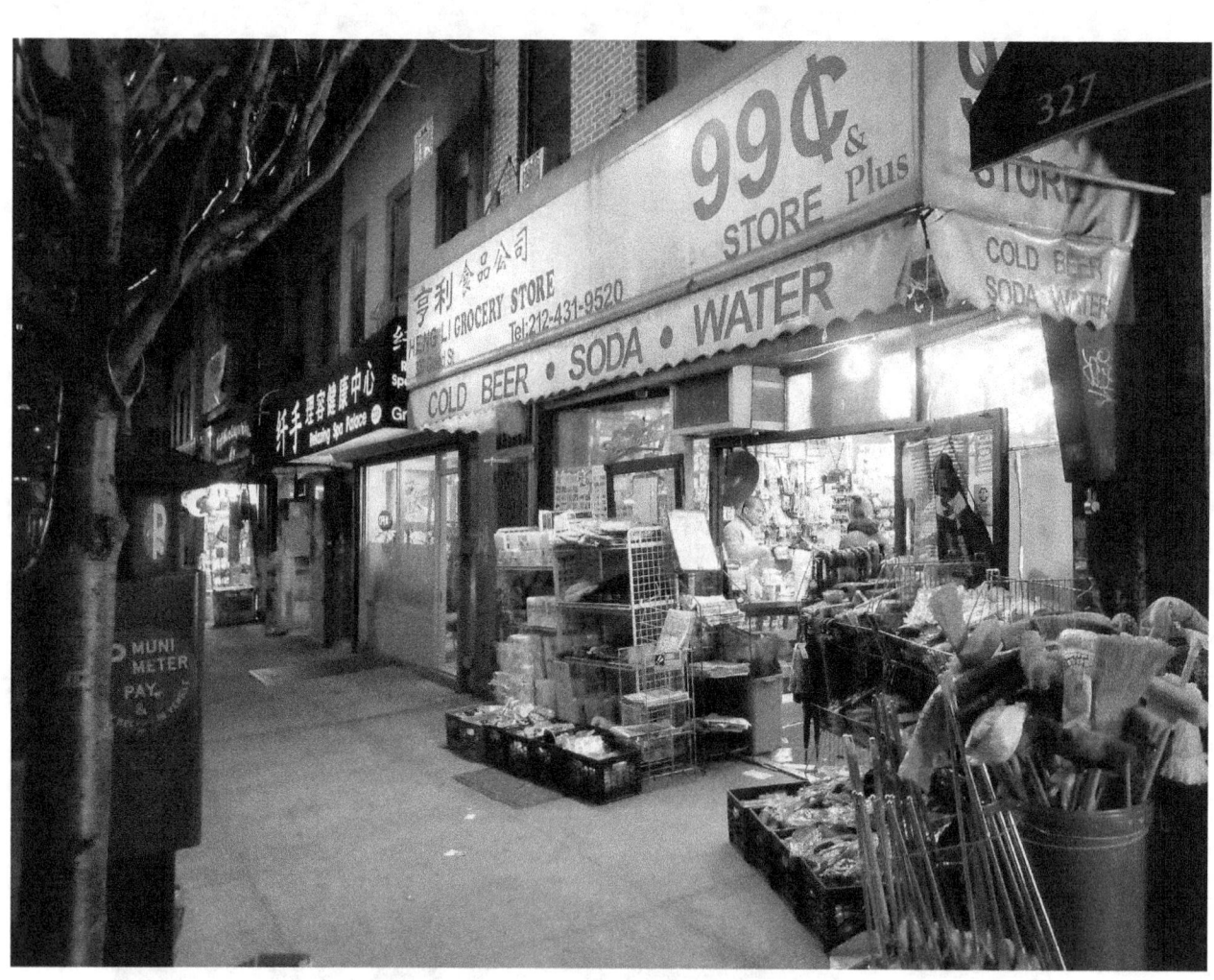

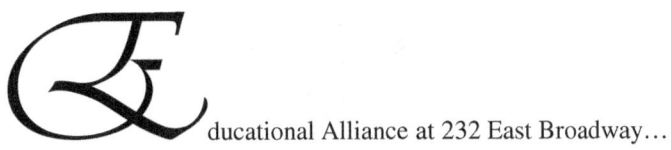

ducational Alliance at 232 East Broadway…

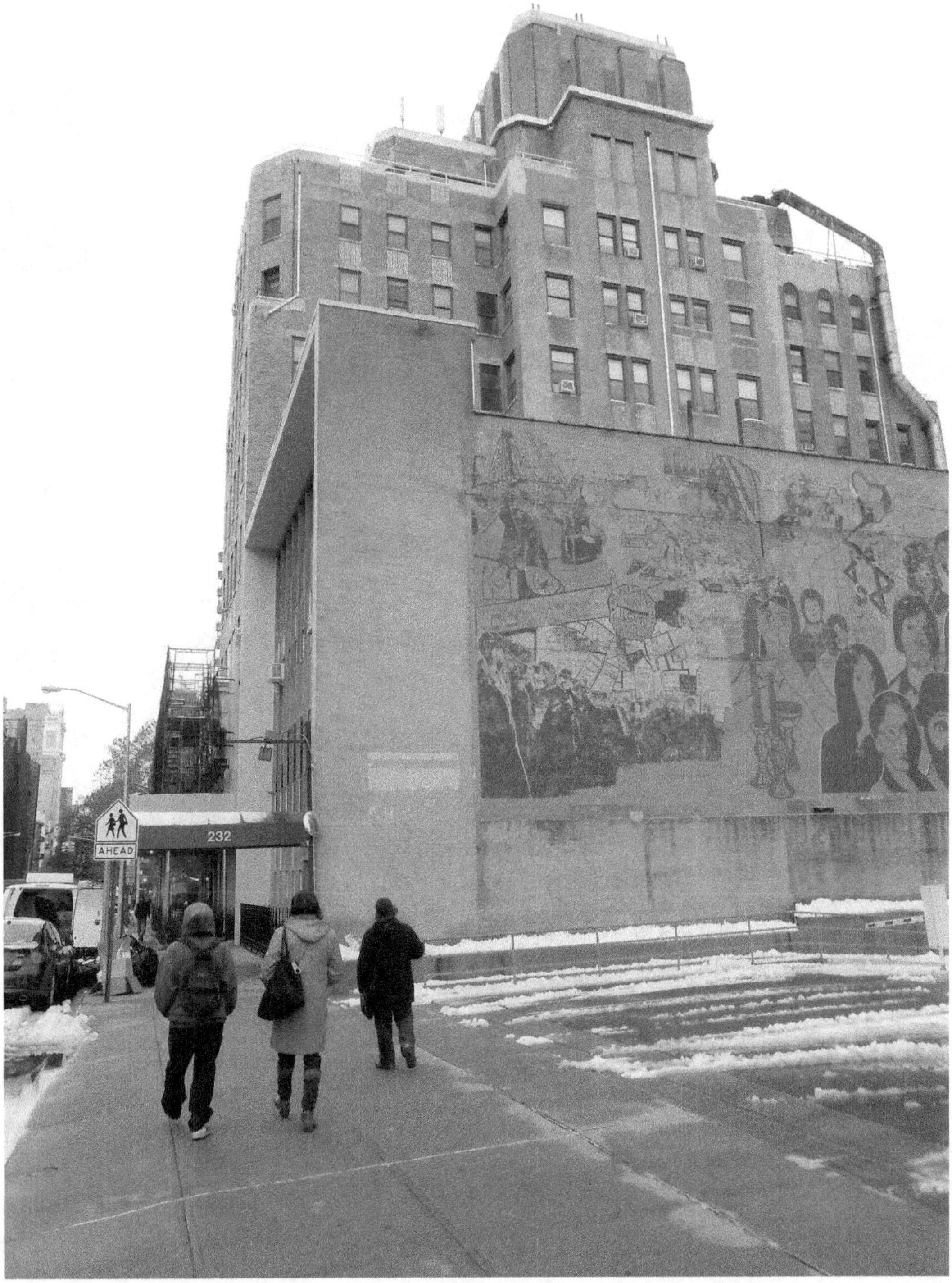

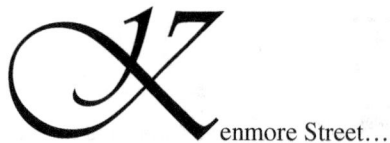

enmore Street…

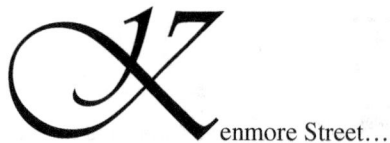

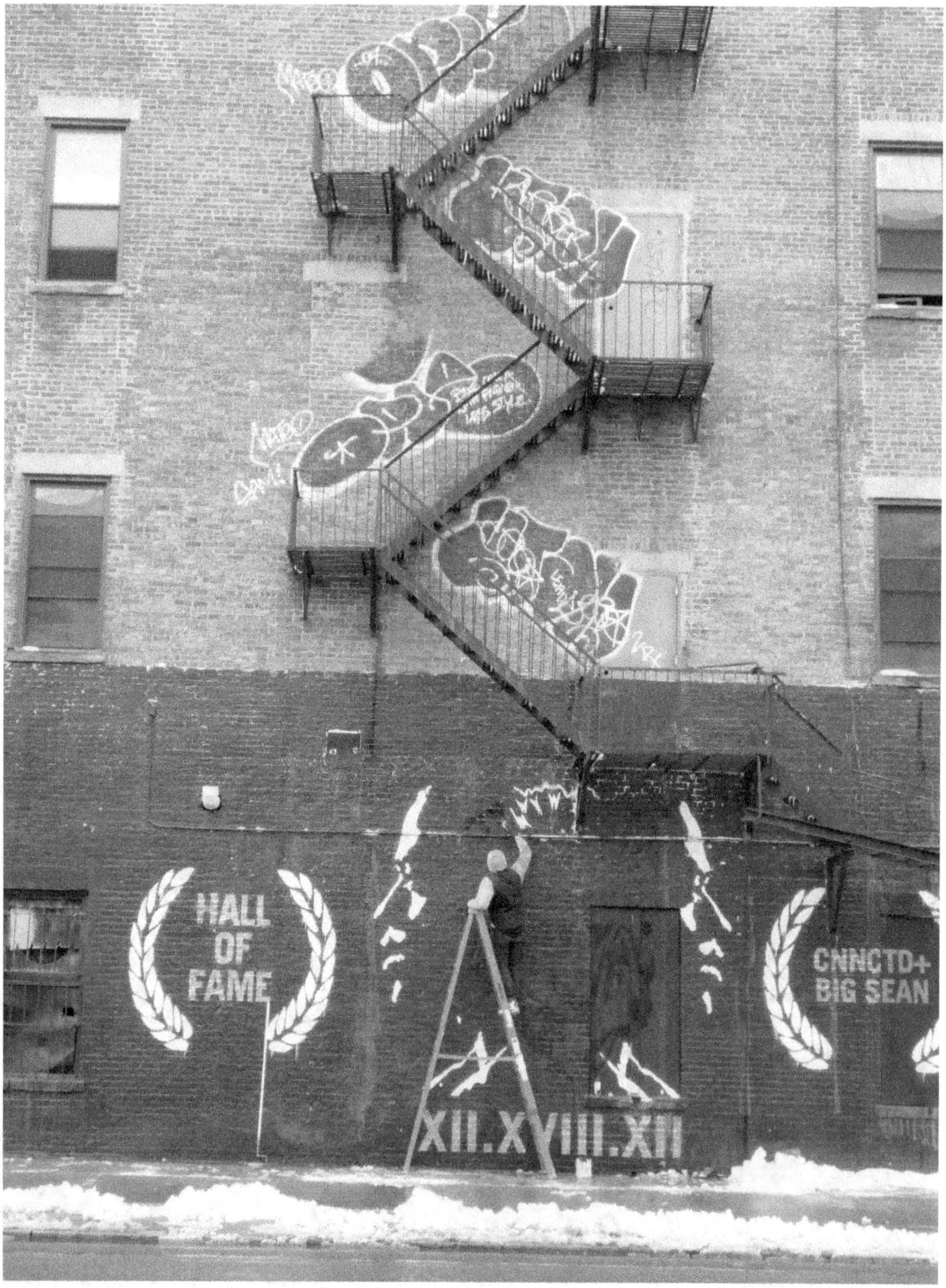

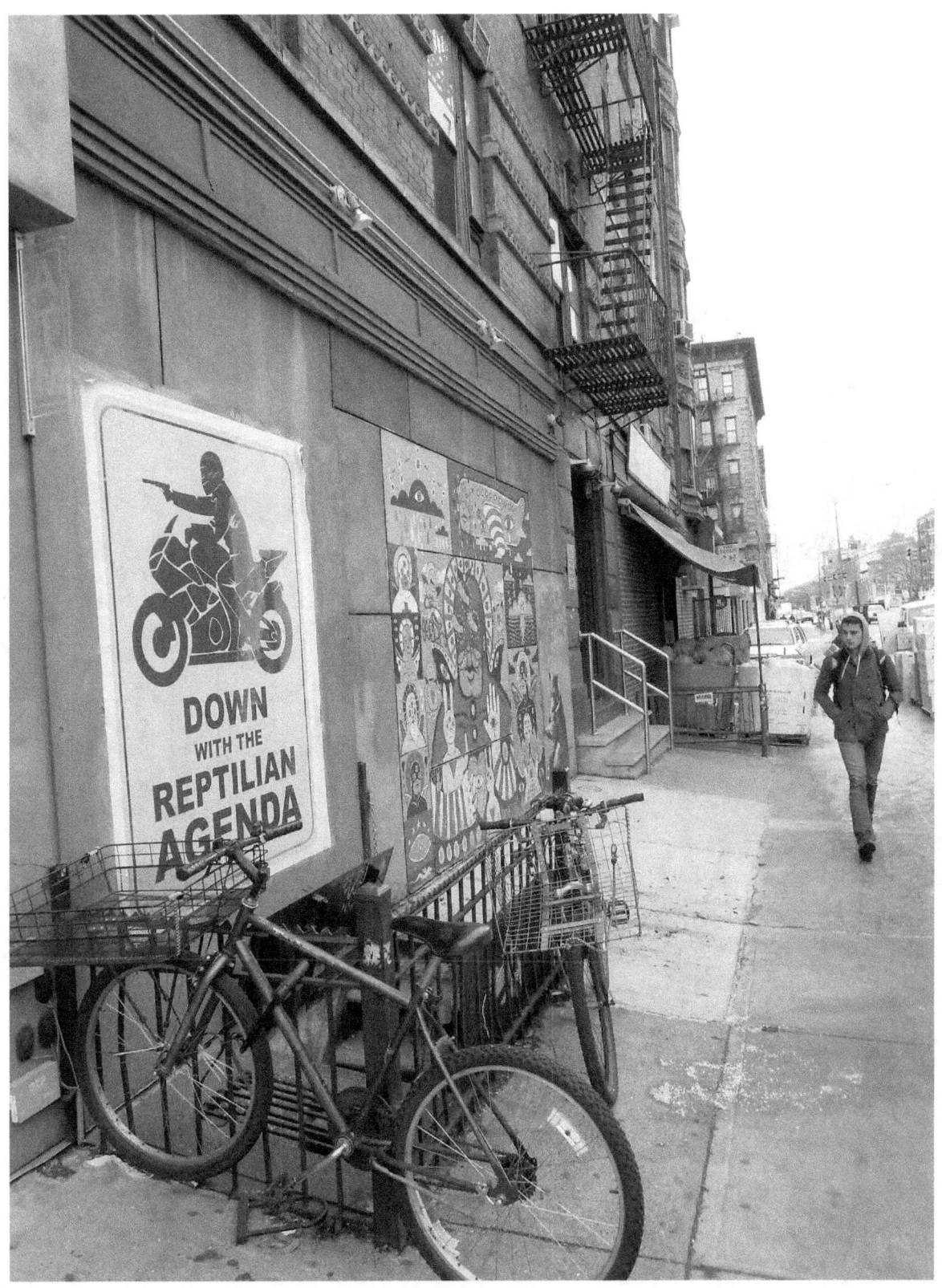

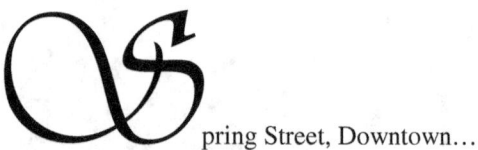pring Street, Downtown…

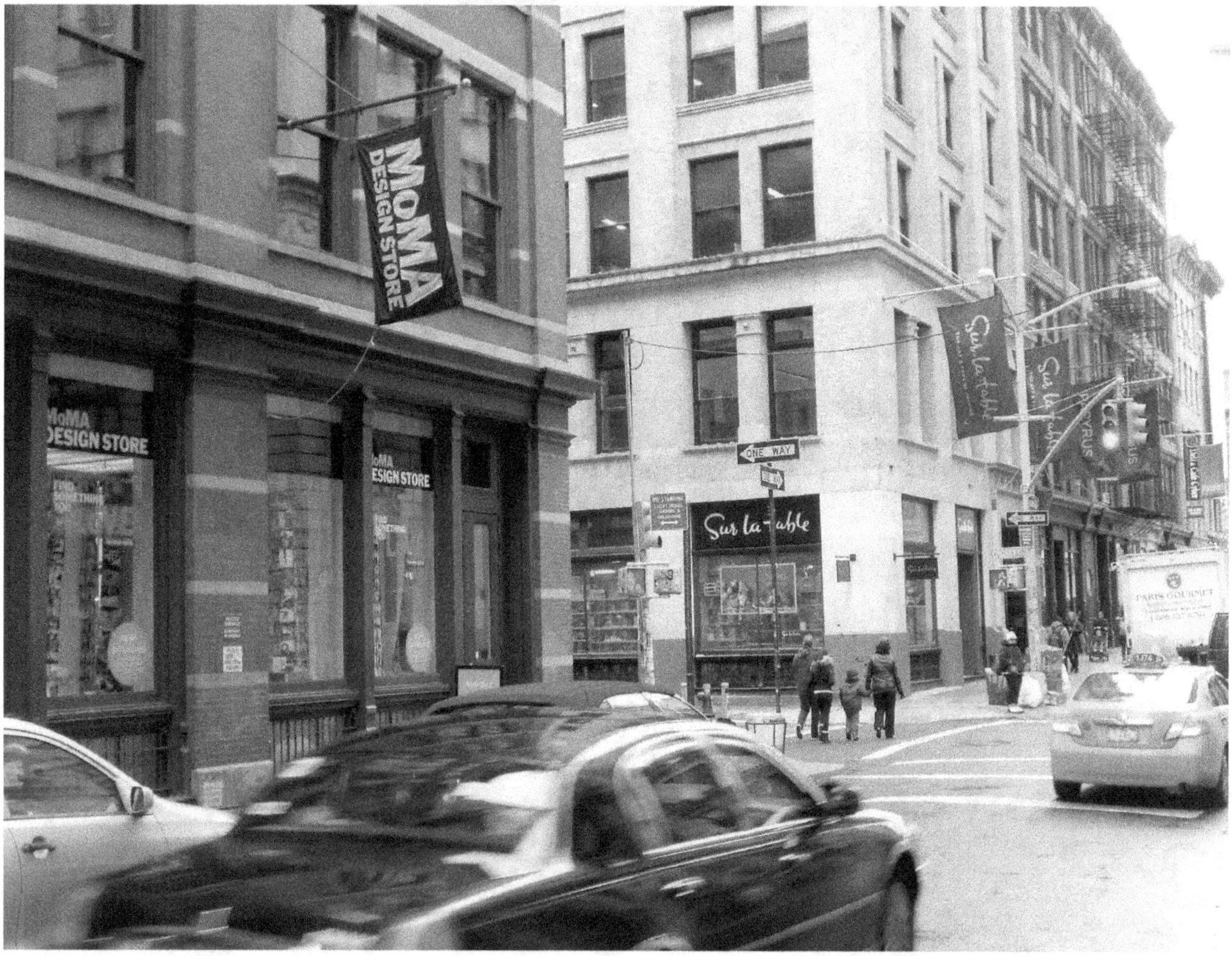

$\mathcal{M}$ercer Hotel at Mercer Street...

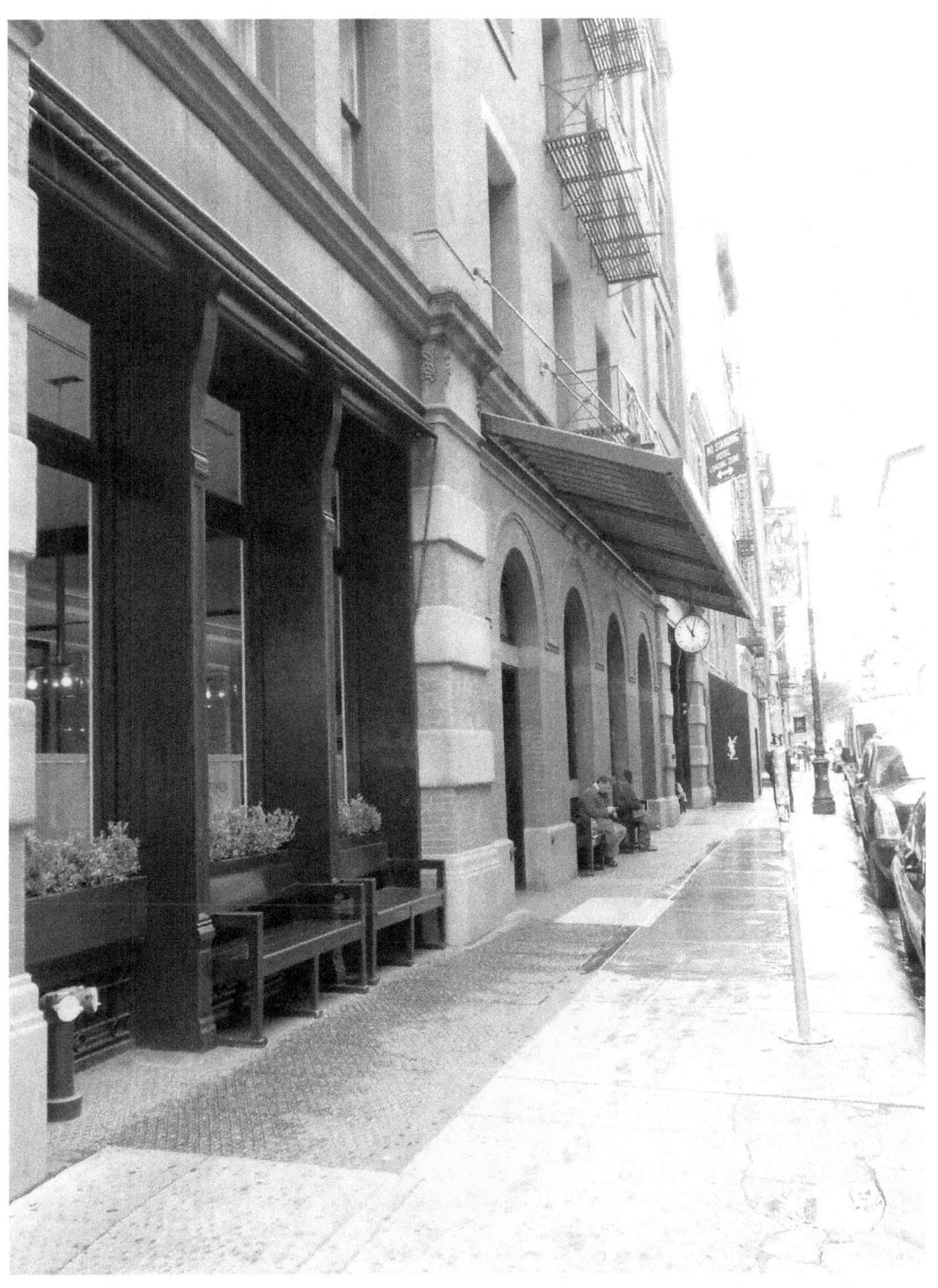

$\mathcal{M}$ercer & Prince Street...

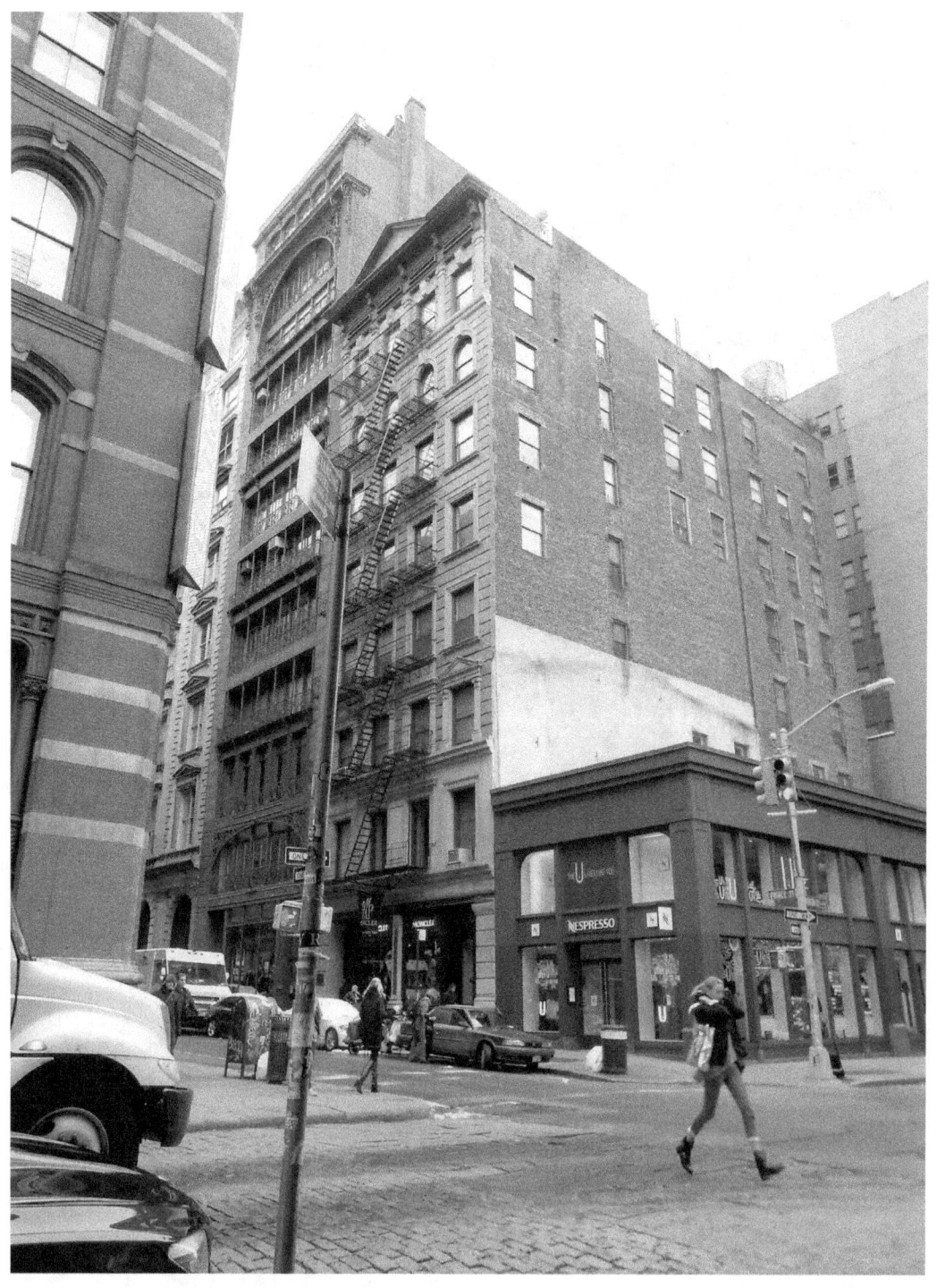

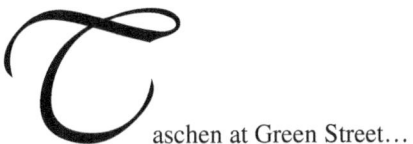 aschen at Green Street…

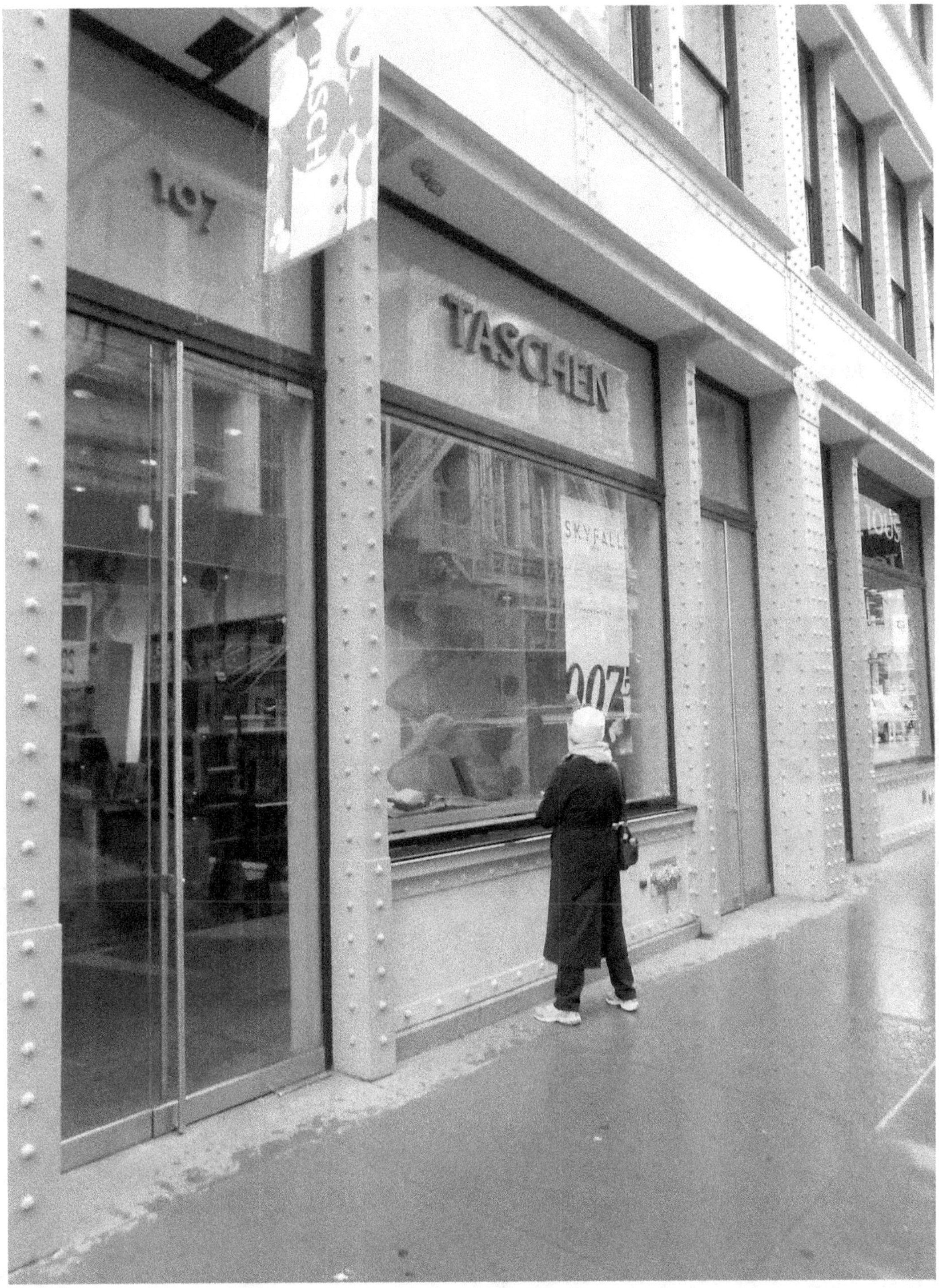

$\mathcal{C}$alvin Klein at Prince Street…

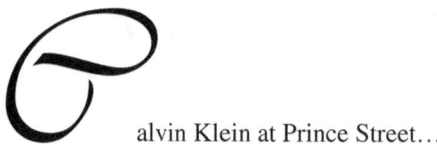

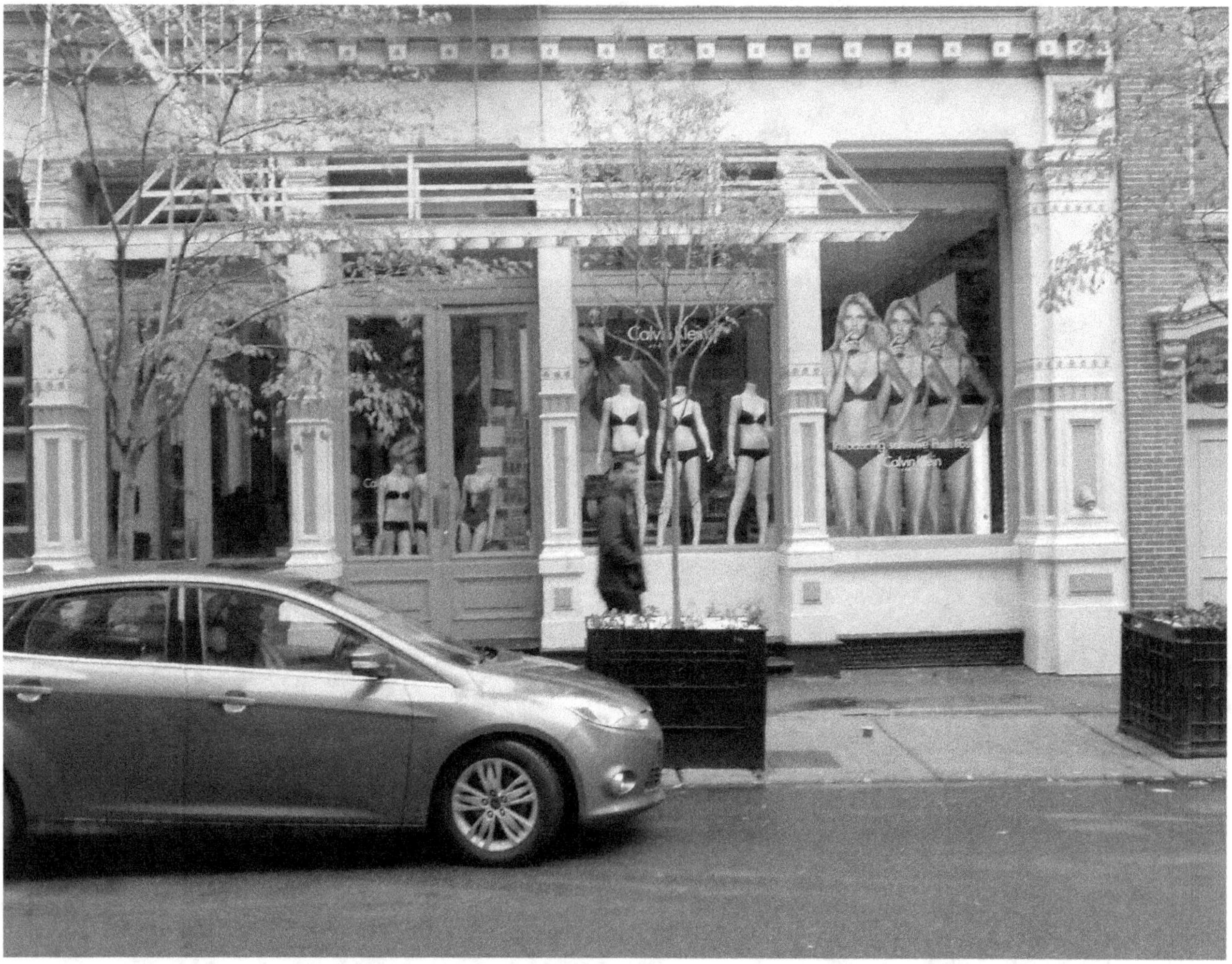

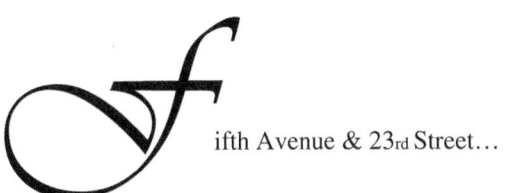

ifth Avenue & 23rd Street…

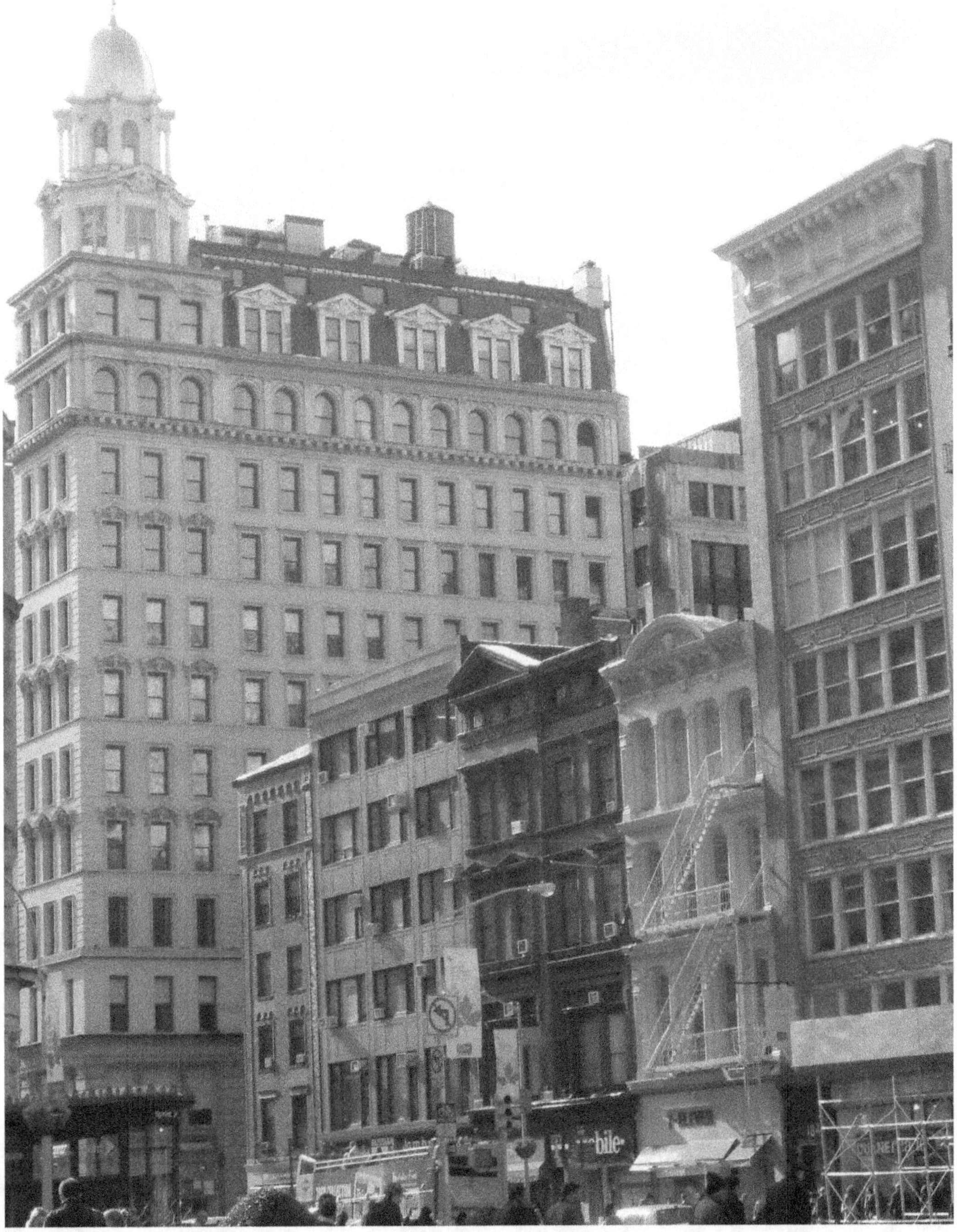

NEW YORK CITY

after sandy & before the end of the world

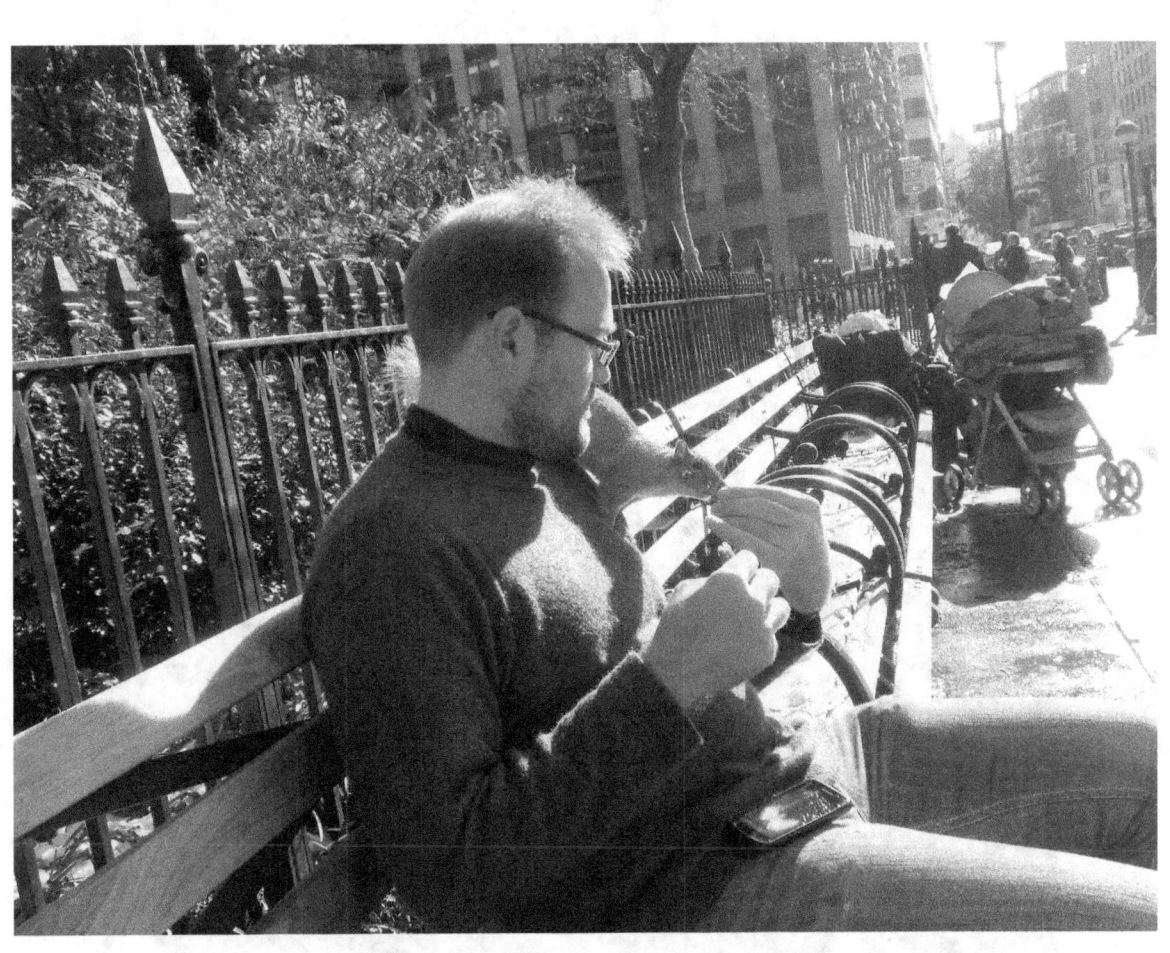

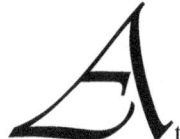t the northern end of Madison Square, on an island bordered by Broadway, 25th Street, and Fifth Avenue,

an obelisk designed by James G. Batterson stands. It was erected in 1857 over the tomb of General William Jenkins Worth who served in the Seminole Wars and the Mexican War. The city's Parks Department designated the area around the monument as a parklet called General Worth Square.

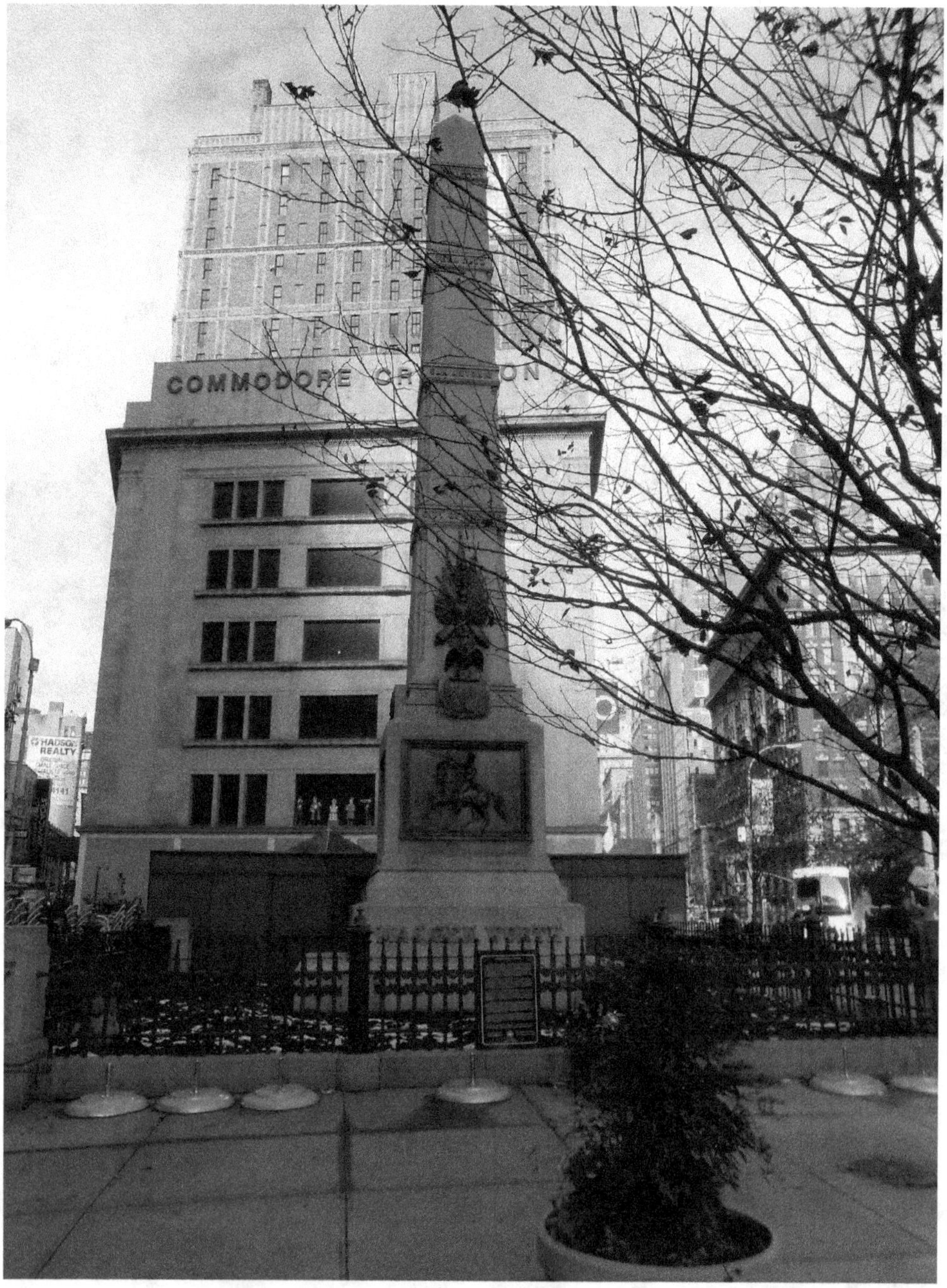

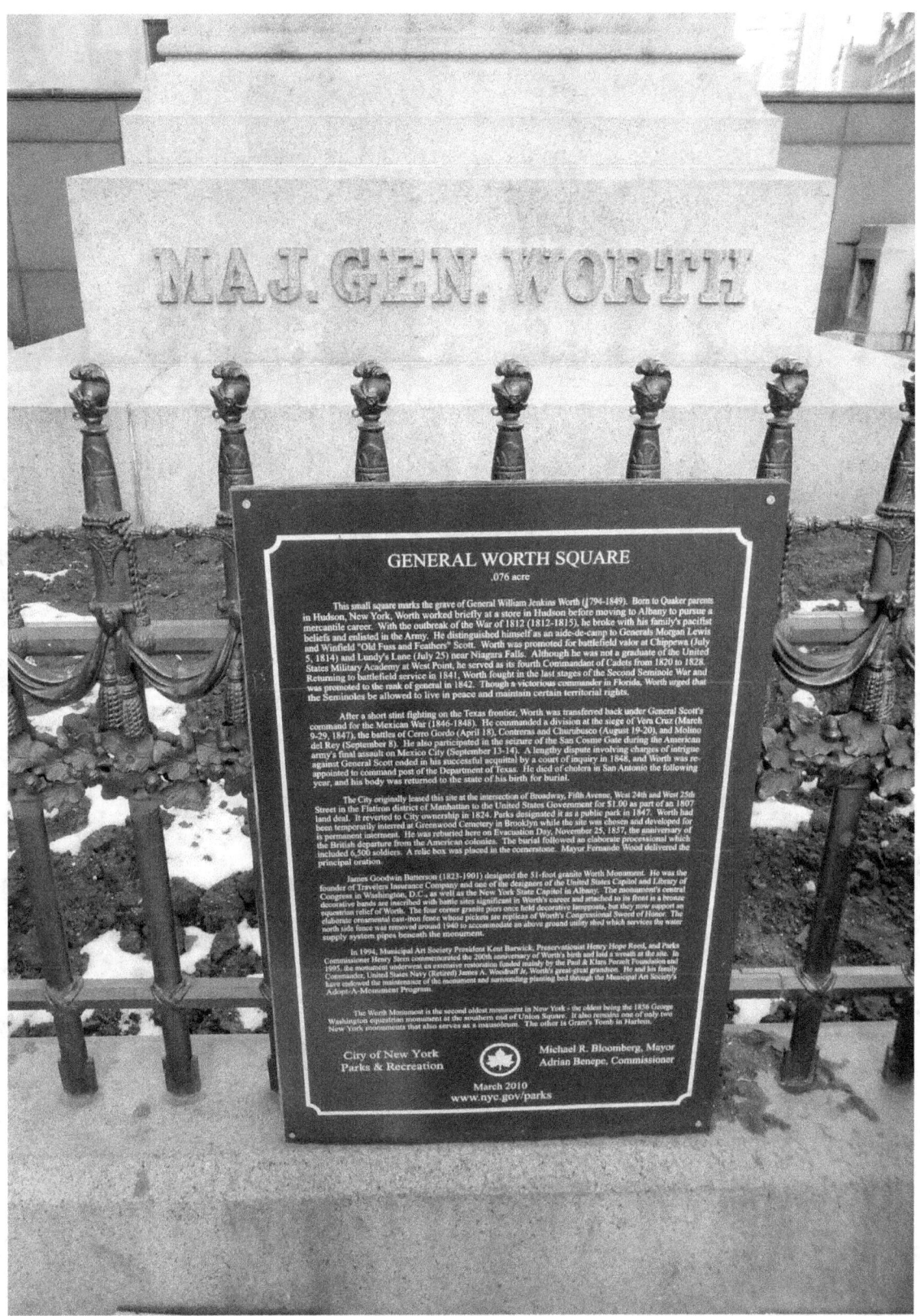

MAJ. GEN. WORTH

GENERAL WORTH SQUARE
.076 acre

This small square marks the grave of General William Jenkins Worth (1794-1849). Born to Quaker parents in Hudson, New York, Worth worked briefly at a store in Hudson before moving to Albany to pursue a mercantile career. With the outbreak of the War of 1812 (1812-1815), he broke with his family's pacifist beliefs and enlisted in the Army. He distinguished himself as an aide-de-camp to Generals Morgan Lewis and Winfield "Old Fuss and Feathers" Scott. Worth was promoted for battlefield valor at Chippewa (July 5, 1814) and Lundy's Lane (July 25) near Niagara Falls. Although he was not a graduate of the United States Military Academy at West Point, he served as its fourth Commandant of Cadets from 1820 to 1828. Returning to battlefield service in 1841, Worth fought in the last stages of the Second Seminole War and was promoted to the rank of general in 1842. Though a victorious commander in Florida, Worth urged that the Seminoles be allowed to live in peace and maintain certain territorial rights.

After a short stint fighting on the Texas frontier, Worth was transferred back under General Scott's command for the Mexican War (1846-1848). He commanded a division at the siege of Vera Cruz (March 9-29, 1847), the battles of Cerro Gordo (April 18), Contreras and Churubusco (August 19-20), and Molino del Rey (September 8). He also participated in the seizure of the San Cosme Gate during the American army's final assault on Mexico City (September 13-14). A lengthy dispute involving charges of intrigue against General Scott ended in his successful acquittal by a court of inquiry in 1848, and Worth was re-appointed to command post of the Department of Texas. He died of cholera in San Antonio the following year, and his body was returned to the state of his birth for burial.

The City originally leased this site at the intersection of Broadway, Fifth Avenue, West 24th and West 25th Street in the Flatiron district of Manhattan to the United States Government for $1.00 as part of an 1807 land deal. It reverted to City ownership in 1824. Parks designated it as a public park in 1847. Worth had been temporarily interred at Greenwood Cemetery in Brooklyn while the site was chosen and developed for his permanent interment. He was reburied here on Evacuation Day, November 25, 1857, the anniversary of the British departure from the American colonies. The burial followed an elaborate processional which included 6,500 soldiers. A relic box was placed in the cornerstone. Mayor Fernando Wood delivered the principal oration.

James Goodwin Batterson (1823-1901) designed the 51-foot granite Worth Monument. He was the founder of Travelers Insurance Company and one of the designers of the United States Capitol and Library of Congress in Washington, D.C., as well as the New York State Capitol in Albany. The monument's central decorative bands are inscribed with battle sites significant in Worth's career and attached to its front is a bronze equestrian relief of Worth. The four corner granite piers once held decorative lampposts, but they now support an elaborate ornamental cast-iron fence whose pickets are replicas of Worth's Congressional Sword of Honor. The north side fence was removed around 1940 to accommodate an above ground utility shed which services the water supply system pipes beneath the monument.

In 1994, Municipal Art Society President Kent Barwick, Preservationist Henry Hope Reed, and Parks Commissioner Henry Stern commemorated the 200th anniversary of Worth's birth and laid a wreath at the site. In 1995, the monument underwent an extensive restoration funded mainly by the Paul & Klara Porzelt Foundation and Commander, United States Navy (Retired) James A. Woodruff Jr., Worth's great-great grandson. He and his family have endowed the maintenance of the monument and surrounding planting bed through the Municipal Art Society's Adopt-A-Monument Program.

The Worth Monument is the second oldest monument in New York - the oldest being the 1856 George Washington equestrian monument at the southern end of Union Square. It also remains one of only two New York monuments that also serves as a mausoleum. The other is Grant's Tomb in Harlem.

City of New York
Parks & Recreation

Michael R. Bloomberg, Mayor
Adrian Benepe, Commissioner

March 2010
www.nyc.gov/parks

$\mathcal{M}$useum of Sex, 233 Fifth Avenue…

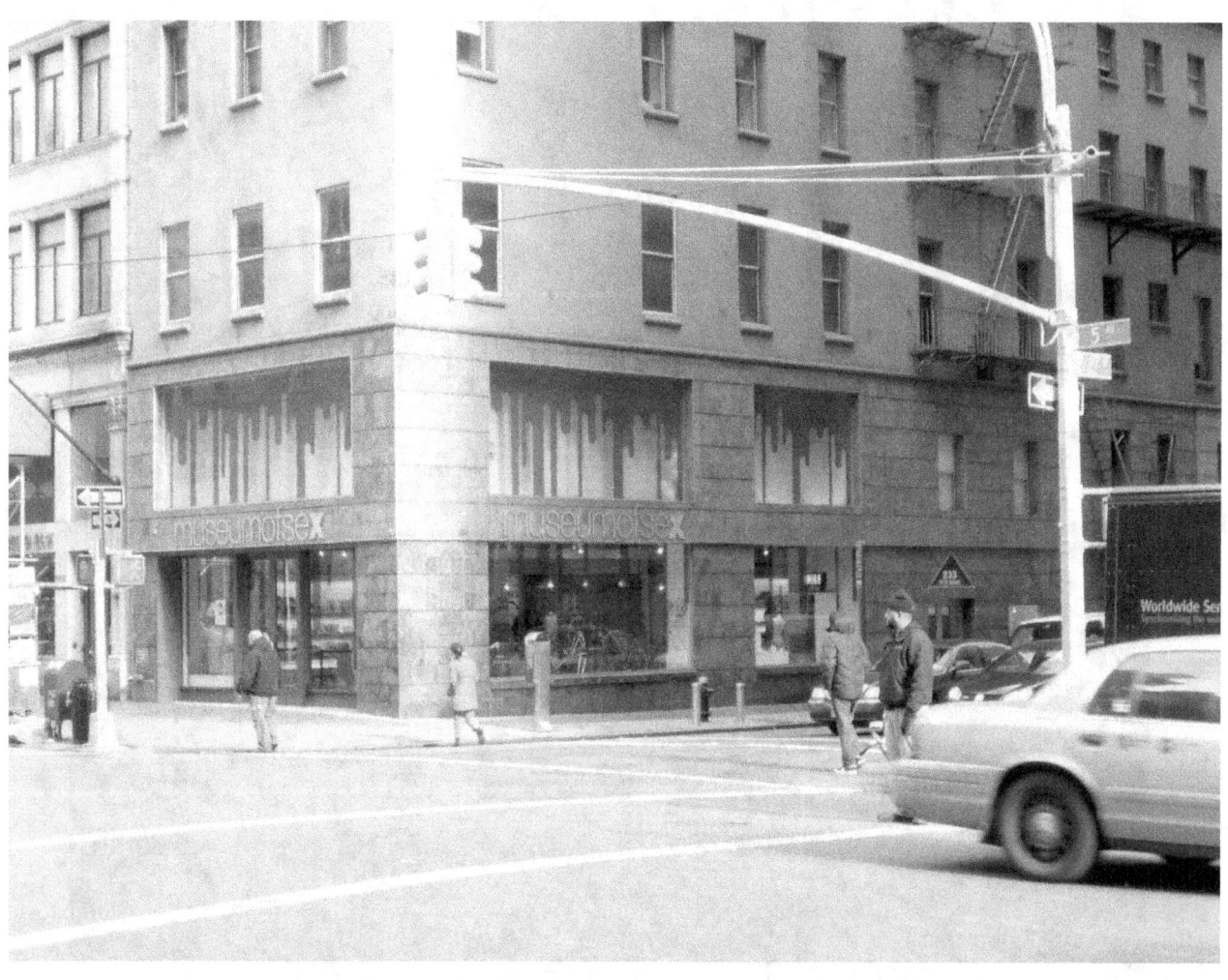

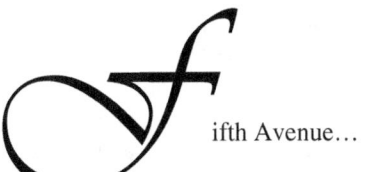

ifth Avenue…

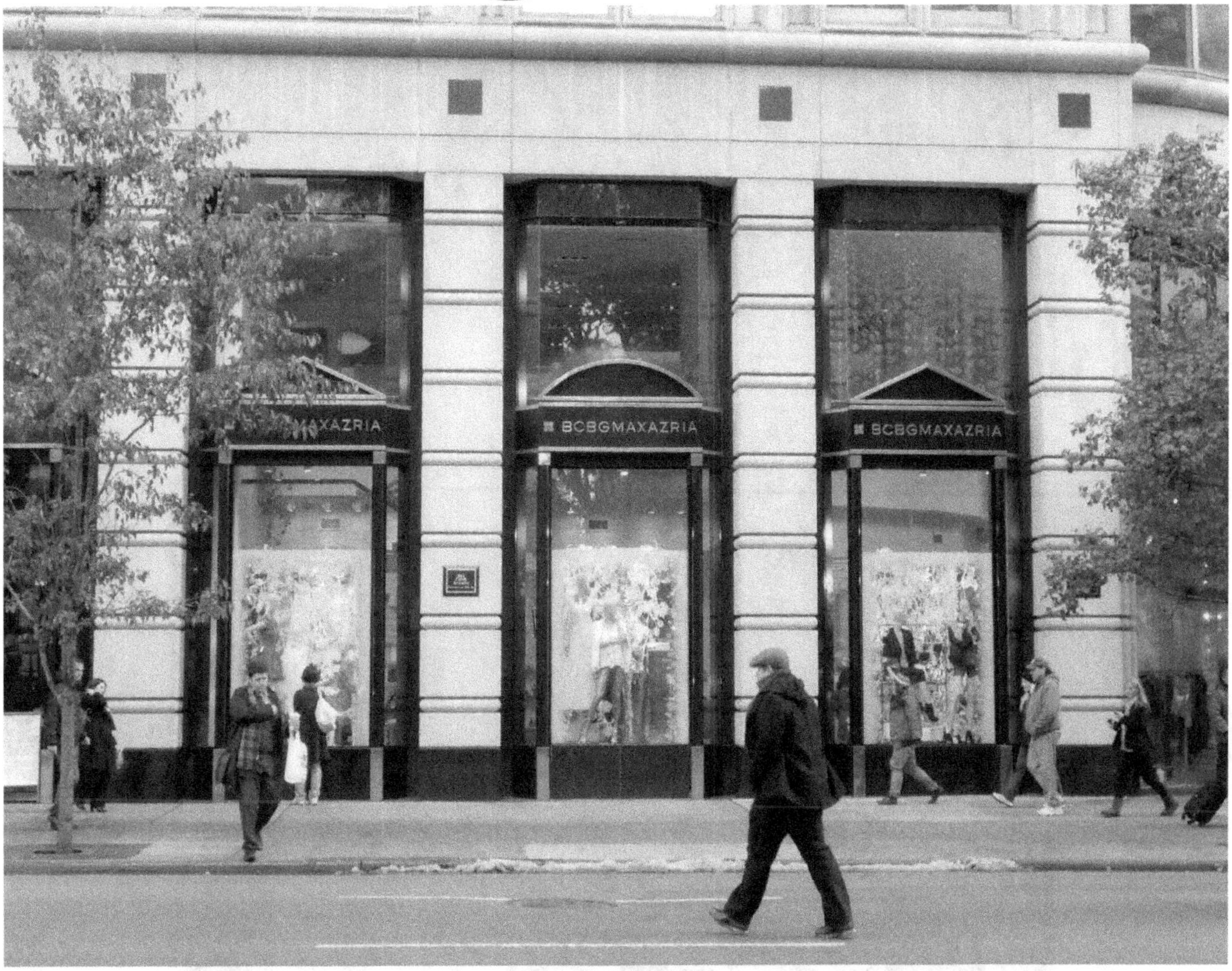

*T*he Marble Collegiate Church was founded in 1628 and is one of the oldest continuous Protestant congregations in North America. The congregation, which is part of the Reformed Church in America, is now located at 272 Fifth Avenue at the corner of West 29th Street in the NoMad neighborhood of Manhattan. It was designed by Samuel A. Warner in Romanesque Revival style with Gothic trim and built in 1851-54. The facade is covered in Tuckahoe marble for which the church, originally called the Fifth Avenue Church, in 1906 was renamed. The building was designated a New York City landmark in 1967, and in 1980 was added to the National Register of Historic Places.

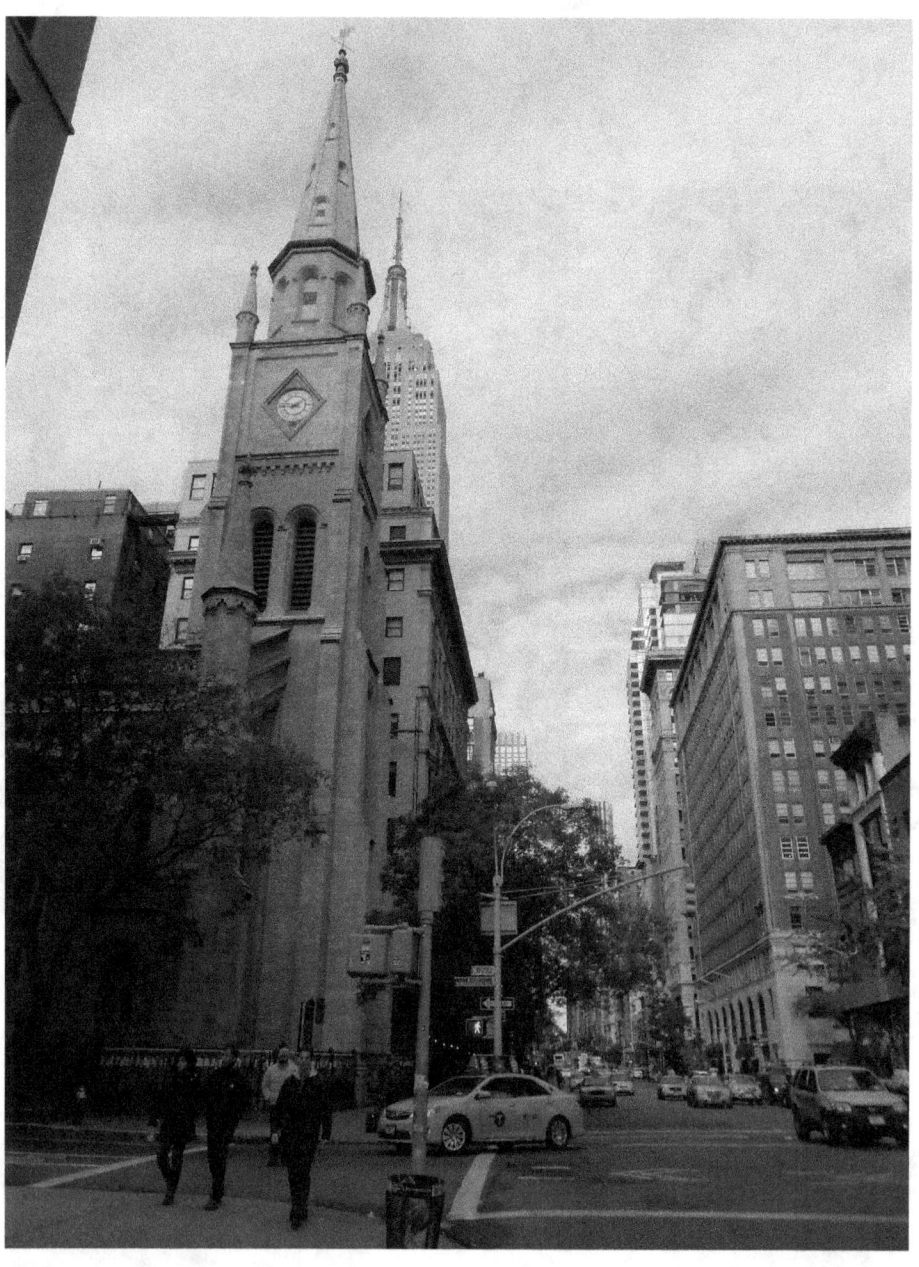

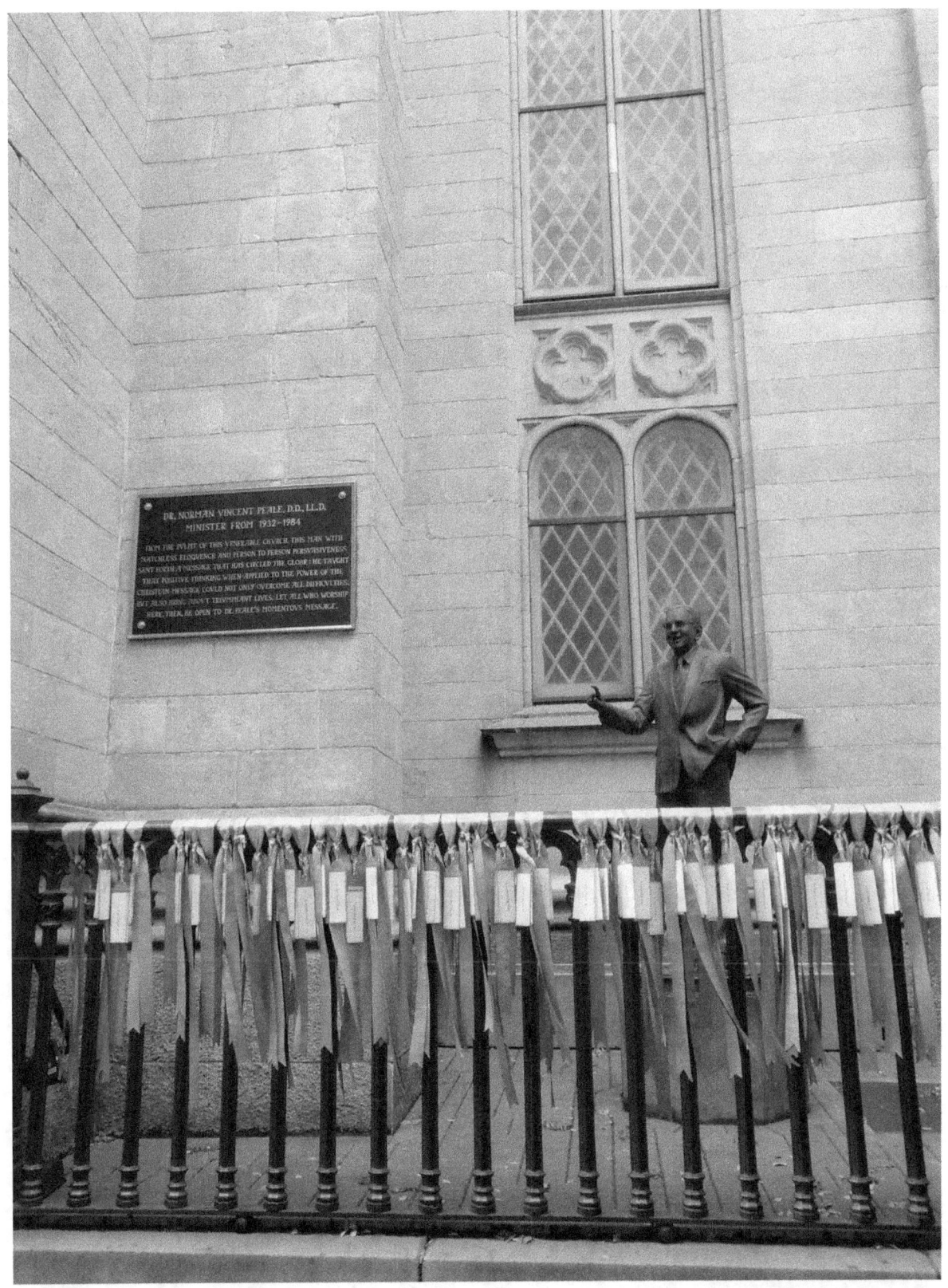

*T*he Empire State Building is a 102-story skyscraper located in Midtown Manhattan, at the intersection of Fifth Avenue and West 34th Street. It has a roof height of 1,250 feet, and with its antenna spire included, it stands a total of 1,454 feet high. The name is derived from the nickname for New York, the Empire State. For 40 years, from its completion in 1931 until construction of the World Trade Center's North Tower in 1972, it stood as the world's tallest building. Following the September 11 attacks in 2001, the Empire State Building was again the tallest building in New York. However, it was no longer the tallest in the U.S. or the world. Currently, the Empire State Building is the third tallest skyscraper in the United States after the Willis Tower and Trump International Hotel and Tower, both in Chicago, and the 15th-tallest in the world. It is also the fourth-tallest freestanding structure in the Americas.

The Empire State Building is designed in the distinctive Art Deco style and has been named as one of the Seven Wonders of the Modern World by the American Society of Civil Engineers. The building and its street floor interior are designated landmarks of the New York City Landmarks Preservation Commission. It was designated as a National Historic Landmark in 1986. In 2007, according to the AIA it was ranked number one on the List of America's Favorite Architecture.

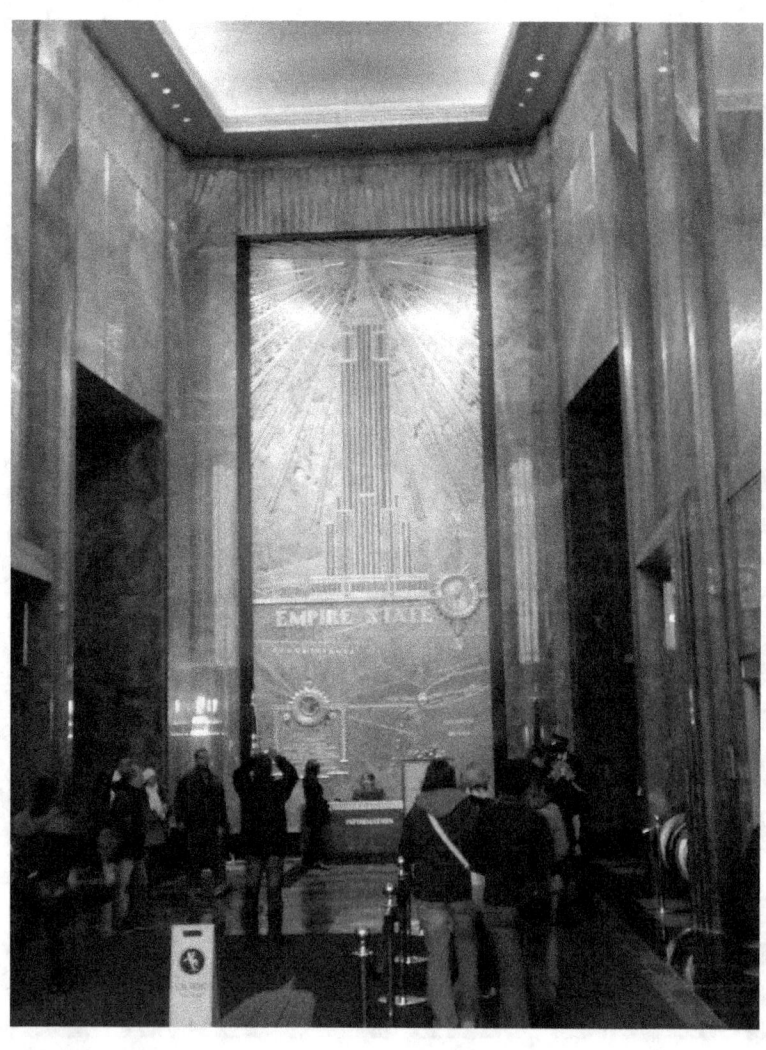

ounder Juliette Gordon Low organized the first Girl Scout Troop on March 12, 1912, in Savannah,

Ga. Girl Scouts of the USA was chartered by the U.S. Congress on March 16, 1950. Today, there are 3.2 million Girl Scouts — 2.3 million girl members and 890,000 adult members working primarily as volunteers. The Girl Scouts of the USA national headquarters located in New York City at 420 Fifth Avenue.

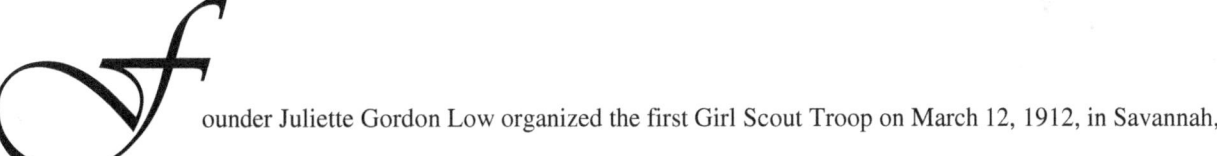

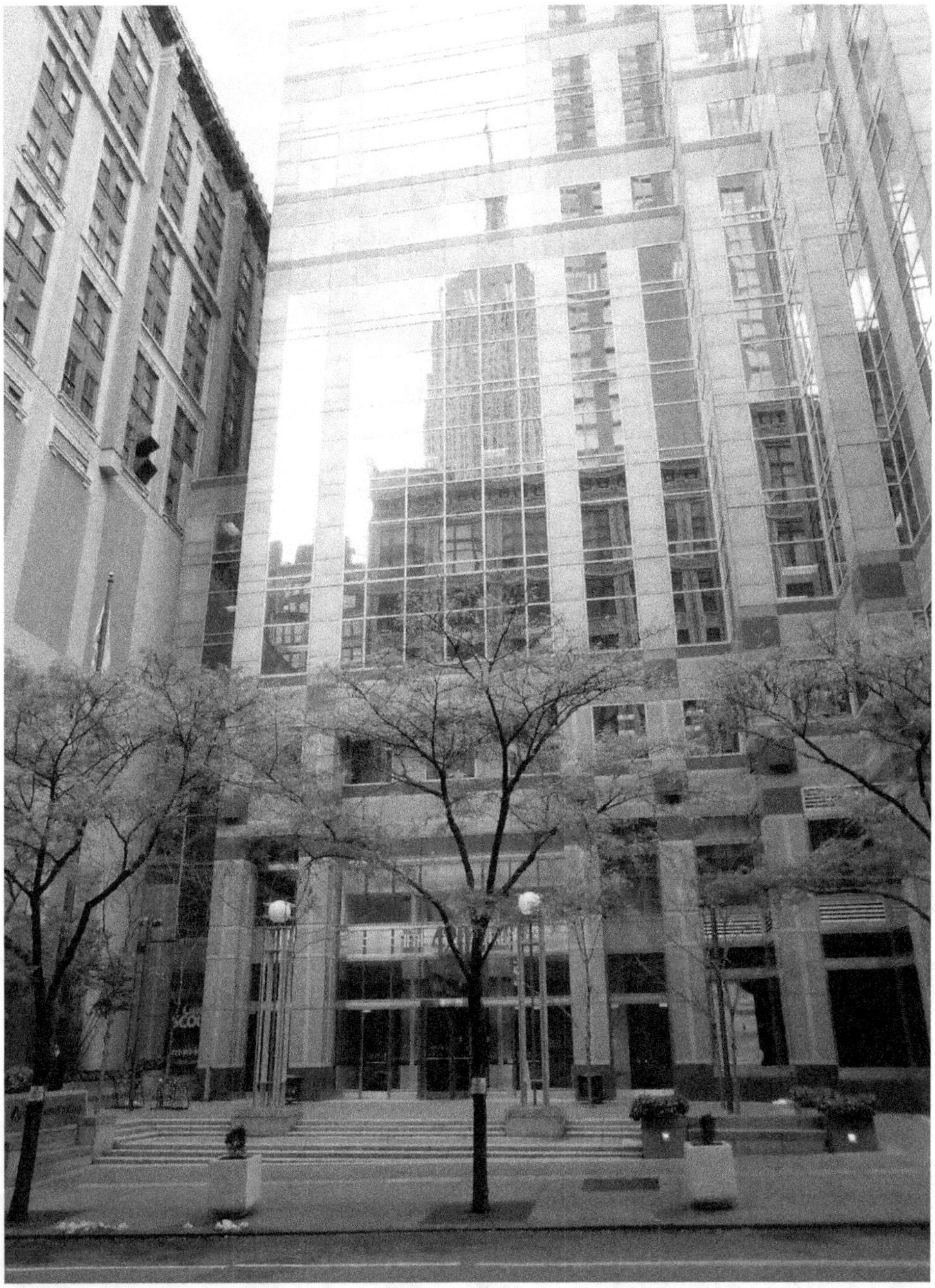

$\mathcal{OS}$tephen A. Schwarzman Building is part of The New York Public Library, which consists of four major research libraries and 87 branch libraries located in the Bronx, Manhattan, and Staten Island. It is located at Fifth Avenue at 42nd Street and is renowned for the comprehensiveness of its historical collections. It houses some 15 million items, including medieval manuscripts, ancient Japanese scrolls, contemporary novels and poetry, baseball cards, dime novels, and comic books and provides free and equal access to its resources and facilities.

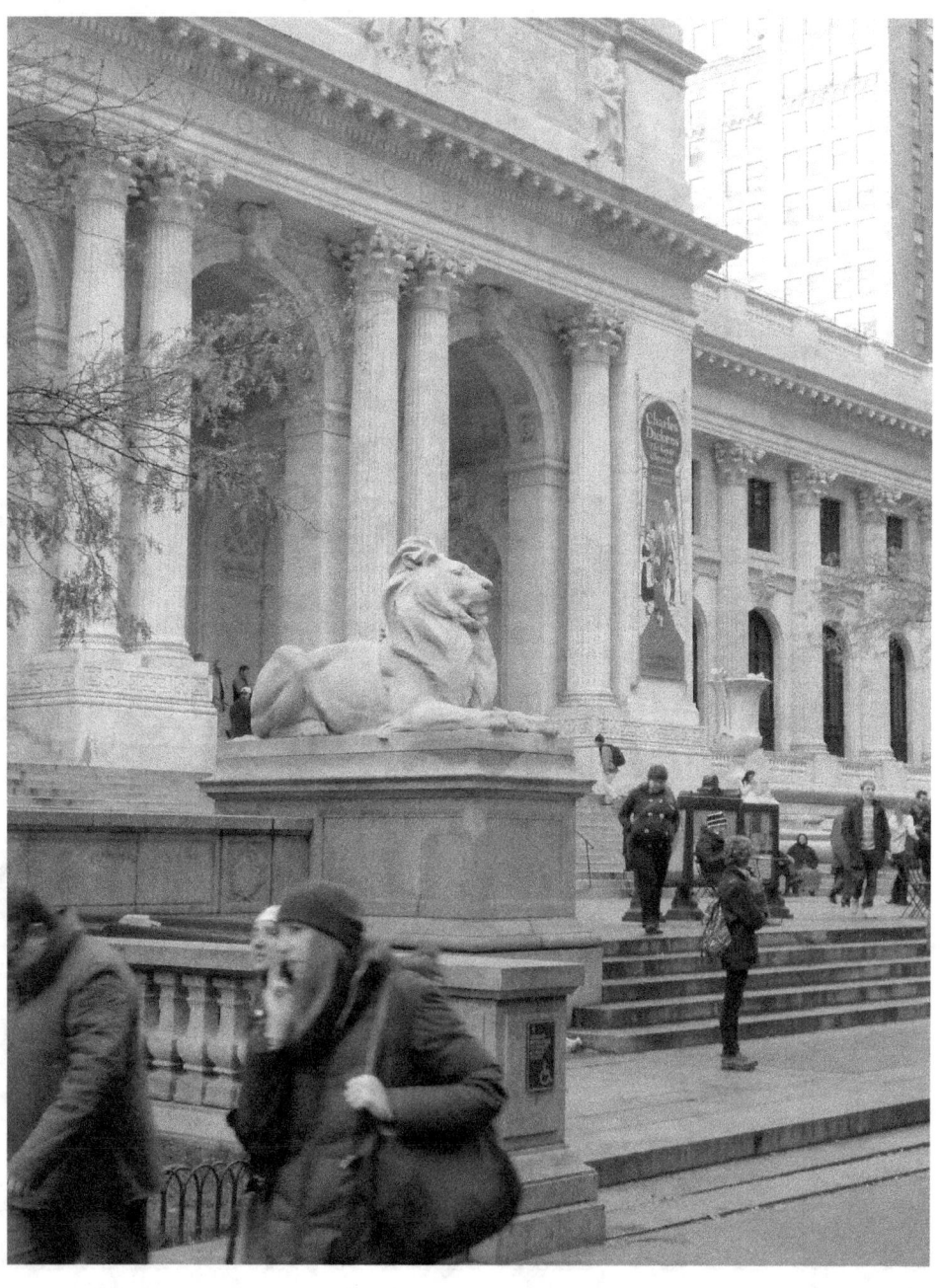

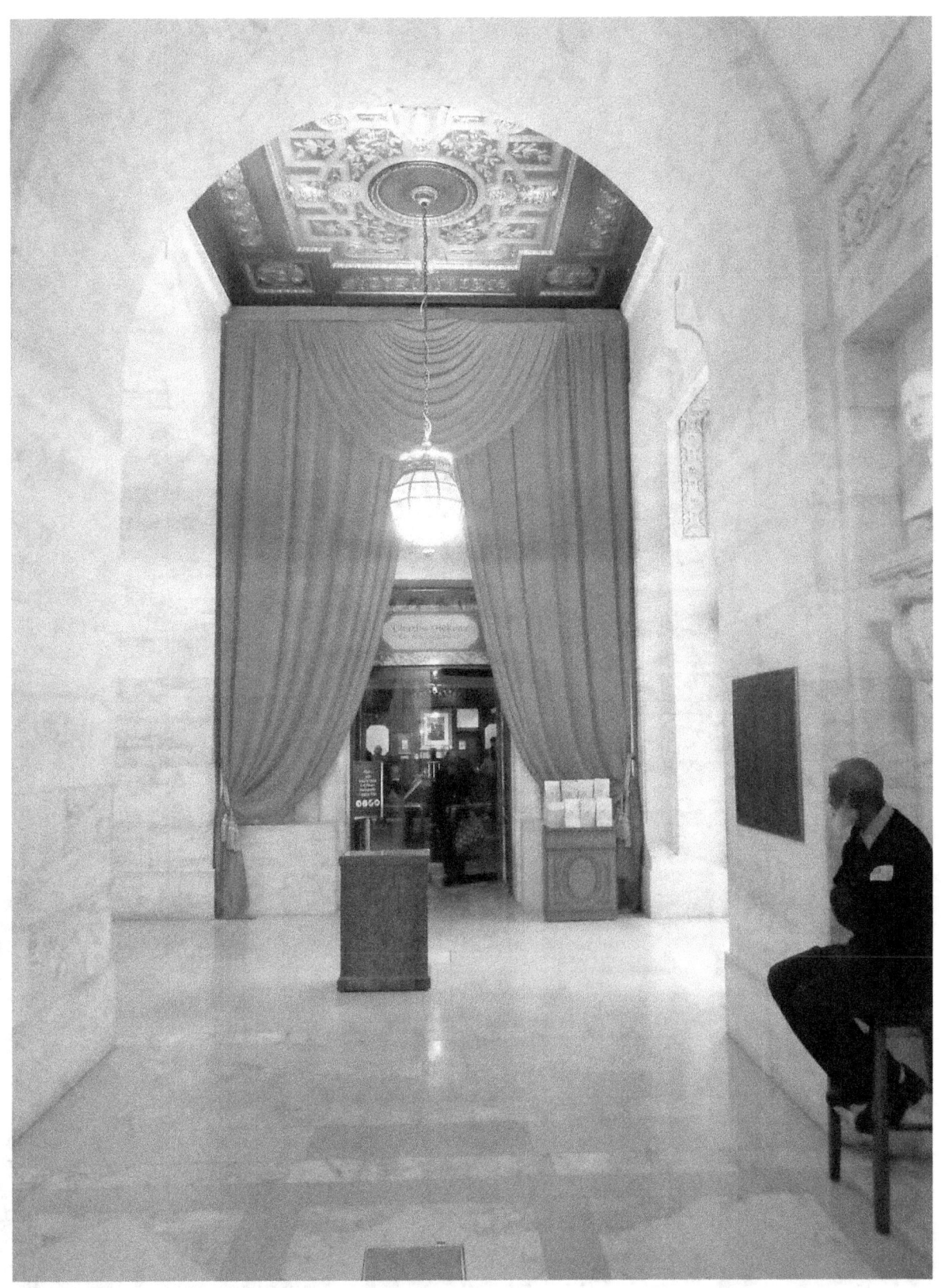

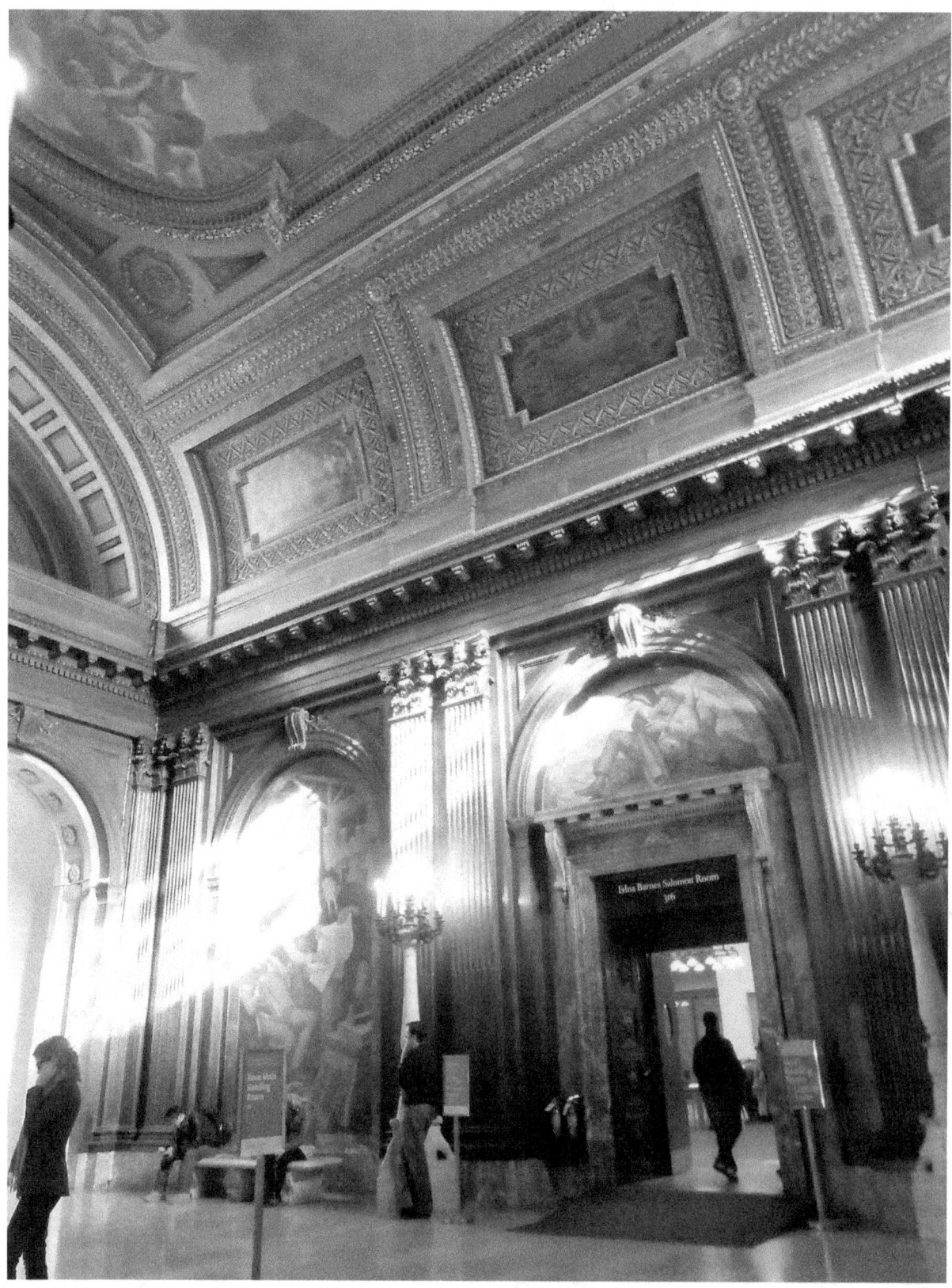

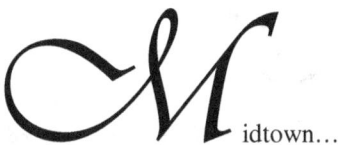

idtown…

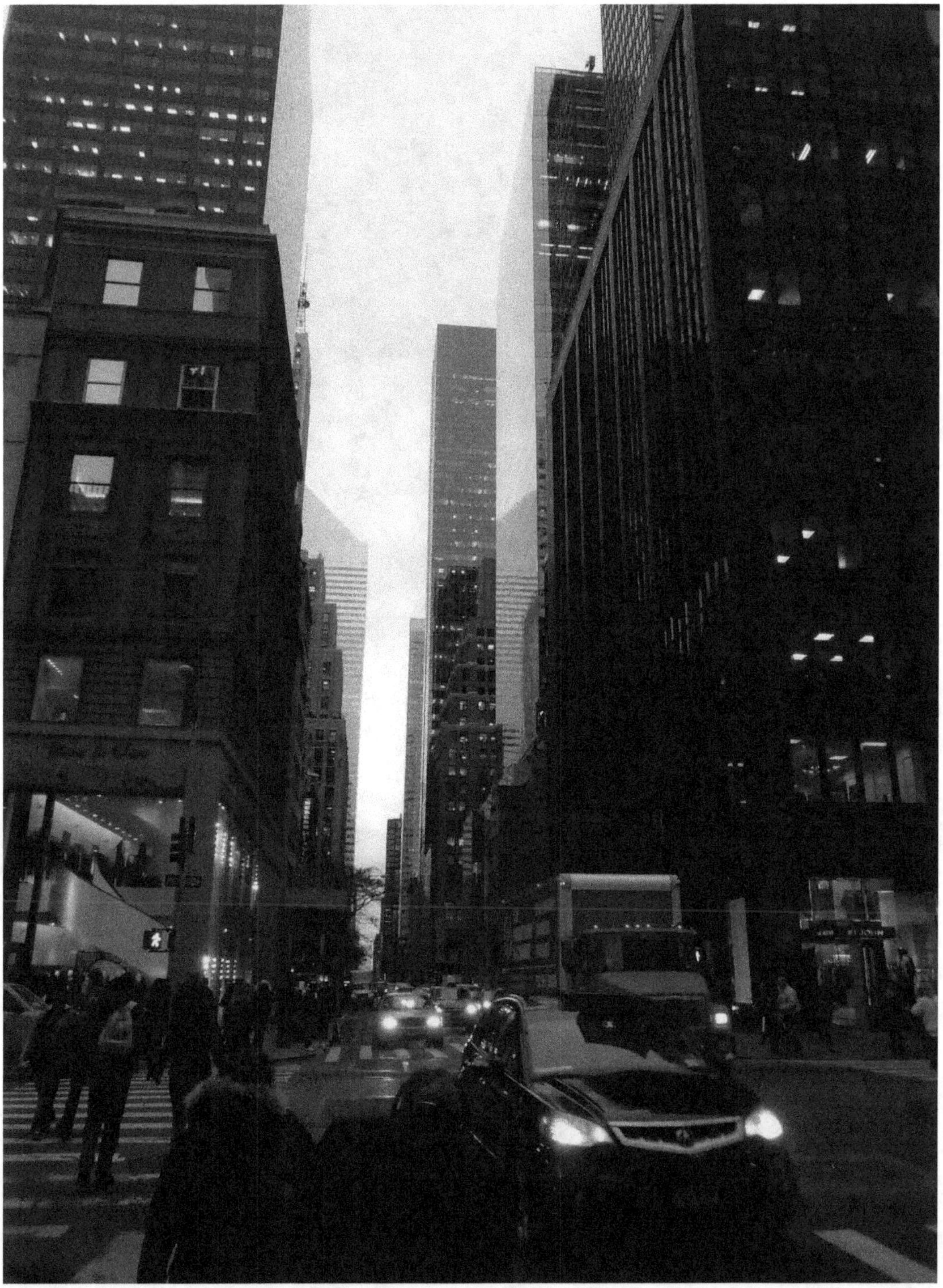

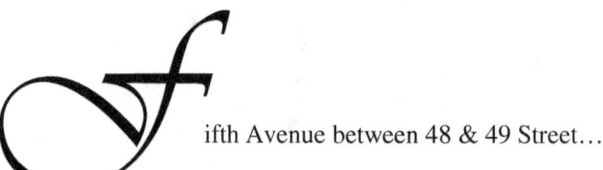 ifth Avenue between 48 & 49 Street…

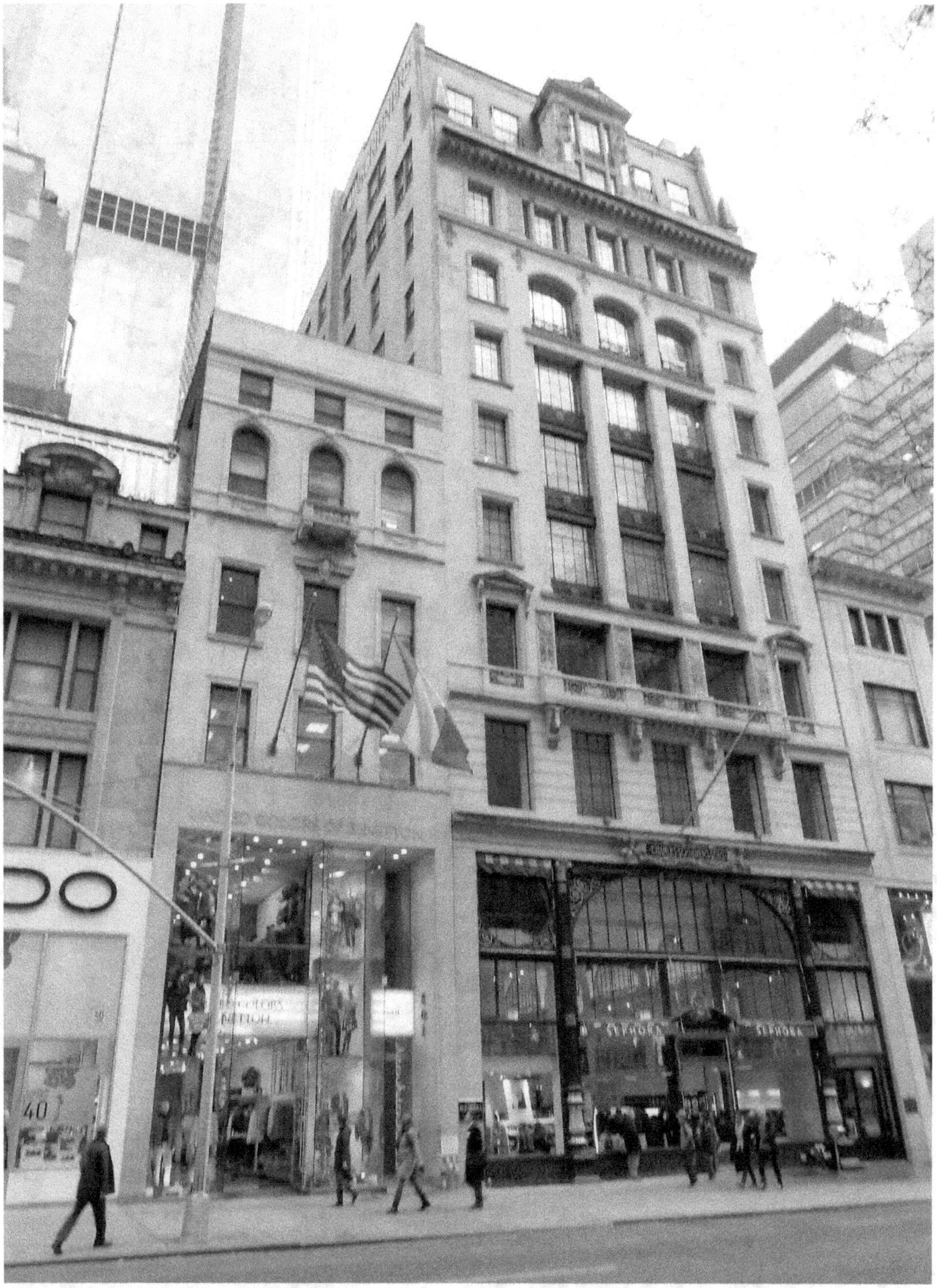

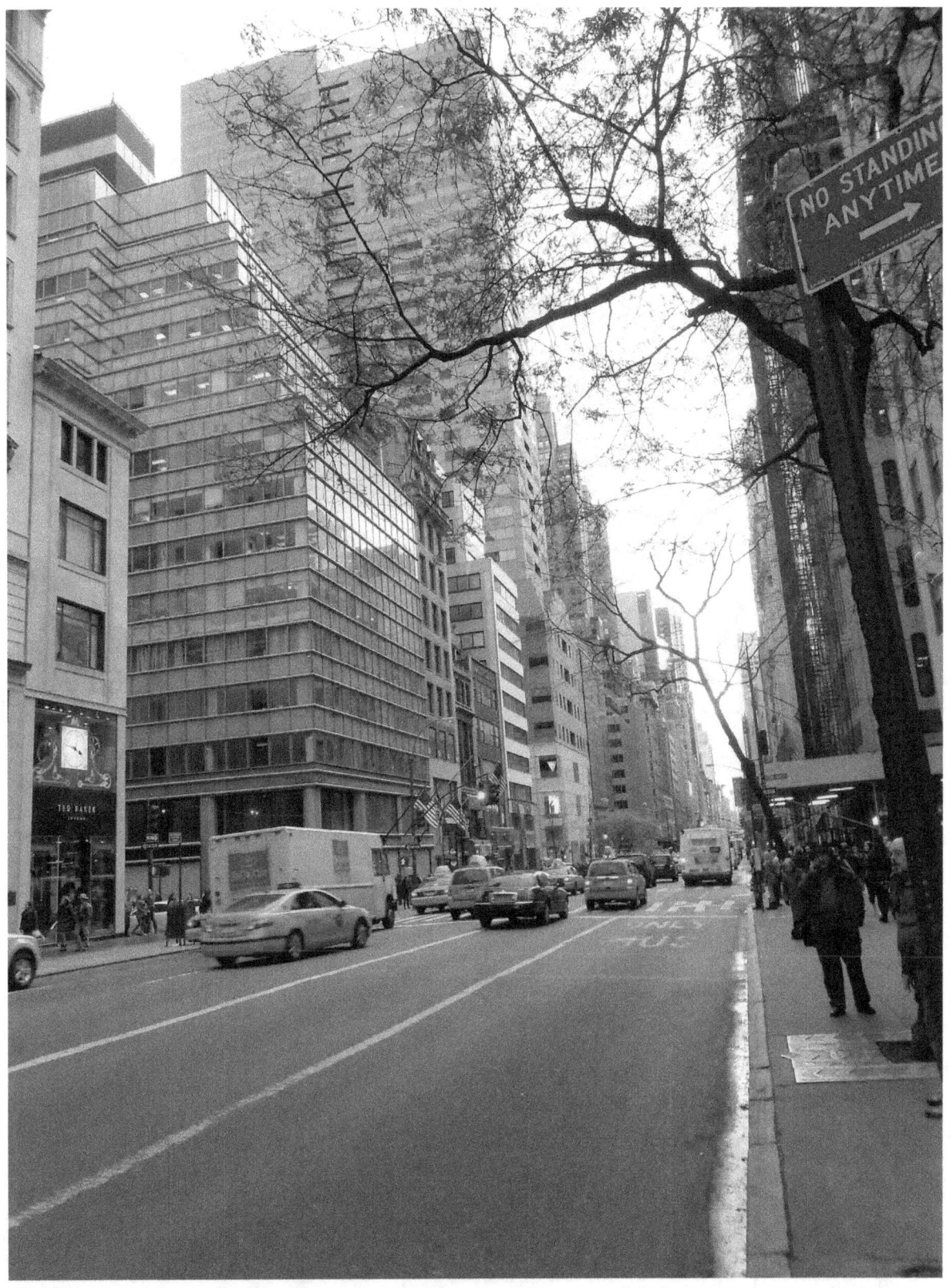

ℳichael Kors, Fifth Avenue…

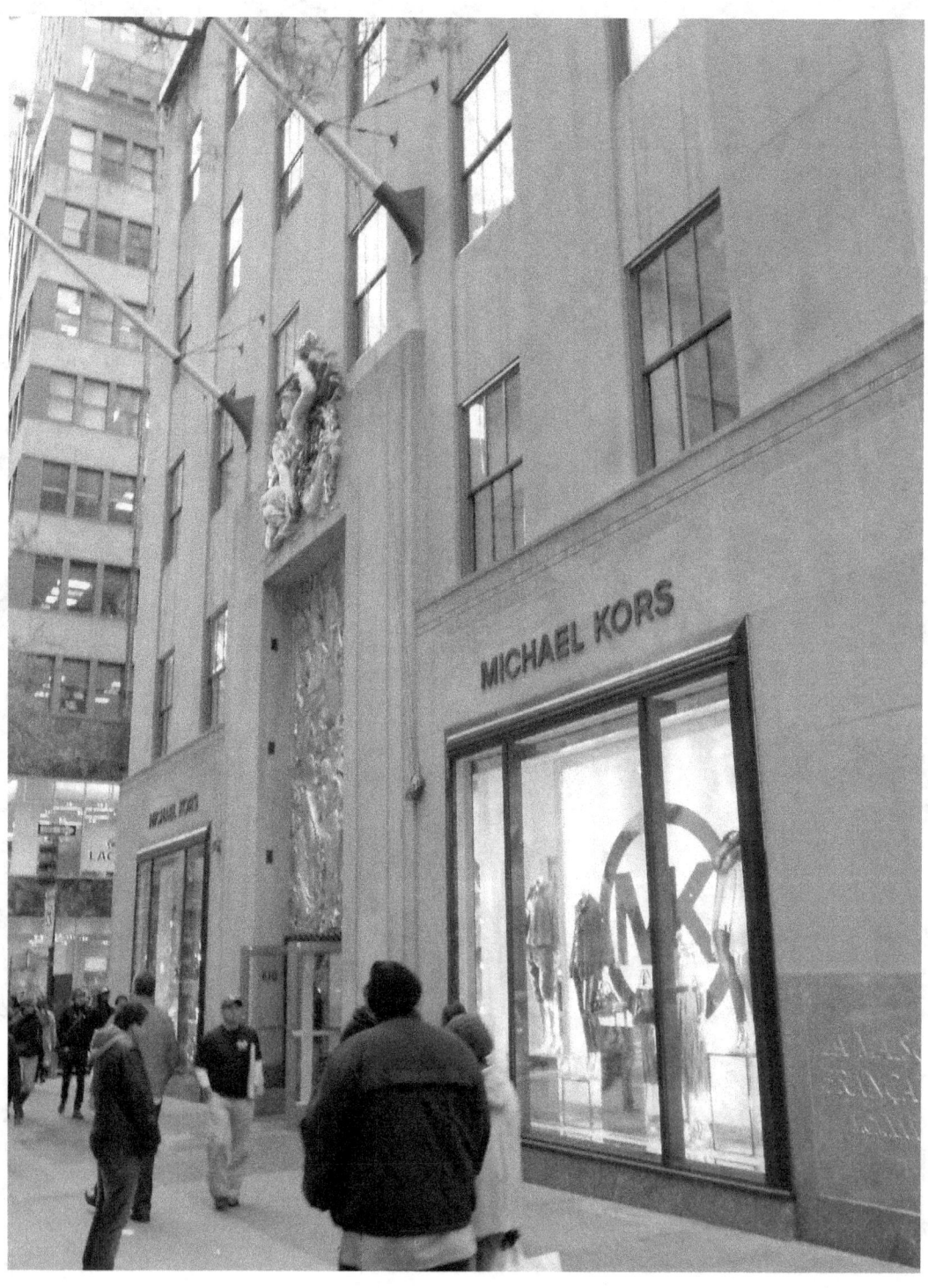

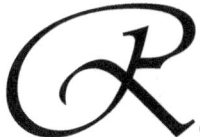ockefeller Center covers 22 acres between 48th and 51st streets, it is located in the center of Midtown Manhattan, spanning the area between Fifth Avenue and Sixth Avenue. Rockefeller Center was named after John D. Rockefeller, Jr.. The Center is a combination of two building complexes: the older and original 14 Art Deco office buildings from the 1930s, and a set of four International-style towers built along the west side of Avenue of the Americas during the 60s and 70s, and the Lehman Brothers Building. The Time-Life Building, McGraw-Hill and News Corporation/ Fox News Channel headquarters are part of the Rockefeller Center extension. In 1987, it was declared a National Historic Landmark.

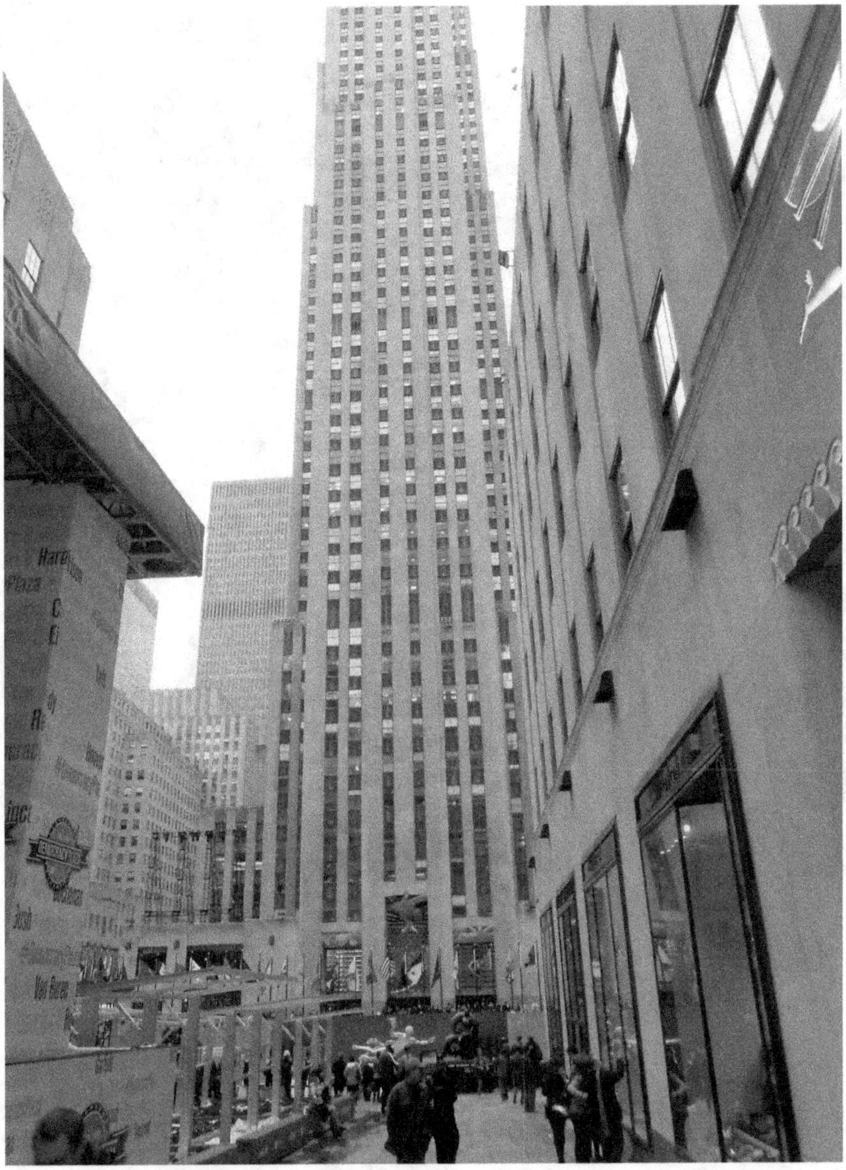

$\mathcal{L}$ower Plaza of Rockefeller Center, ice skating…

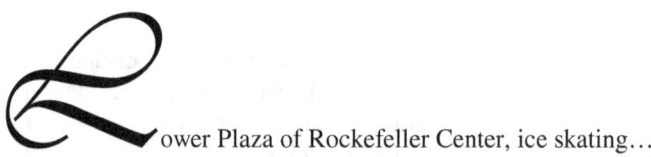

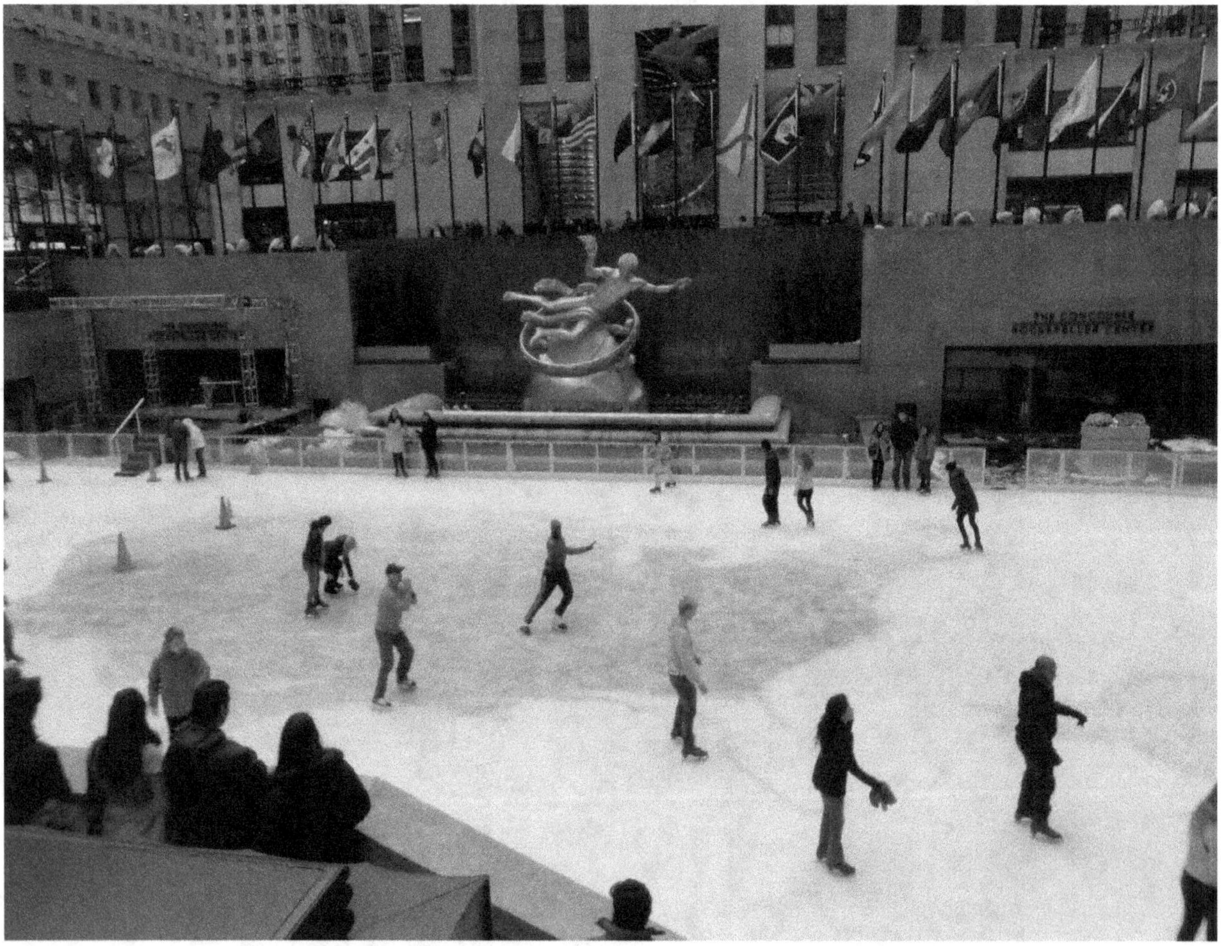

$\mathcal{T}$he Metropolitan Museum of Art Shop

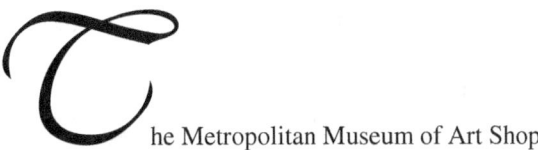

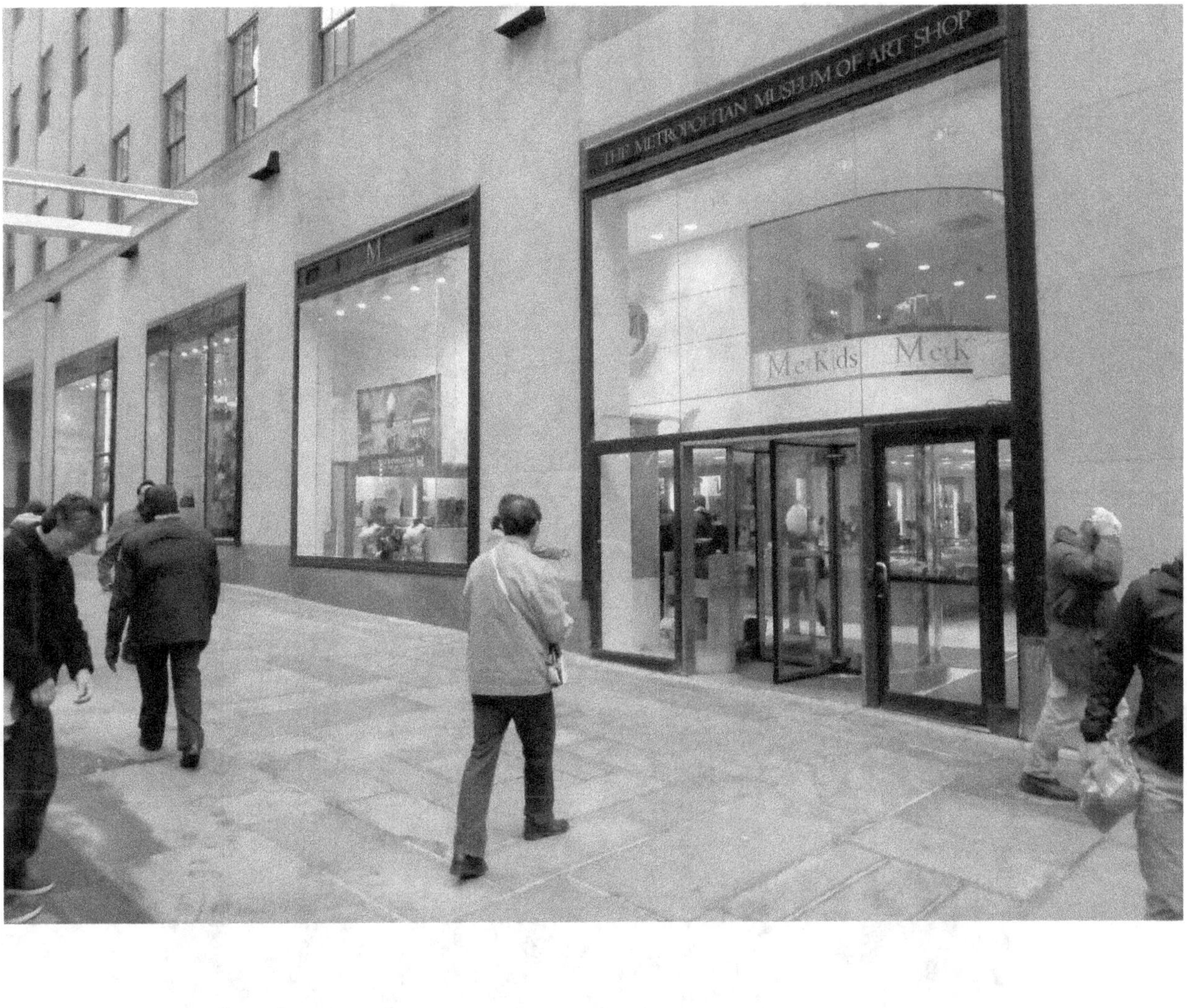

𝒯he Cathedral of St. Patrick is the 135-year-old Roman Catholic cathedral church in Neo-Gothic-style. It is located on the east side of Fifth Avenue between 50th and 51st Streets in midtown Manhattan, directly across the street from Rockefeller Center facing the Atlas statue. It was announced by Cardinal Timothy Michael Dolan that the Cathedral would undergo a massive five-year, three-phase, $175 million renovation. The first phase began in March 2012. This involves repairing, restoring, and cleaning the soot-covered exterior, and an extensive cleaning of the outside and inside surfaces of the stained glass windows. The Cathedral remains open during the renovations.

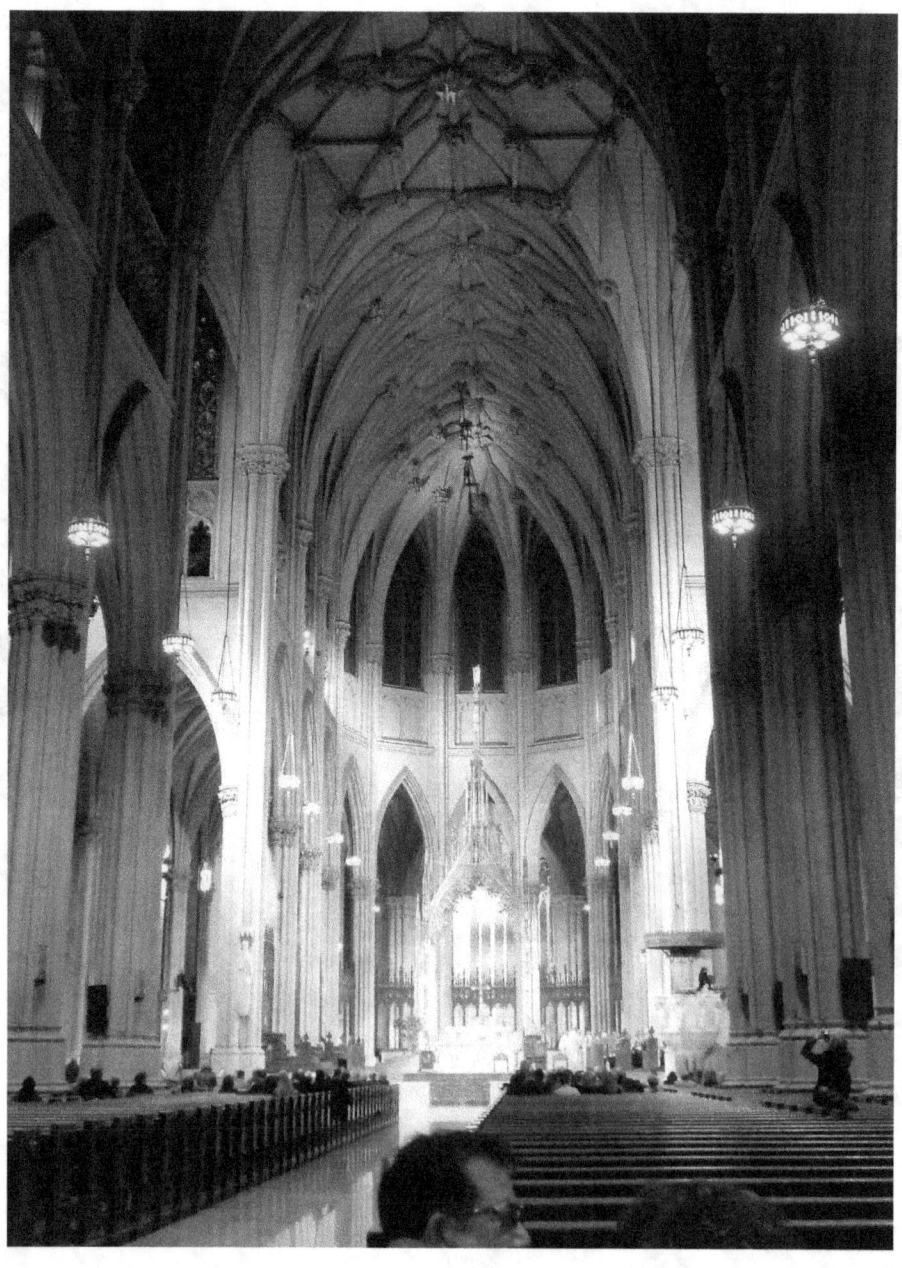

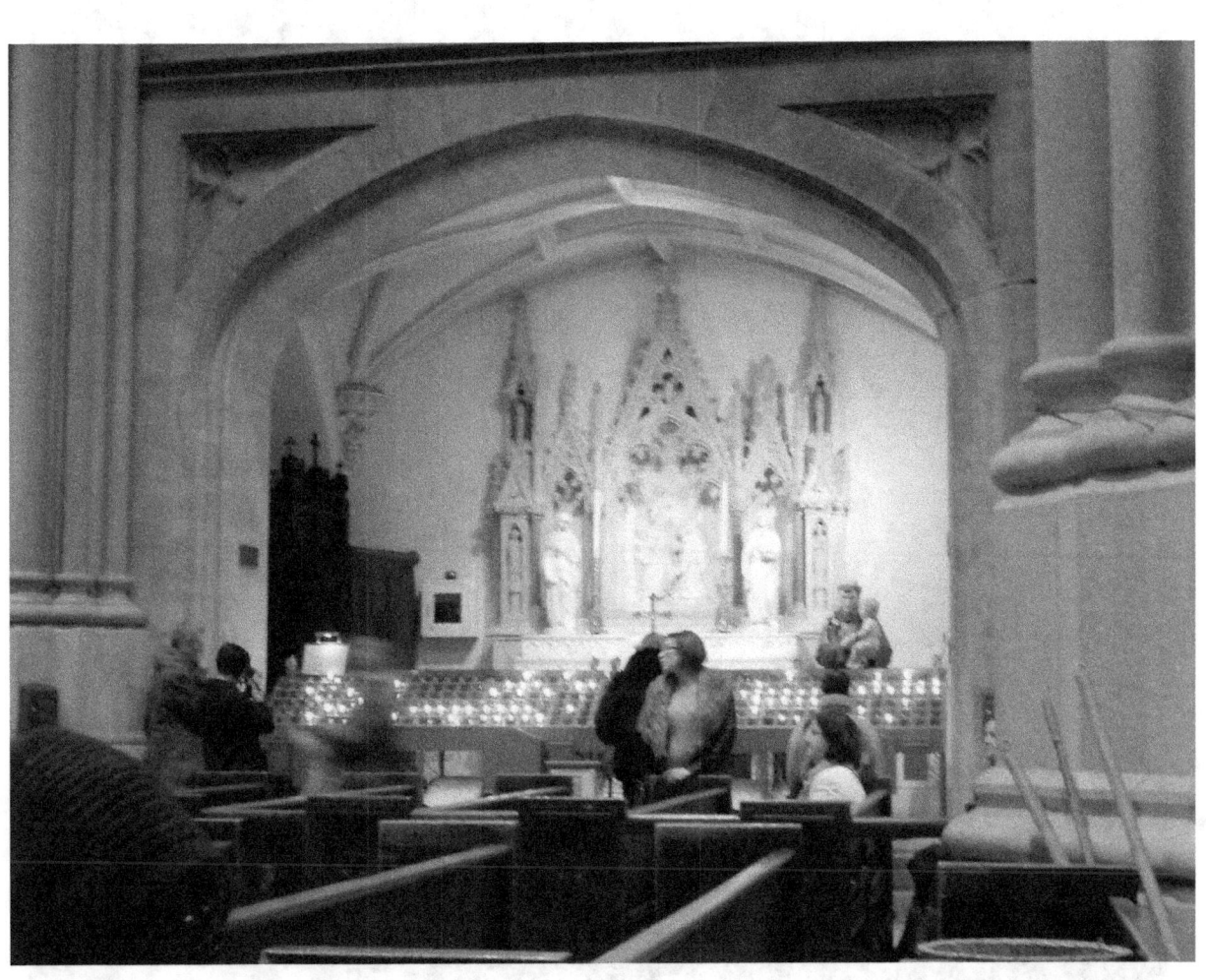

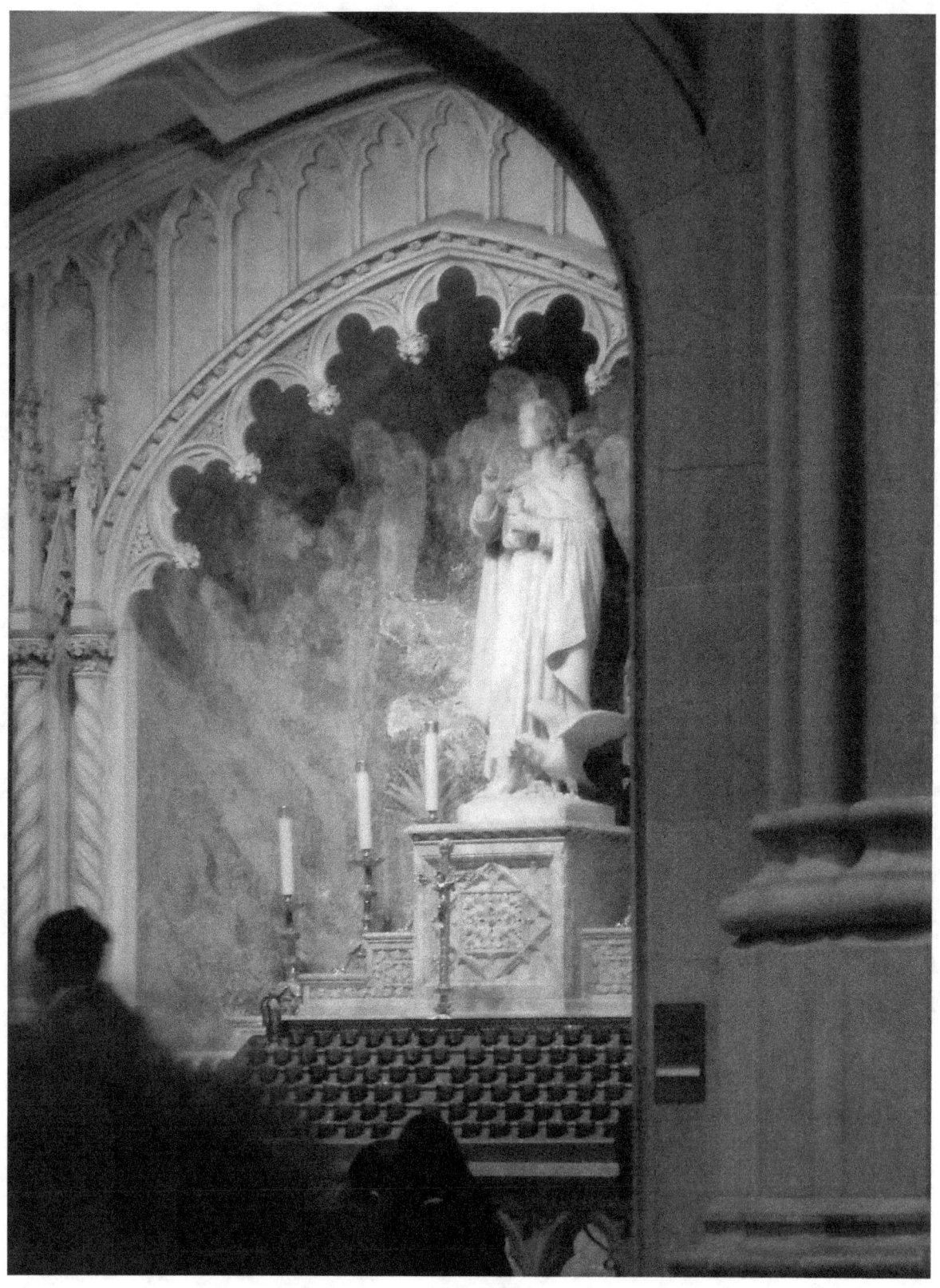

*S*aint Thomas Church is an Episcopal parish church of the Episcopal Diocese of New York also known as Saint Thomas Church Fifth Avenue. It was incorporated on 9 January 1824 and is located at the corner of 53rd Street and Fifth Avenue in the borough of Manhattan. The current structure, completed in 1914, is the fourth church built to house this congregation and was designed in the French High Gothic style by the architects Ralph Adams Cram and Bertram Grosvenor Goodhue. The church is home to the Saint Thomas Choir of Men and Boys a choral ensemble comprising men and boys, which performs music of the Anglican tradition at worship services. It offers a full concert series during the course of the year. The boys of the Saint Thomas Choir are enrolled at the Saint Thomas Choir School, the only church-affiliated residential choir school in the United States.

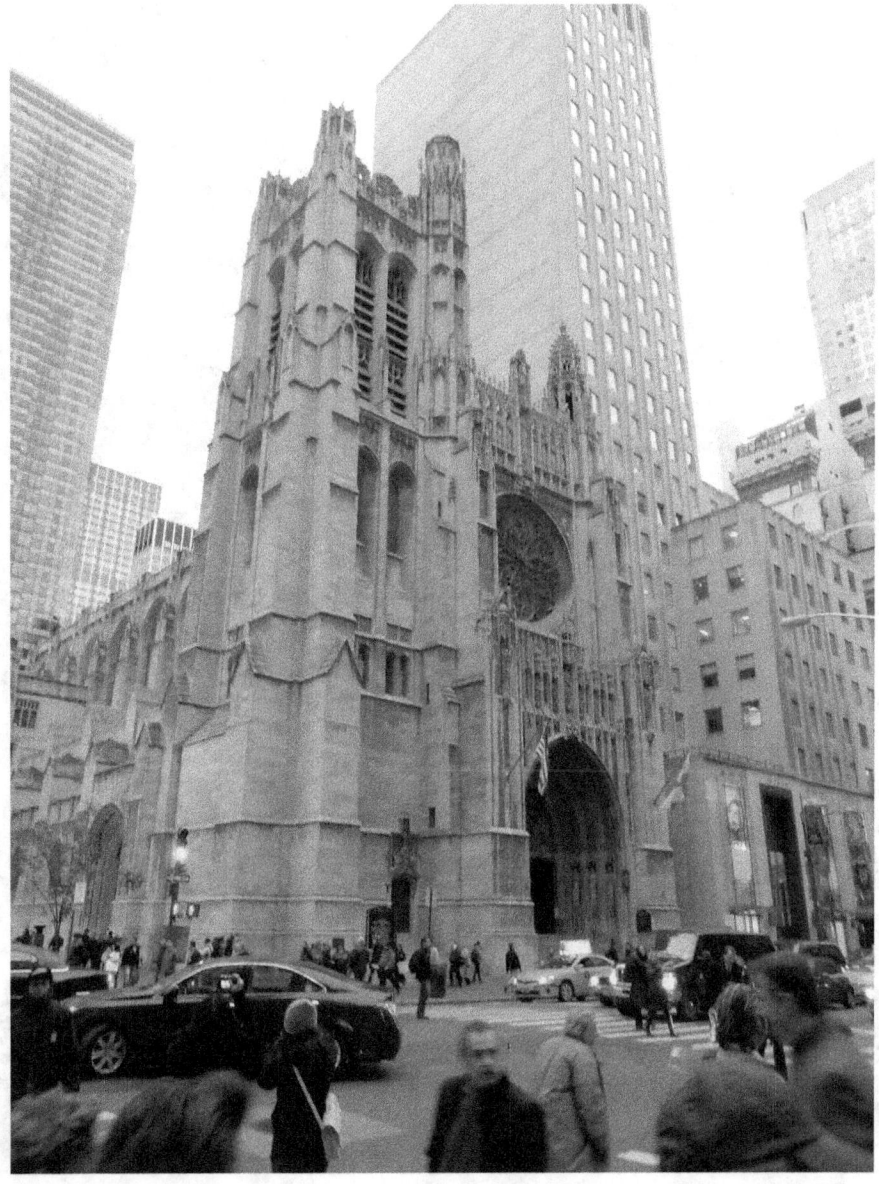

$\mathcal{M}$useum of Modern Art…

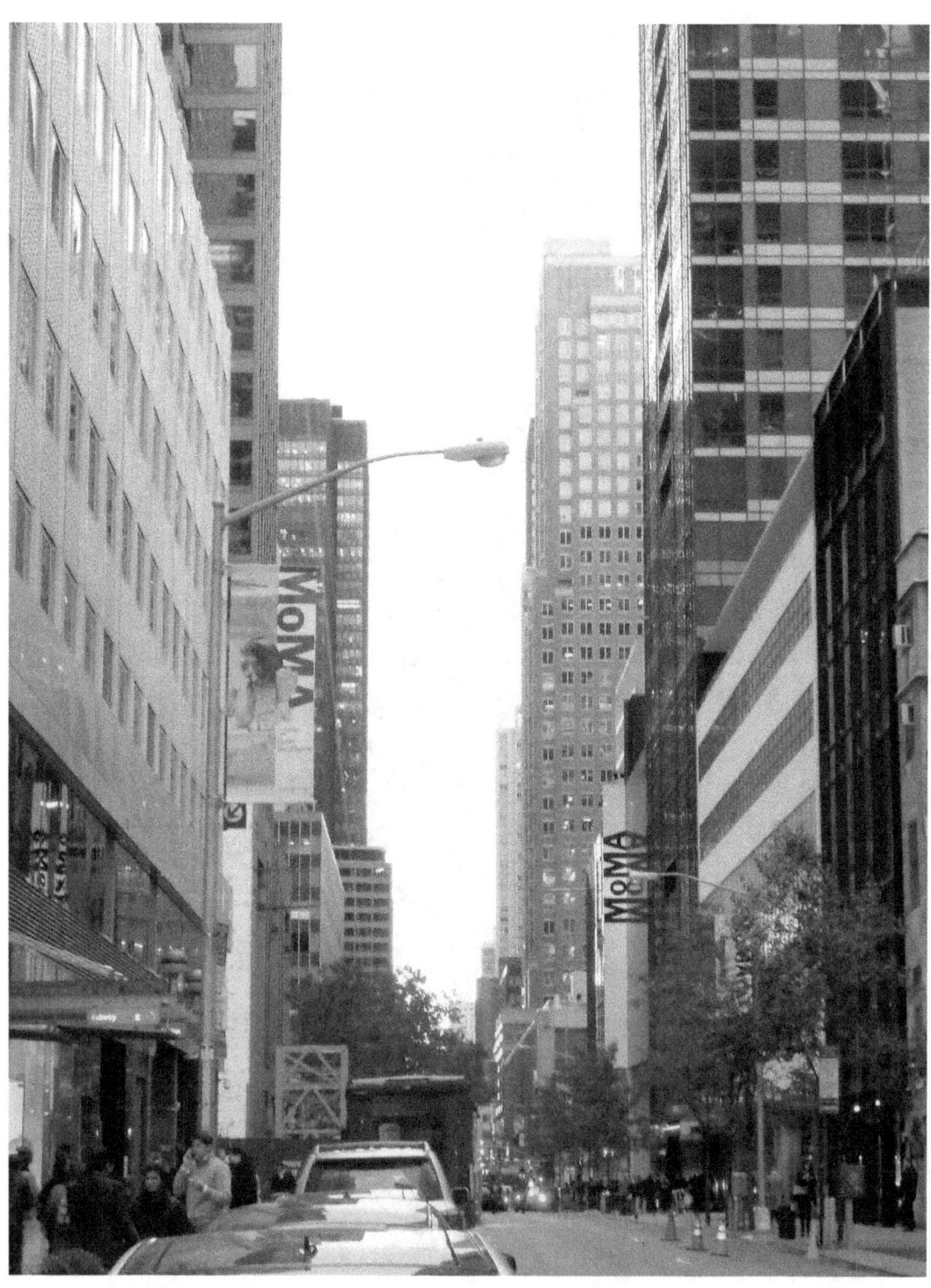

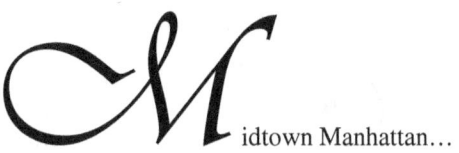

idtown Manhattan…

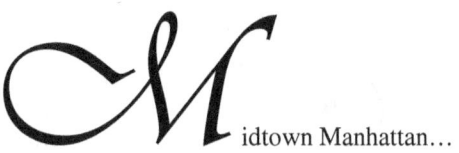

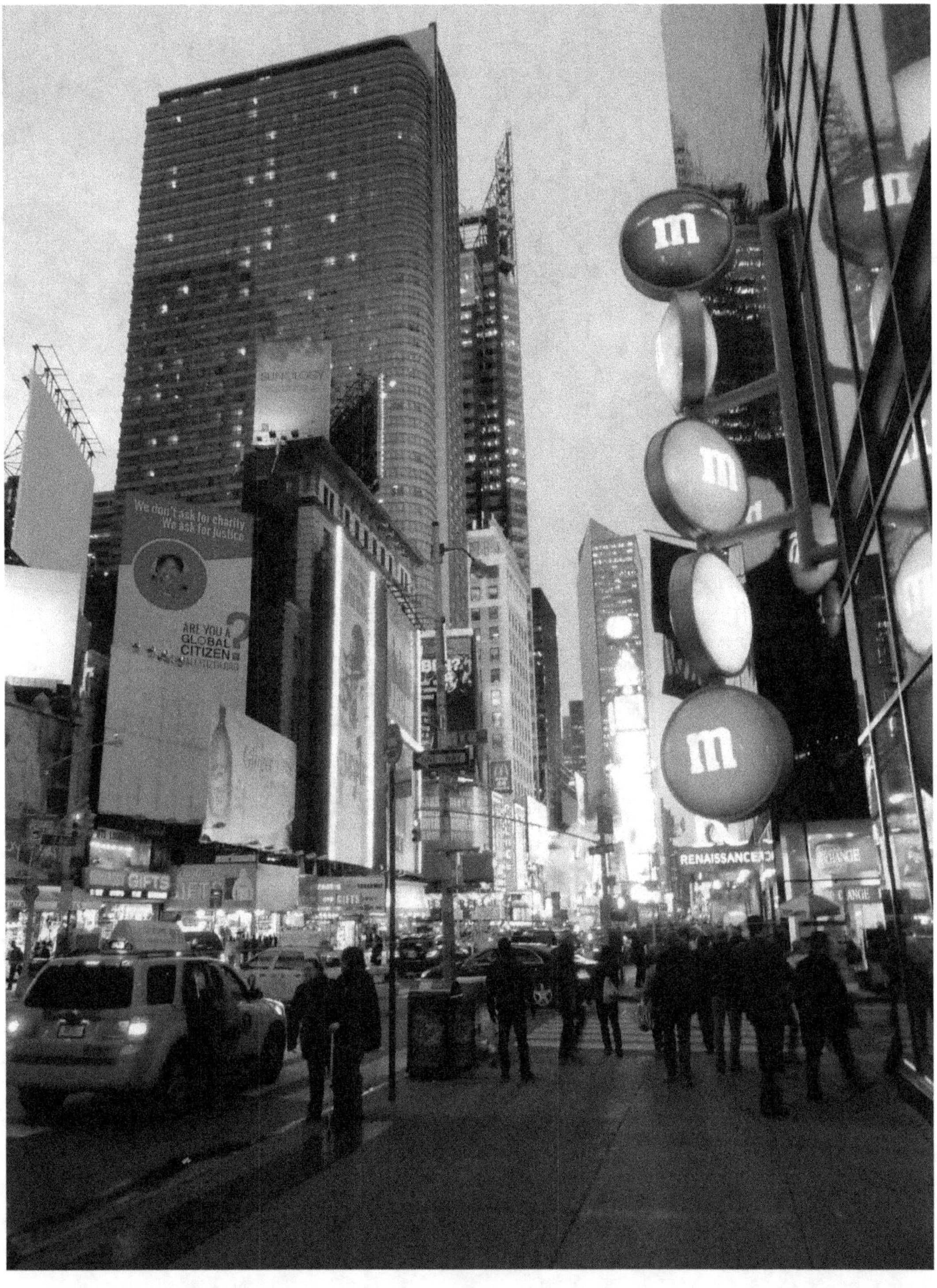

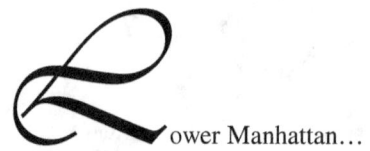

ower Manhattan…

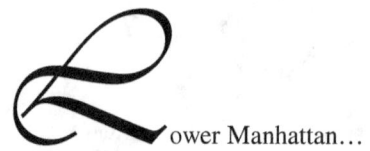

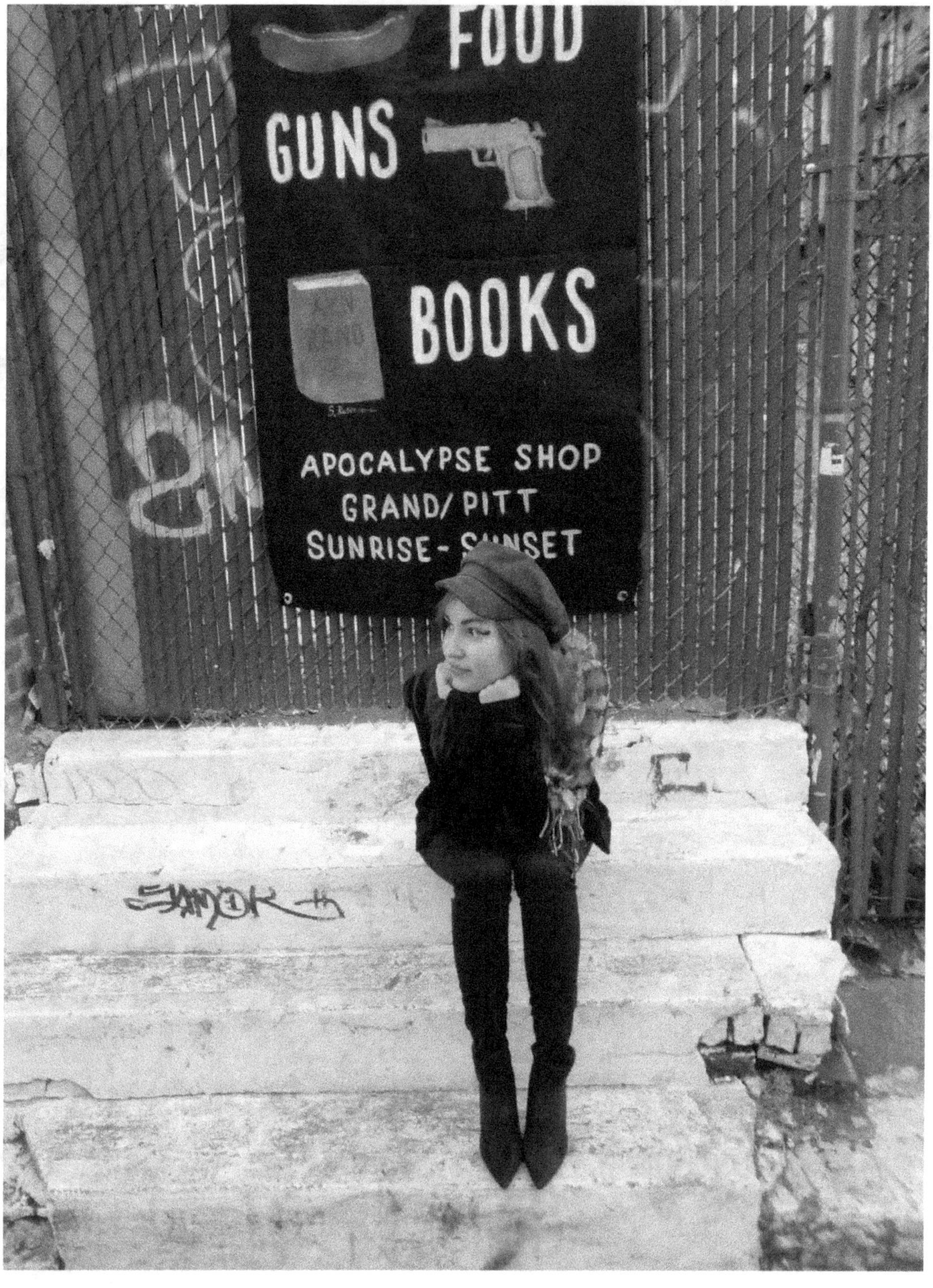

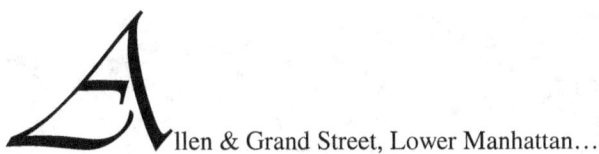
llen & Grand Street, Lower Manhattan…

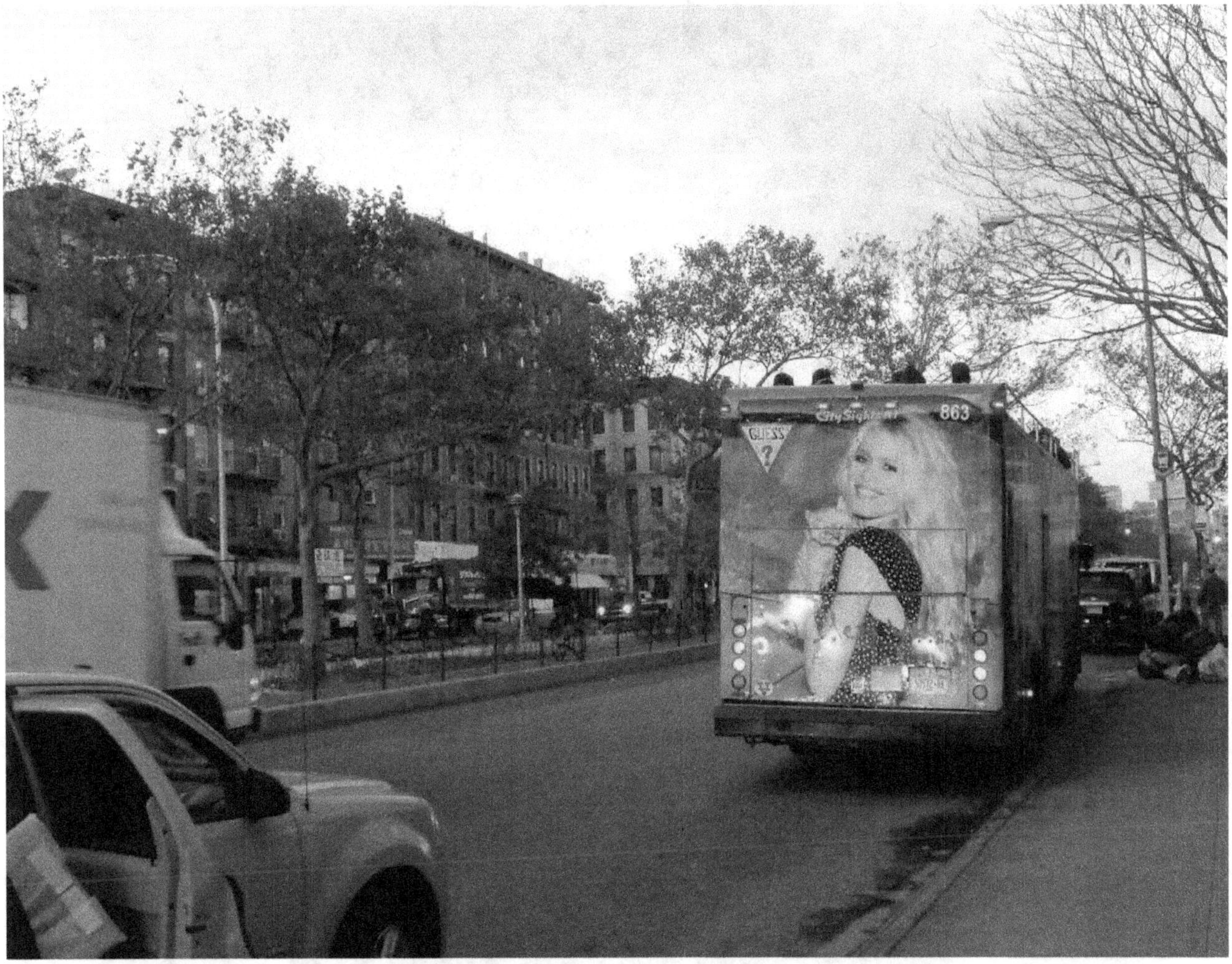

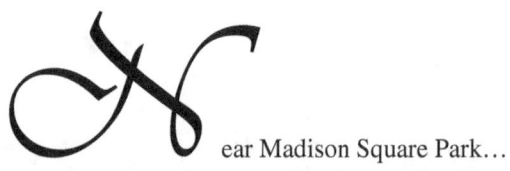 ear Madison Square Park…

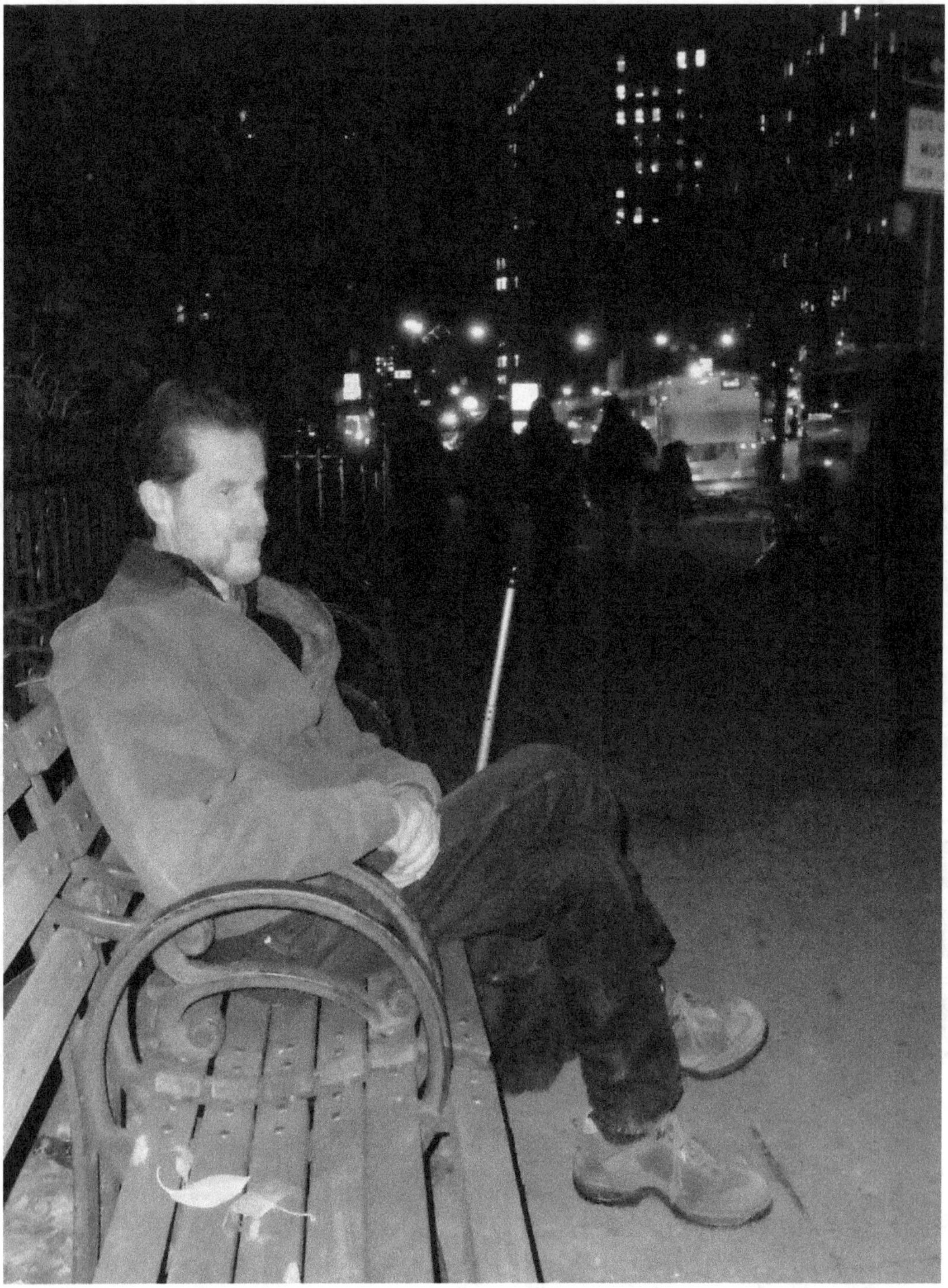

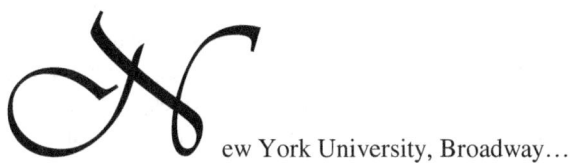

ew York University, Broadway…

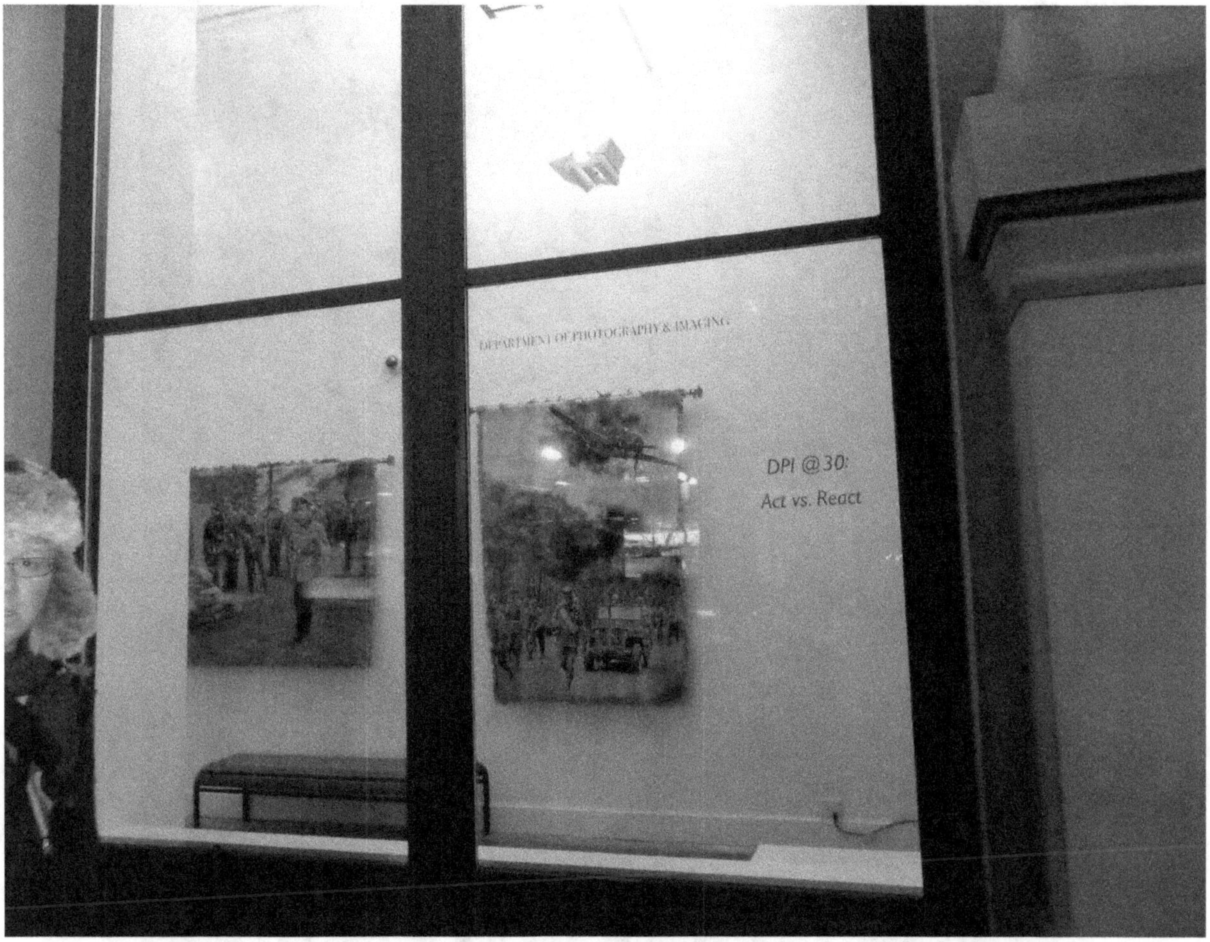

$\mathcal{S}$ubway is a rapid transit system owned by the City of New York and leased to the New York City

Transit Authority. It is one of the most extensive public transportation system in the world. The New York City Subway is also one of the world's oldest public transit systems. In 2011, the subway delivered over 1.64 billion rides, averaging approximately 5.3 million rides on weekdays, about 3.0 million rides on Saturdays, and about 2.4 million rides on Sundays. By annual ridership, the NYC Subway is the 7th busiest rapid transit rail system in the world.

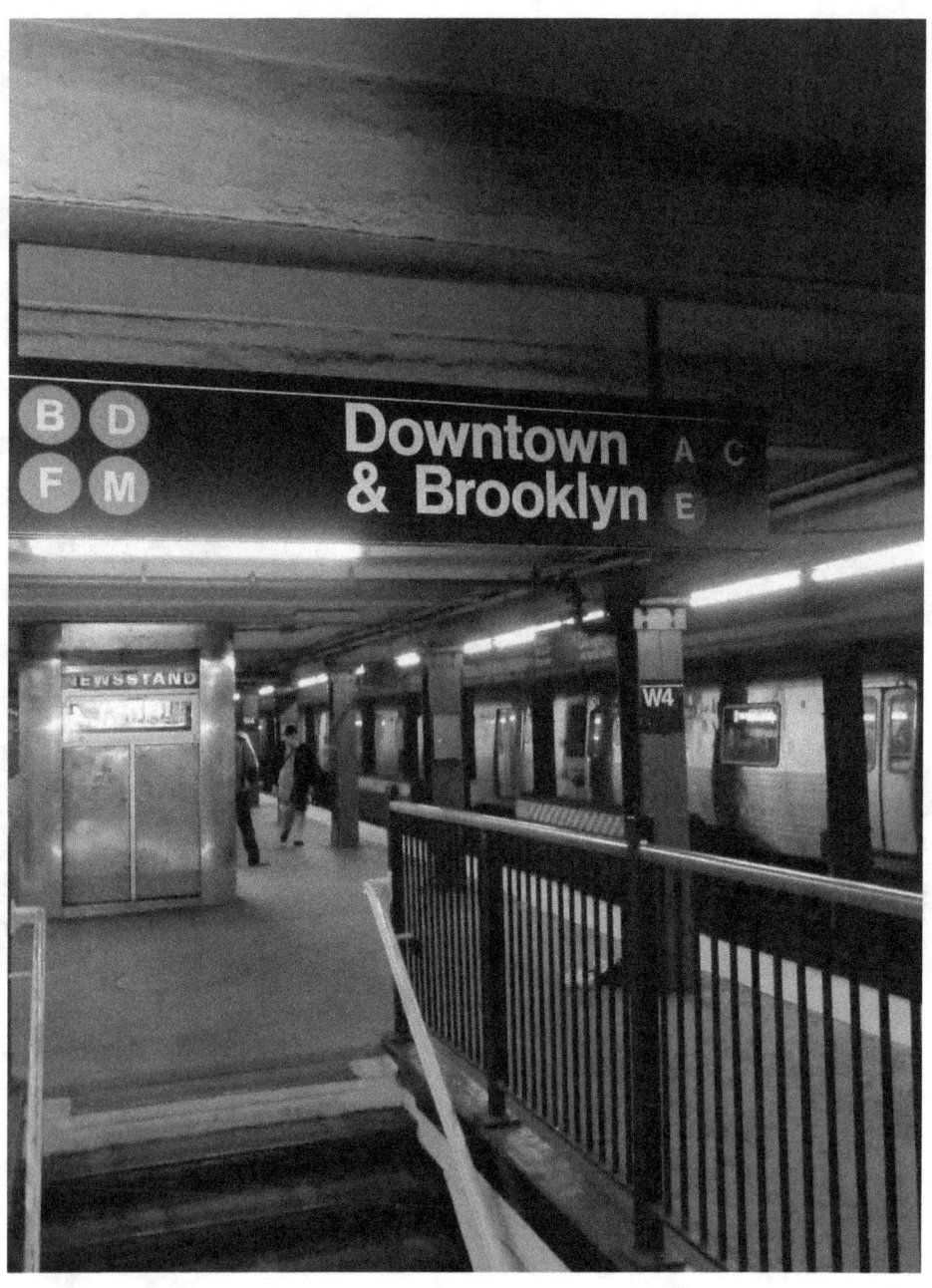

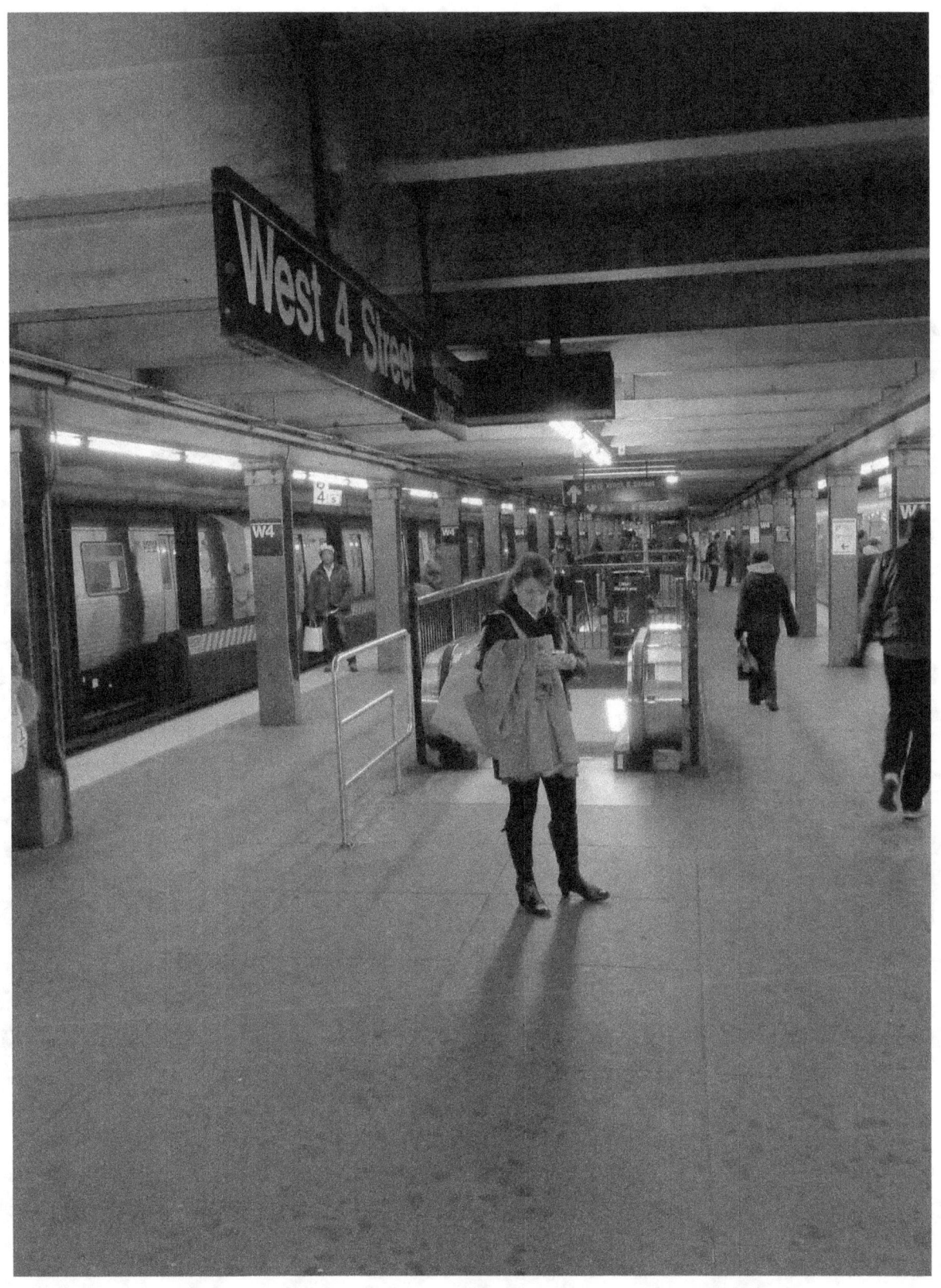

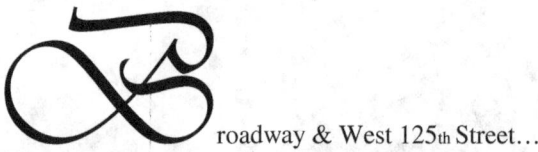

roadway & West 125th Street…

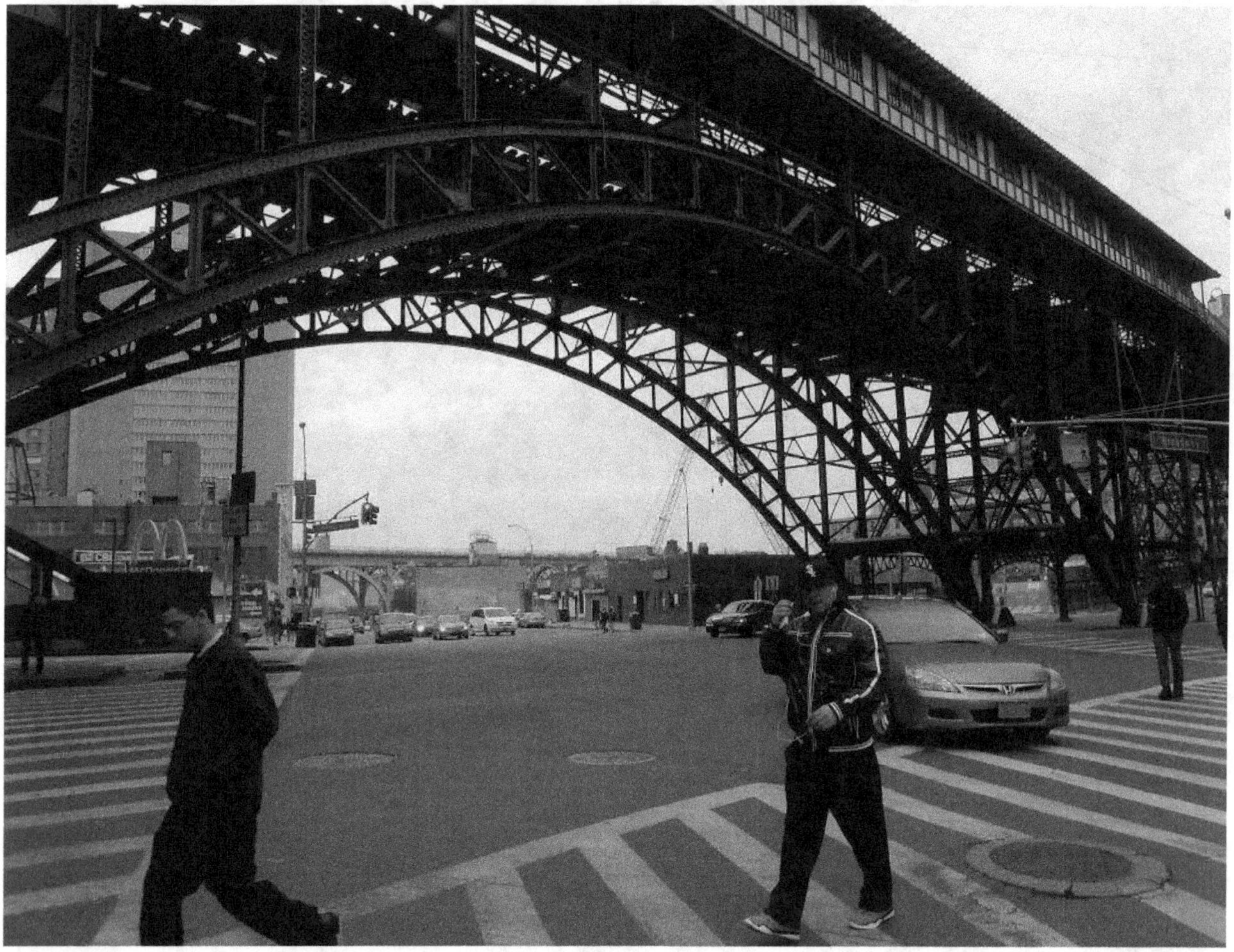

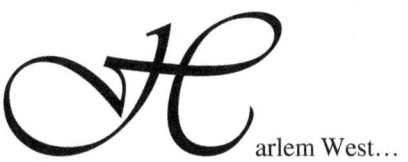

arlem West…

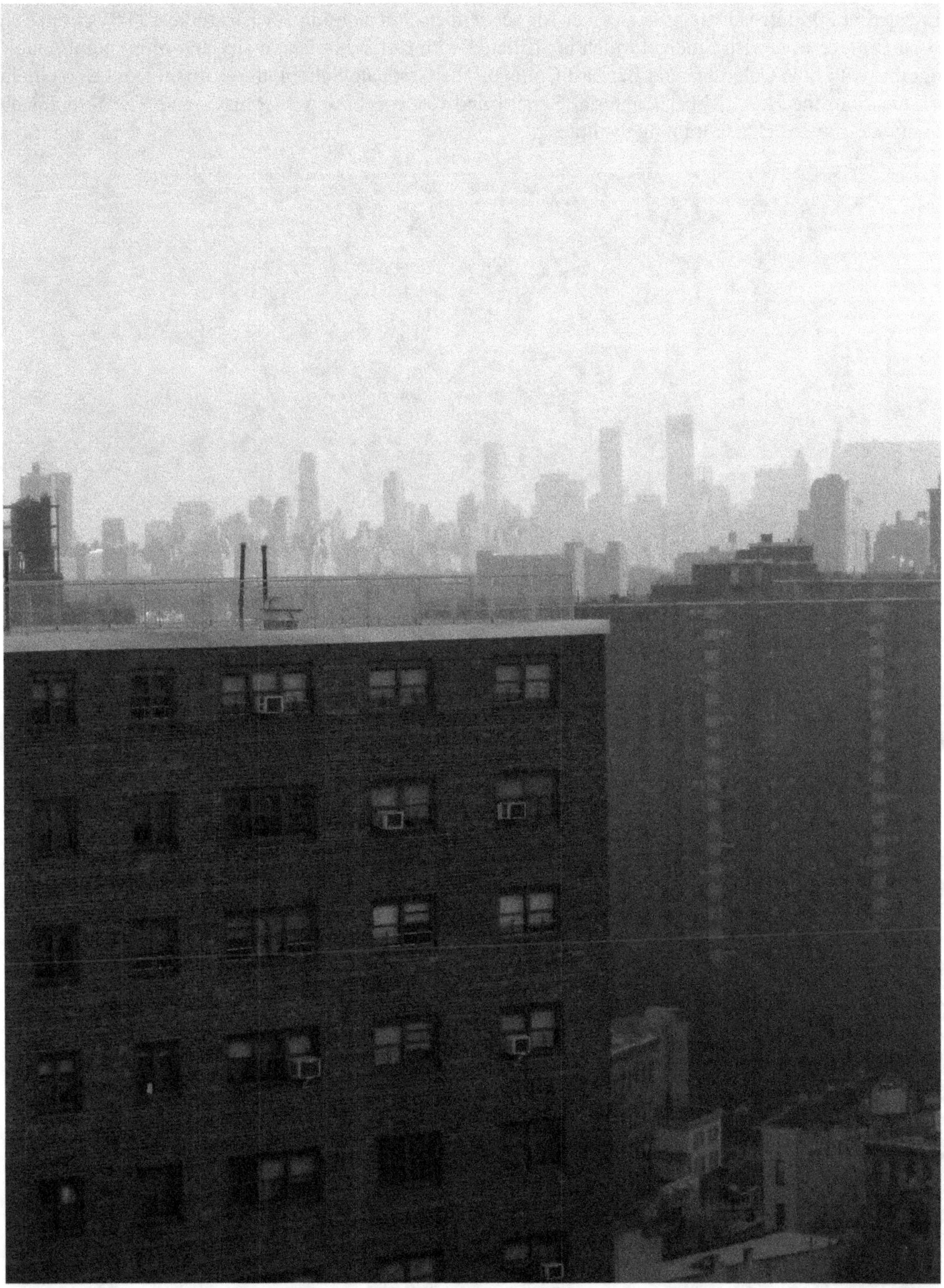

*T*he Jewish Theological Seminary of America is one of the spiritual and academic centers of Conservative Judaism. Located at 3080 Broadway, it is a center for academic scholarship in Jewish studies. JTS operates five schools: Albert A. List College of Jewish Studies, which is affiliated with Columbia University and offers joint/double bachelors degree programs with both Columbia and Barnard College, The Graduate School, the William Davidson Graduate School of Jewish Education, the H. L. Miller Cantorial School and College of Jewish Music, and The Rabbinical School. It operates a number of research and training institutes.

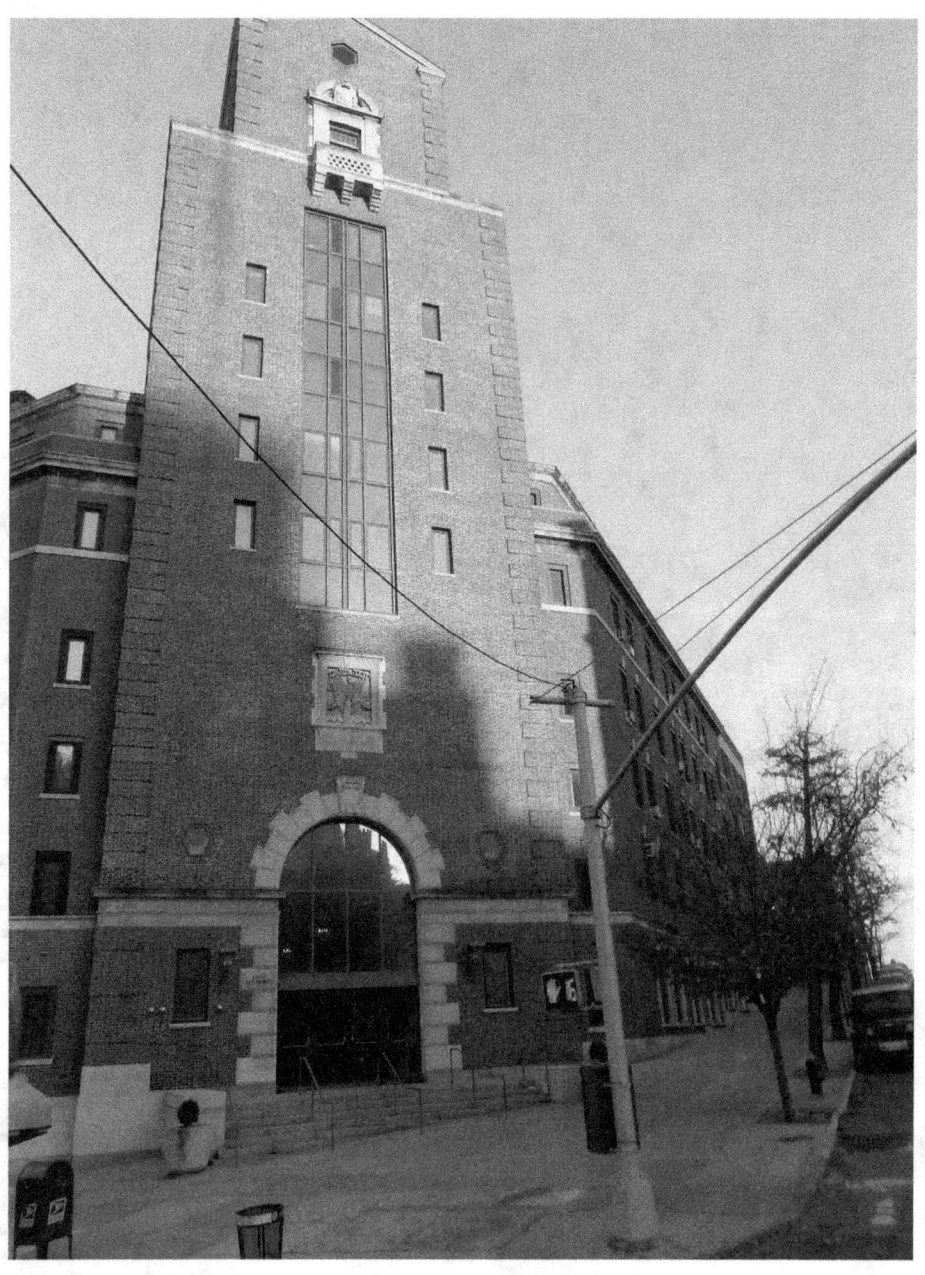

*U*nion Theological Seminary is an independent seminary in New York City. The school is located in

Manhattan between Broadway and Claremont Avenue, 120th to 122nd Streets. The seminary was founded in 1836 under the Presbyterian Church. In the 20th century, Union was world renowned as a center of liberal Christianity and neoorthodoxy. It is the birthplace of the Black Liberation Theology, Womanist Theology and Mujerista Theology movements. It is affiliated with nearby Columbia University. Union houses the largest theological library in the Western Hemisphere. The brick and limestone English Gothic architecture, by Francis R. Allen and Collins, completed in 1910, includes the tower, which adapts features of the crossing tower of Durham Cathedral. The Seminary is also adjacent to Barnard College, Teachers College, the Jewish Theological Seminary of America and the Manhattan School of Music. On April 23, 1980, the building was added to the National Register of Historic Places.

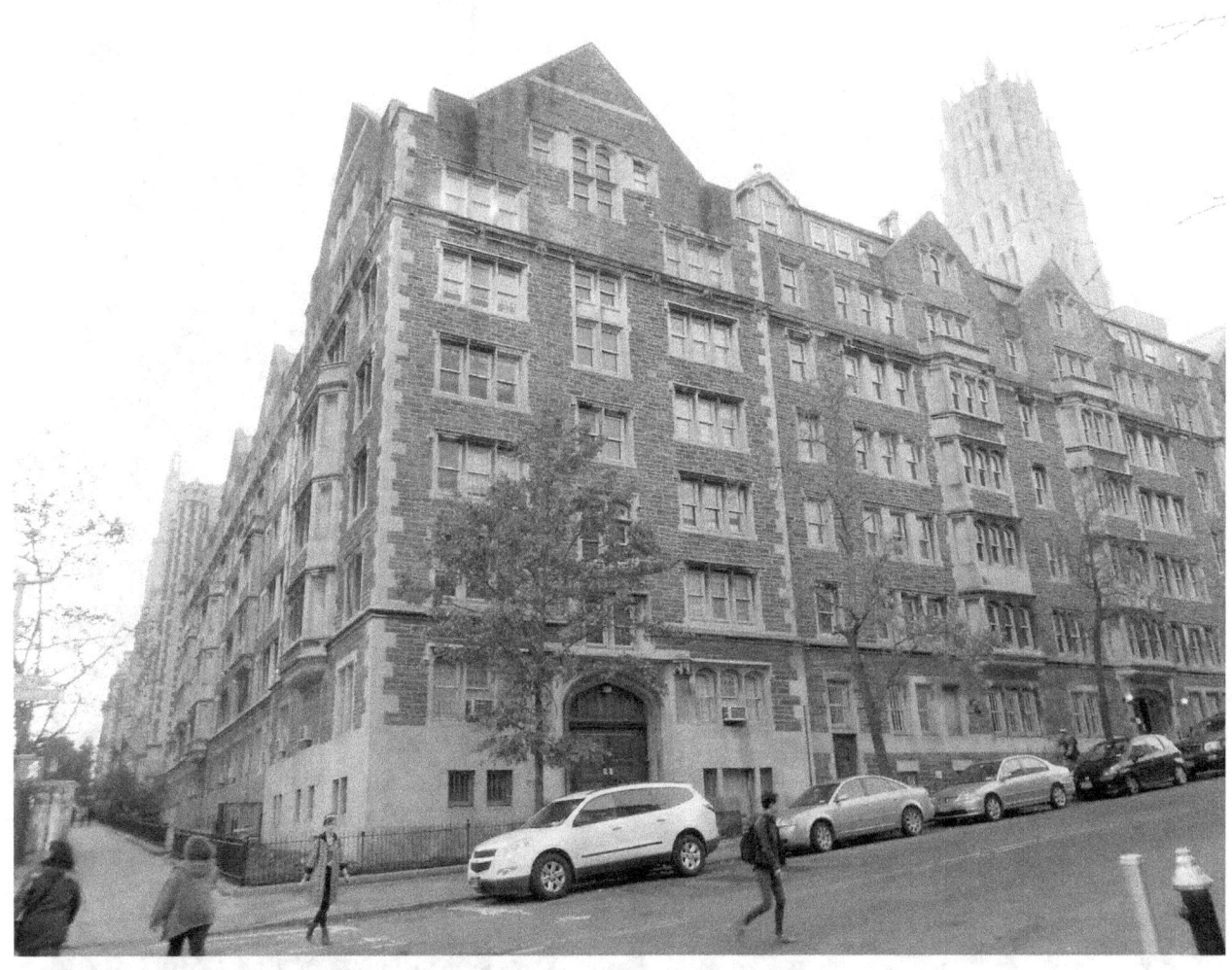

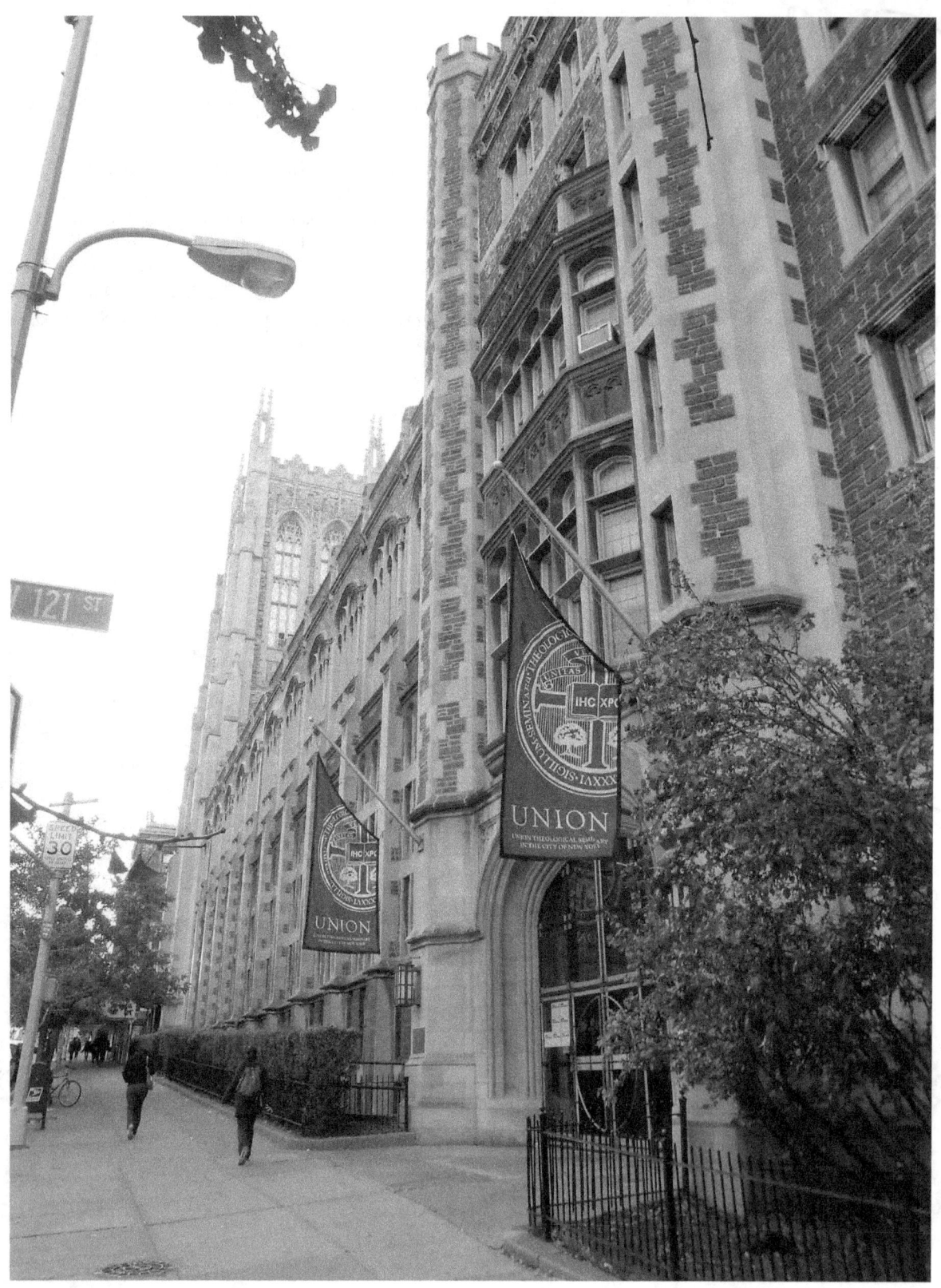

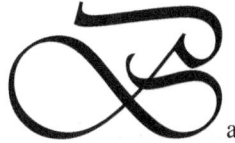arnard College is a private women's liberal arts college. A member of the Seven Sisters, it was founded in 1889. Barnard College has been affiliated with Columbia University since 1900. Its 4-acre campus stretches along Broadway between 116th and 120th Streets in the Morningside Heights neighborhood in Manhattan. It is adjacent to several academic institutions.

The college was named after Frederick Augustus Porter Barnard, an American educator and mathematician who advocated equal educational privileges for men and women. Barnard served as the president of the then-Columbia College from 1864 to 1889.

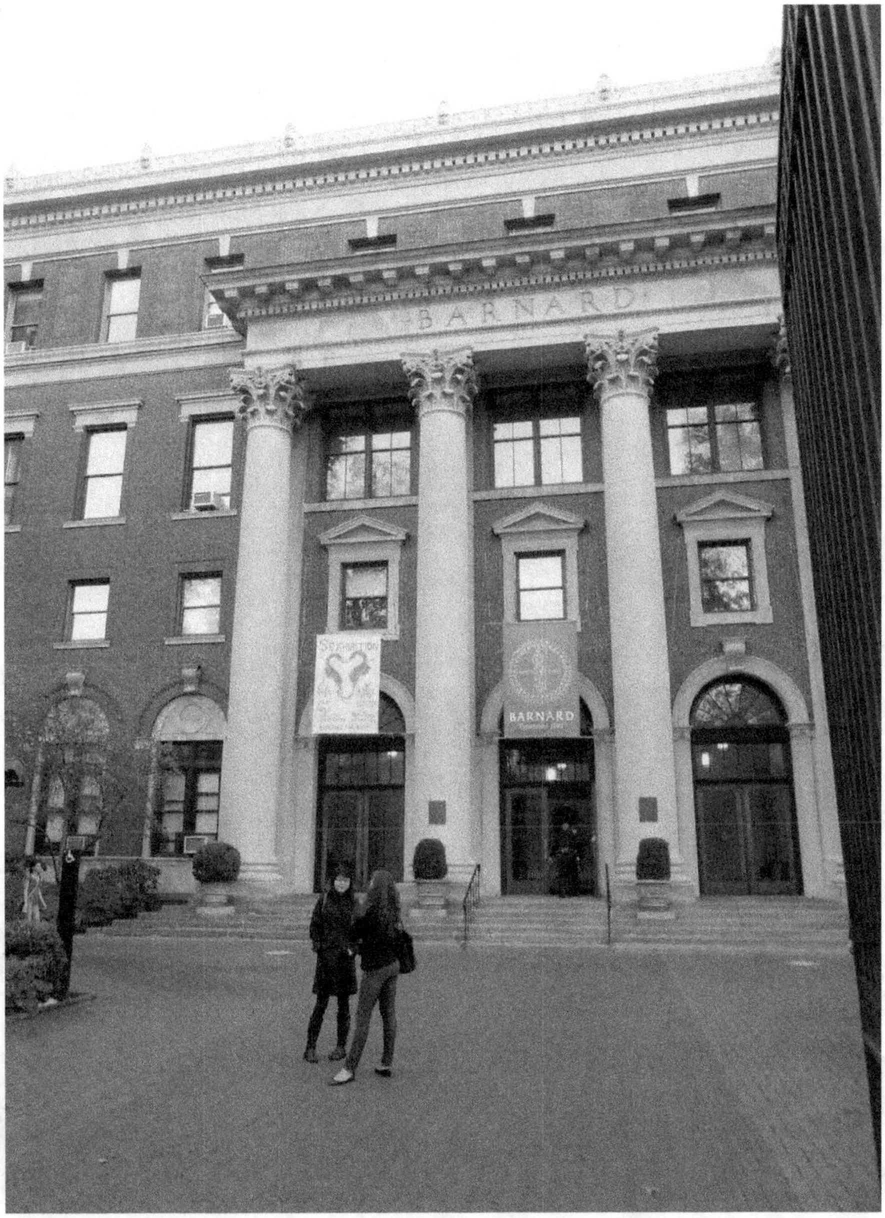

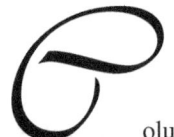olumbia University is an American private Ivy League research university, the oldest institution of higher

learning in the state of New York. The university was founded in 1754 by royal charter of George II of Great Britain as King's College. After the American Revolutionary War, King's College briefly became a state entity, and in 1784 was renamed Columbia College. In 1896 it was renamed Columbia University. Same year, its campus was moved from Madison Avenue to the Morningside Heights Manhattan. It occupies more than six city blocks - 32 acres. The university encompasses 20 schools and is affiliated with numerous institutions.

Columbia annually administers the Pulitzer Prize and has been affiliated with more Nobel Prize laureates than any other academic institution in the world. The university is one of 14 founding members of the Association of American Universities. It was the first school in the U.S. to grant the M.D. degree. The alumni include 25 Academy Award winners; nine Justices of the U.S. Supreme Court; 20 living billionaires; and 29 heads of state, including three U.S. Presidents.

The Low Memorial Library is the administrative center of Columbia University. The steps leading to the library's facade is a home to Daniel Chester French's sculpture, Alma Mater, a university symbol. The Avery Architectural and Fine Arts Library - the largest architecture library in the world - is one of 25 libraries in the Columbia University Library System. It is named for New York architect Henry Ogden Avery. In 2012, the library's building, designed by the architectural firm McKim, Mead, and White, celebrated its 100th anniversary. The Nicholas Murray Butler Library is the largest single library in the Columbia University Library System and is one of the largest buildings on the campus.

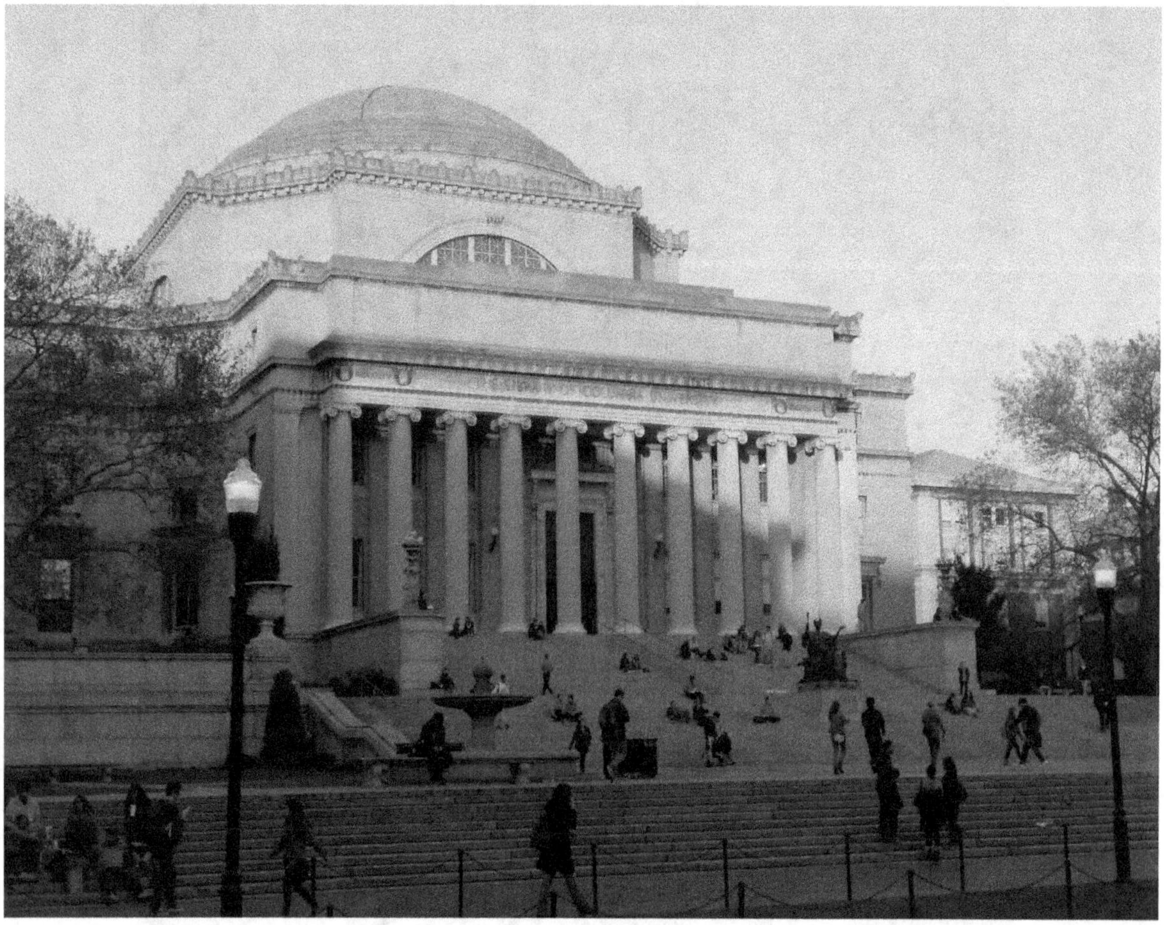

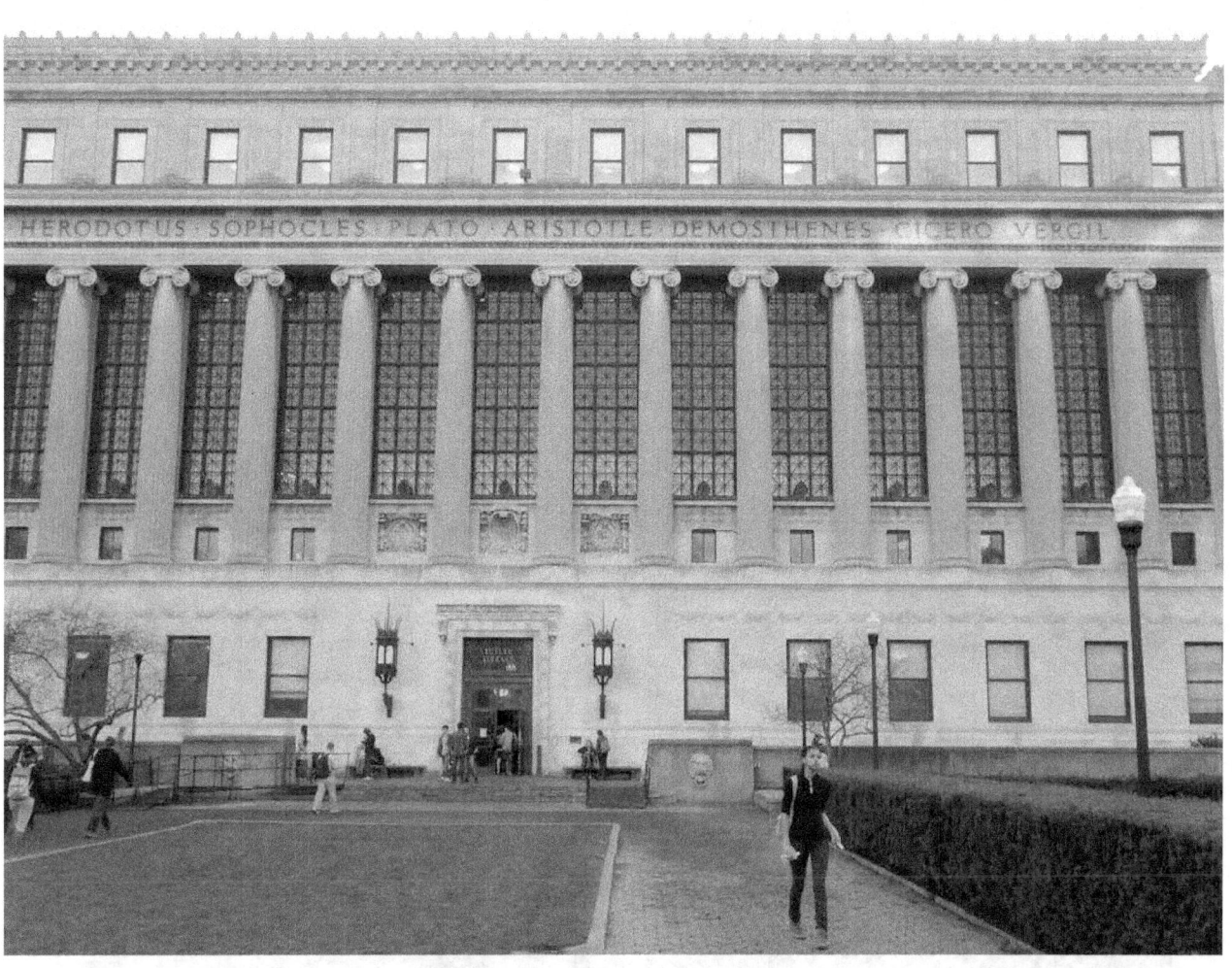

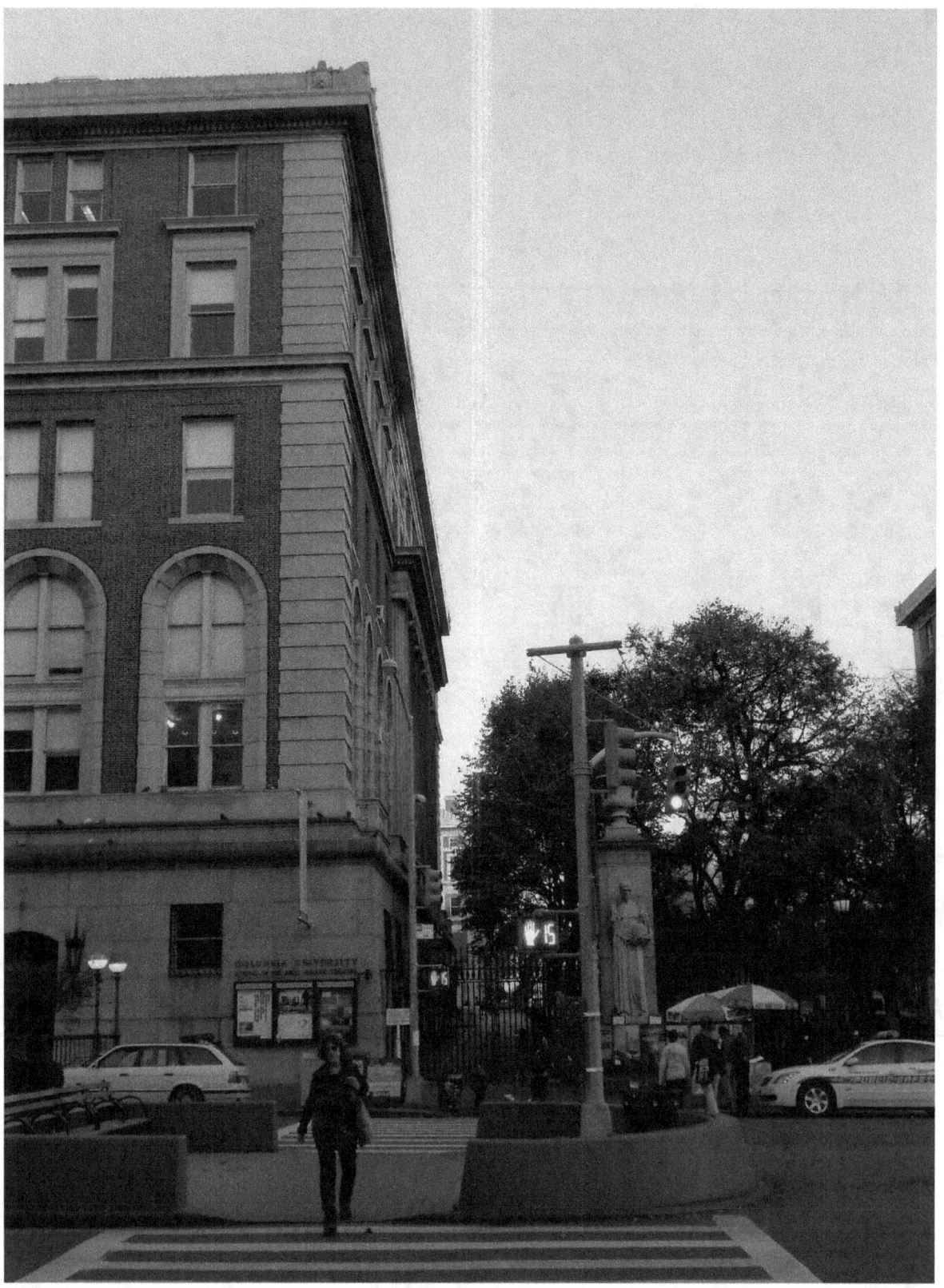

roadway, Upper West…

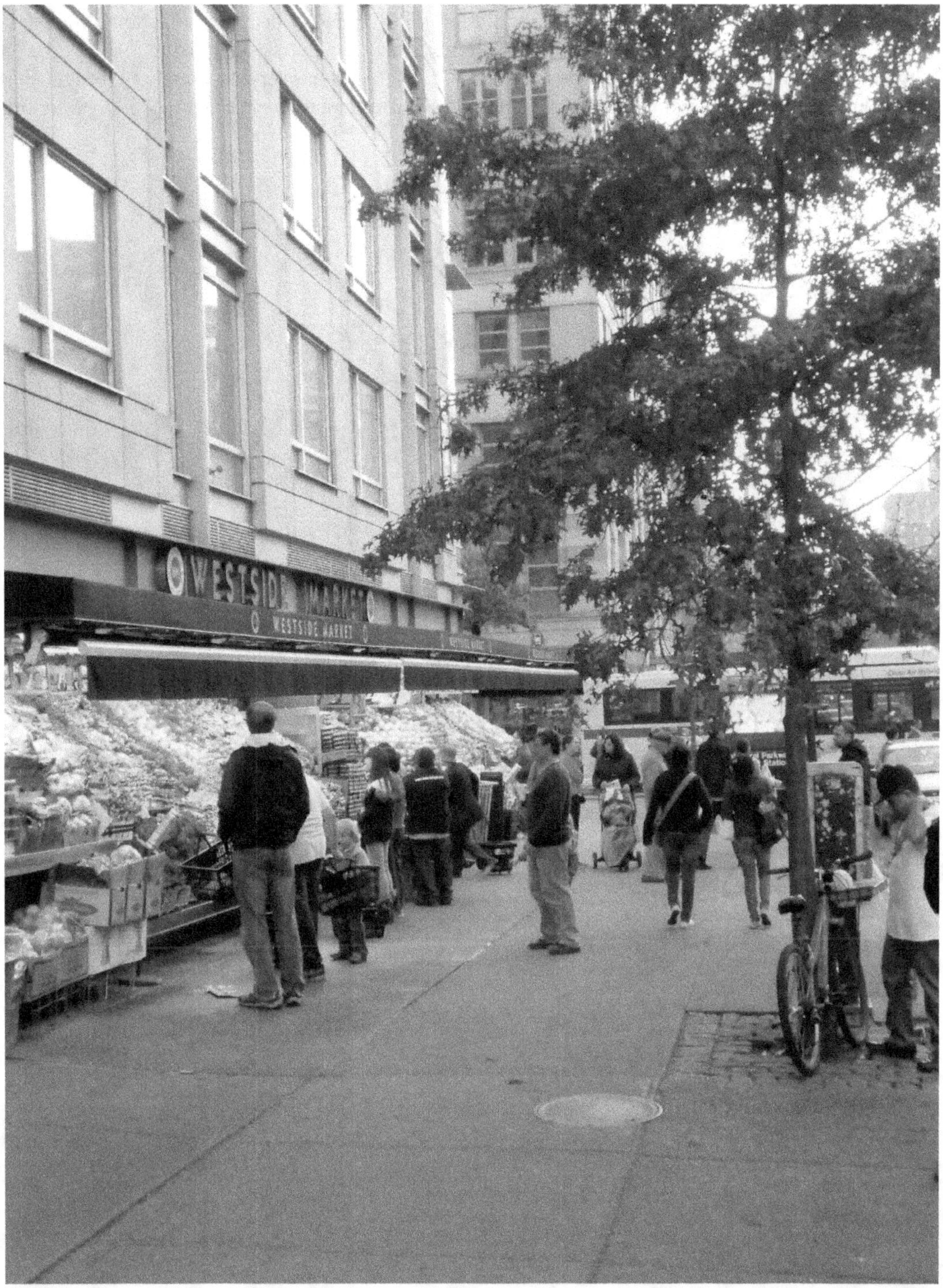

*S*t. Michael's Church - a historic Episcopal church - was founded in January 1807. It is located at 225 West 99th Street. The present Romanesque building was built in 1890 and added to the National Register of Historic Places in 1996. The church building is famous for its two tracker-action pipe organs built in 1967 by the Rudolph von Beckerath Organ Company (Germany), and its fine acoustics. St. Michael's has services traditional Anglican services and prayer groups influenced by the emerging church movement. It is also famous for the many works of art created for the congregation by Tiffany studios.

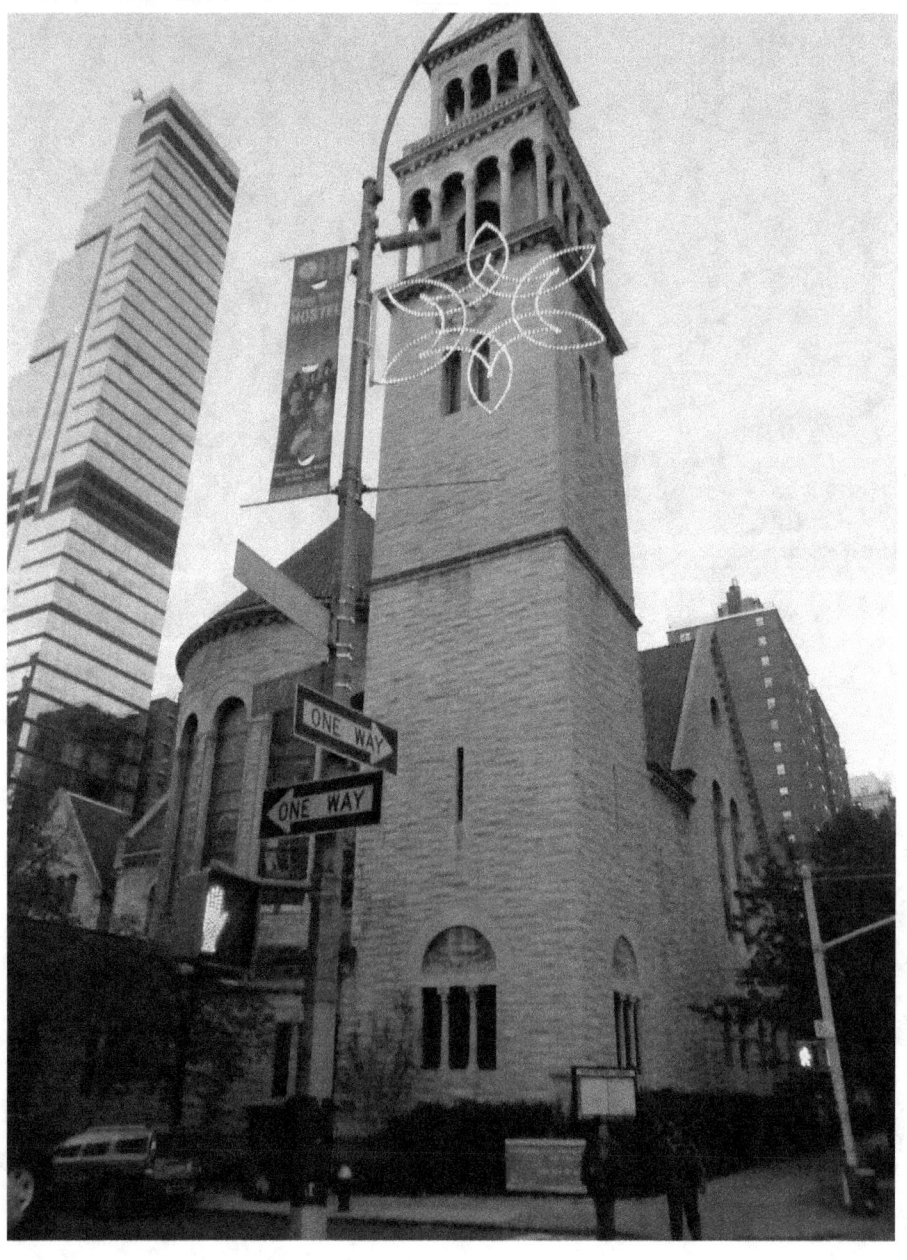

*H*oly Name of Jesus Parish was established on the upper West Side of Manhattan in 1868. It is an urban ministry in the Roman Catholic Church within the Franciscan tradition. Holy Name of Jesus Church was designed by the architect Thomas Henry Poole. It is located in the old Bloomingdale Village on the Upper West Side on the northwest corner of 96th Street and Amsterdam Avenue.

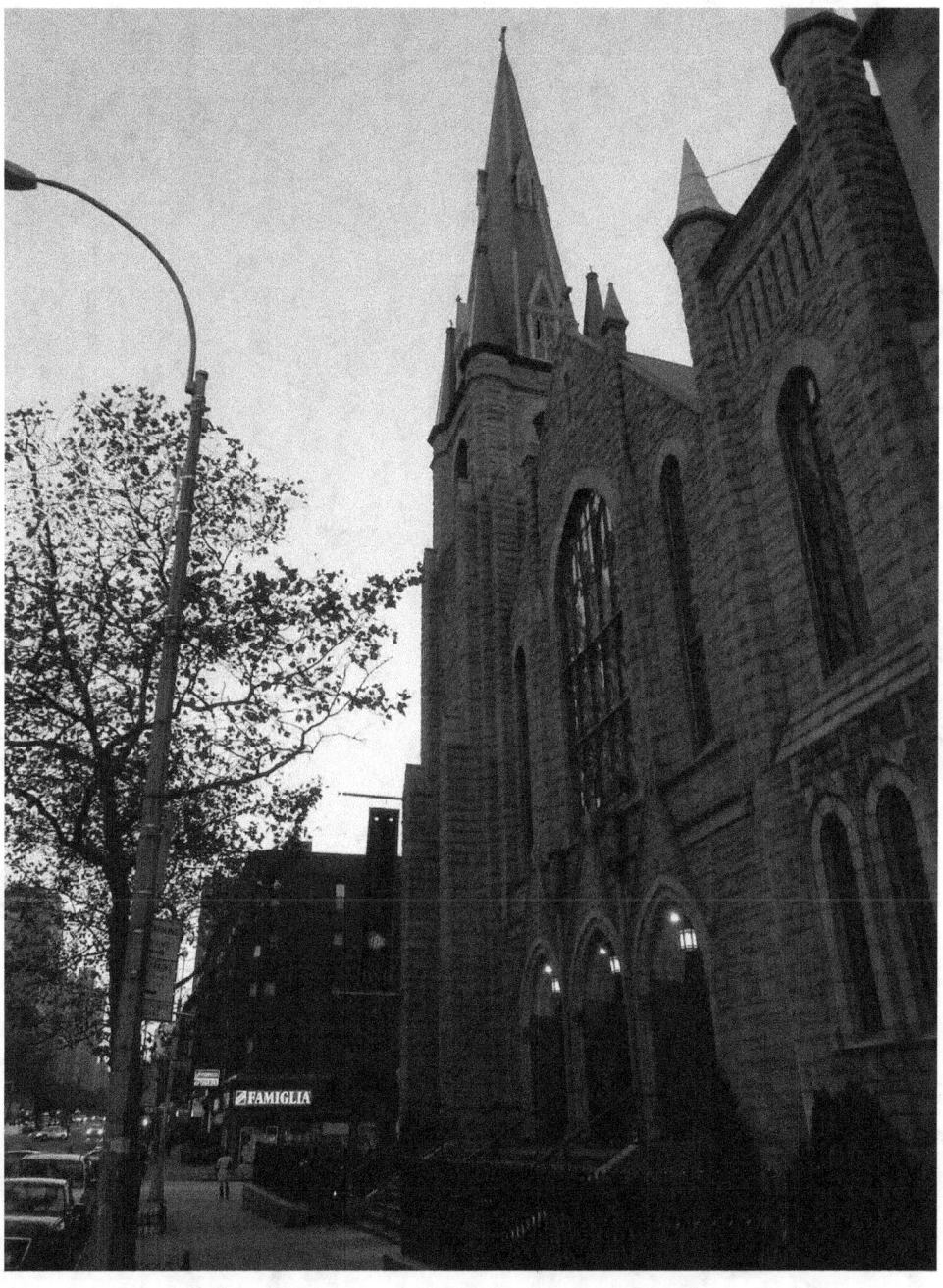

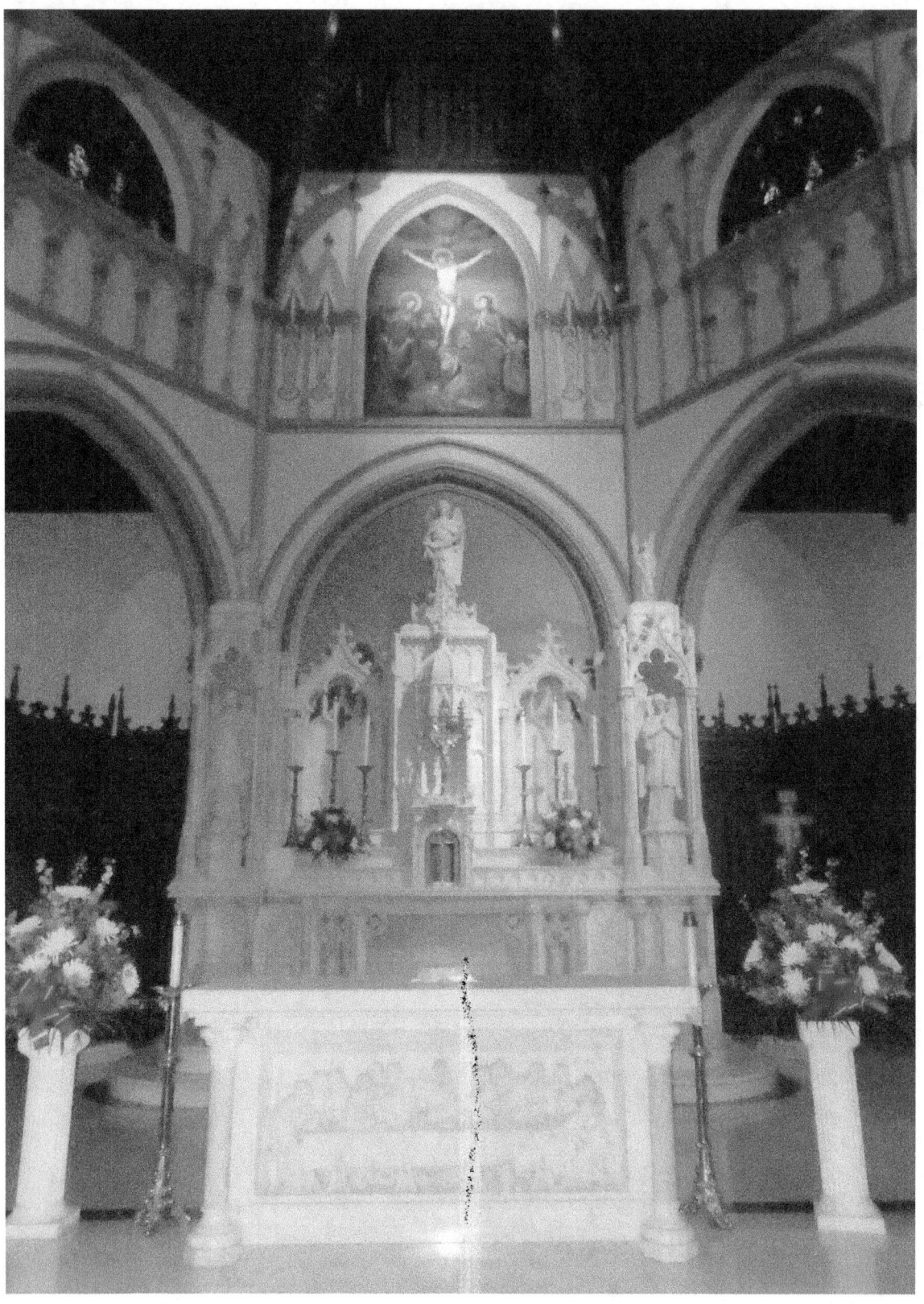

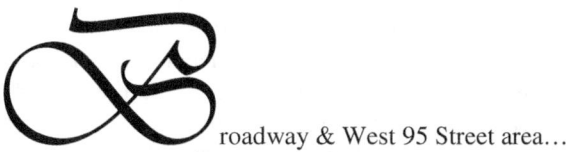

roadway & West 95 Street area…

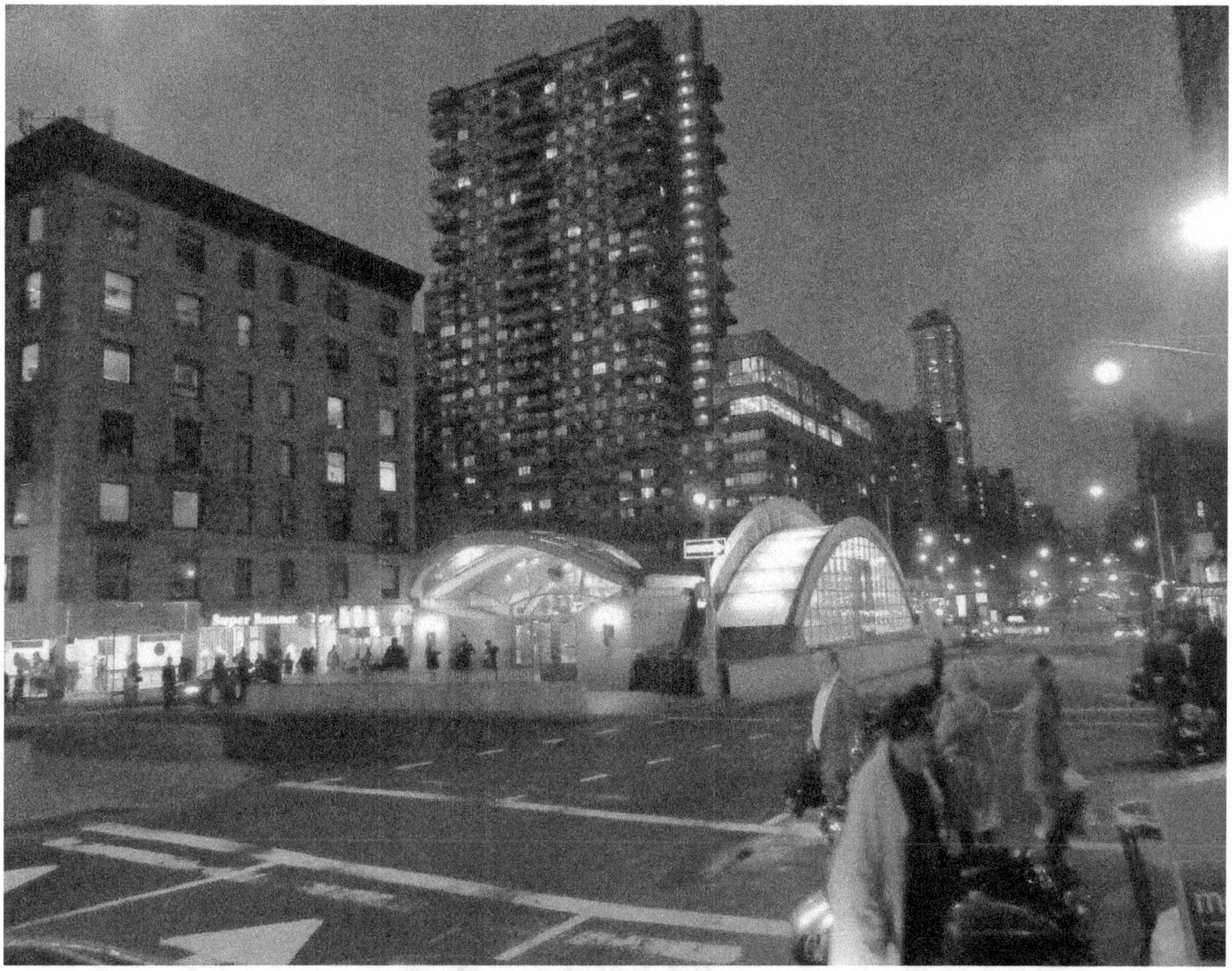

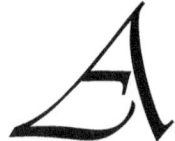dvent Lutheran Church located in the Upper West Side, Manhattan. The church's building was designed

by the architectural firm of William Appleton Potter (1842–1909) and has occupied the corner of 93rd and Broadway in New York City since 1900. It has a pitched slate roof, a double-height brick and stone structure over a basement. It has all of its stained glass in the nave and clerestory designed by Louis Comfort Tiffany and manufactured by the Tiffany Studios. Tiffany Studios was also responsible for the sanctuary lamps, the pews, the ceramic mosaic behind the altar, and the painted decorative organ frontal pipes in the front of the sanctuary. The nave and clerestory windows feature St. Paul preaching at Athens and Christ returning in glory with angels.

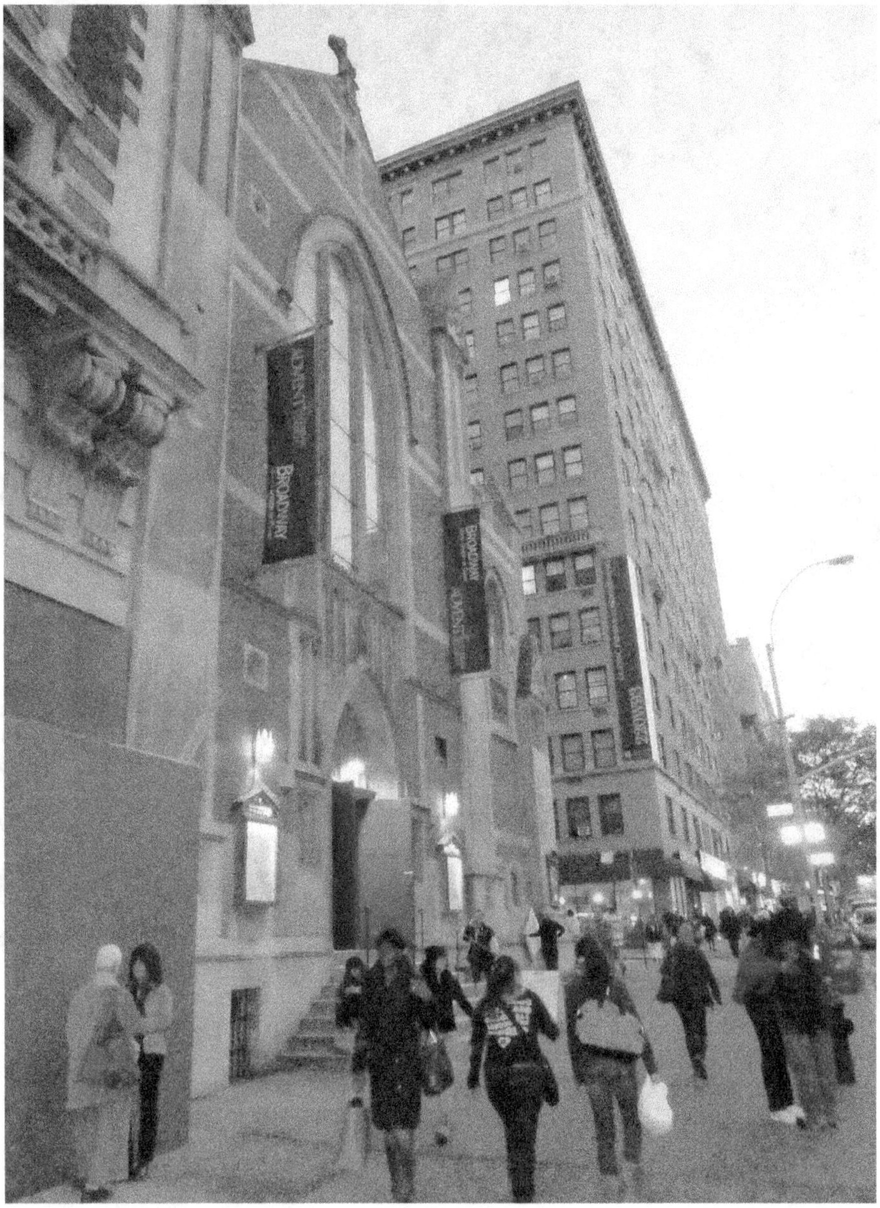

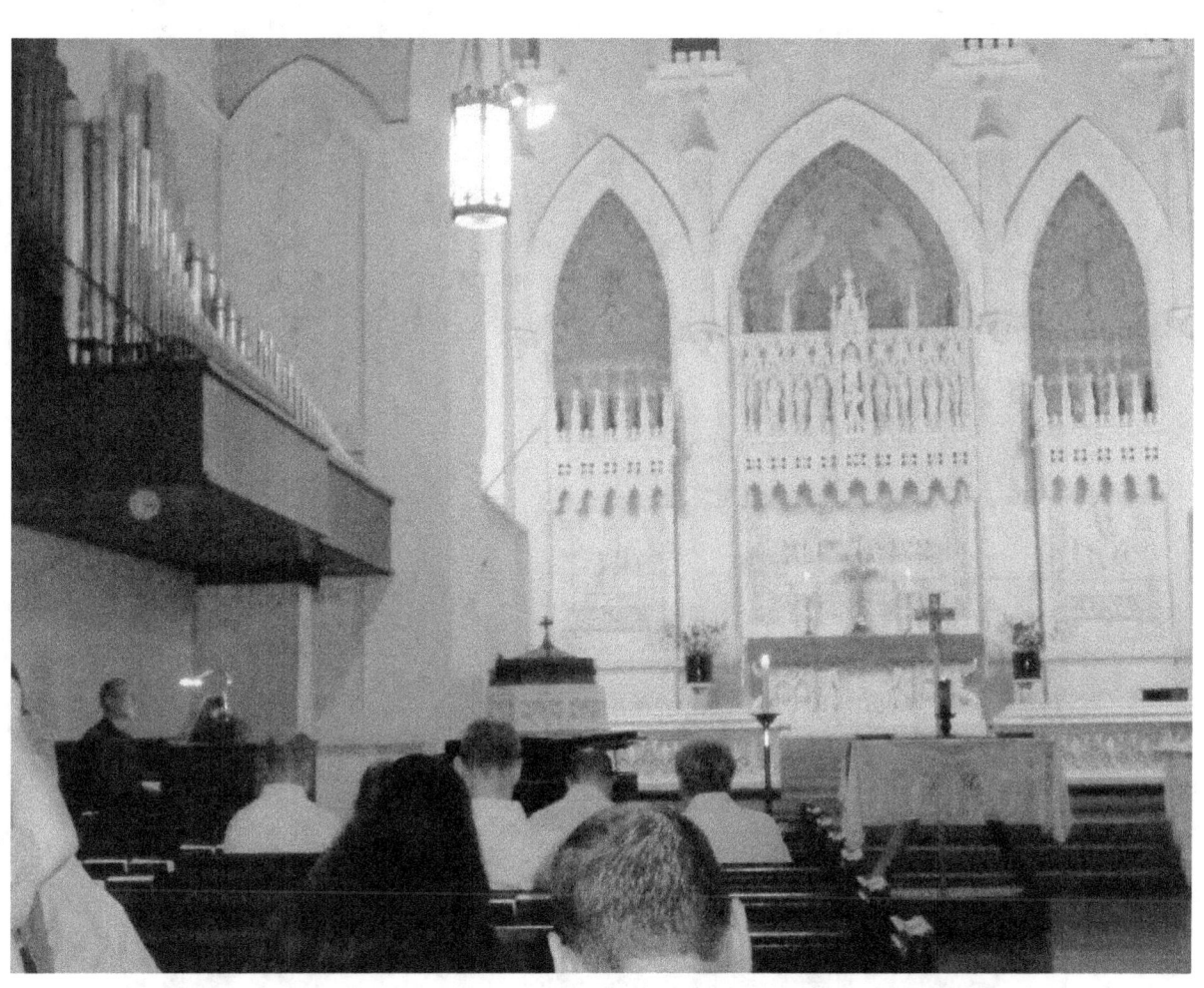

The Manhattan School of Music (MSM) is a conservatory founded by Janet D. Schenck, pianist and philanthropist in 1917. It is located on Claremont Avenue in the Morningside Heights adjacent to Broadway and West 122nd Street. The MSM campus was originally the home to The Juilliard School, until Juilliard migrated to the Lincoln Center area of Midtown Manhattan.

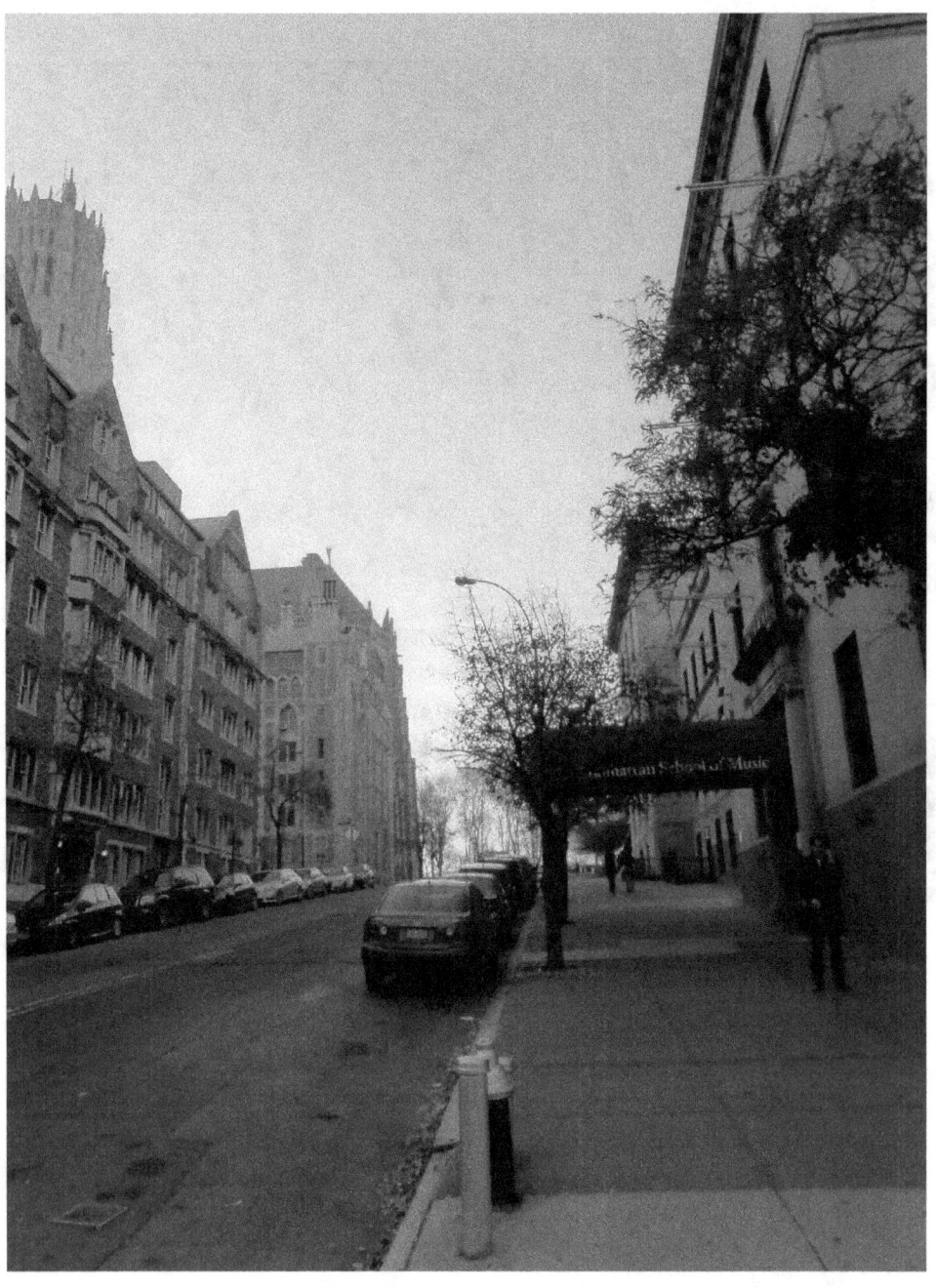

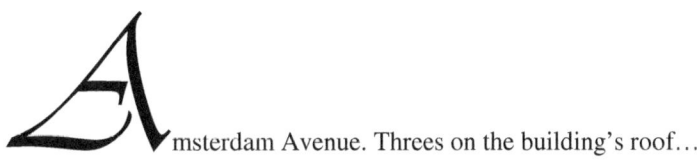

msterdam Avenue. Threes on the building's roof…

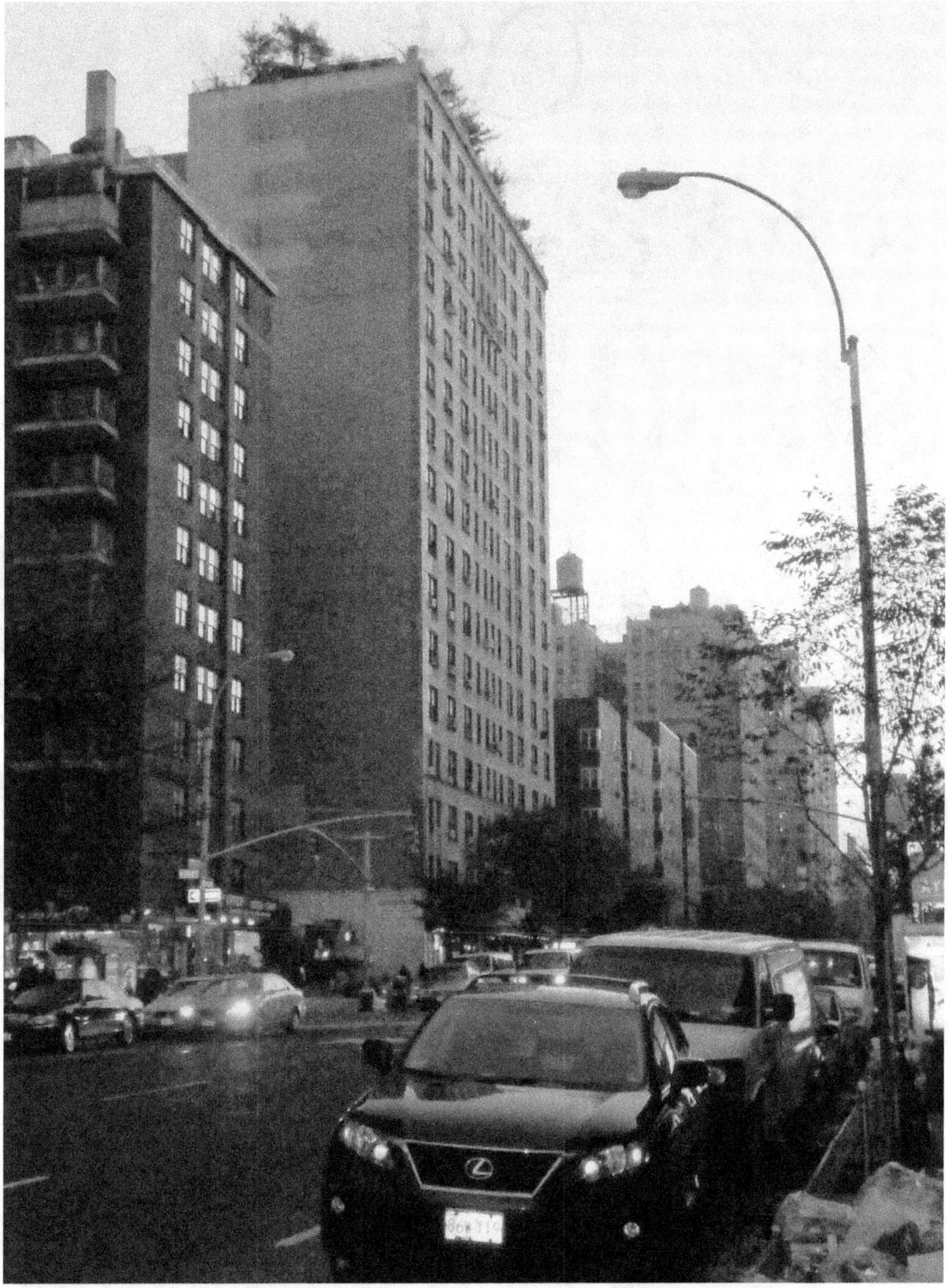

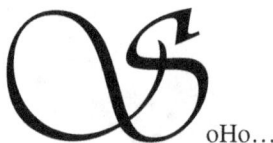

oHo…

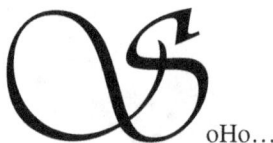

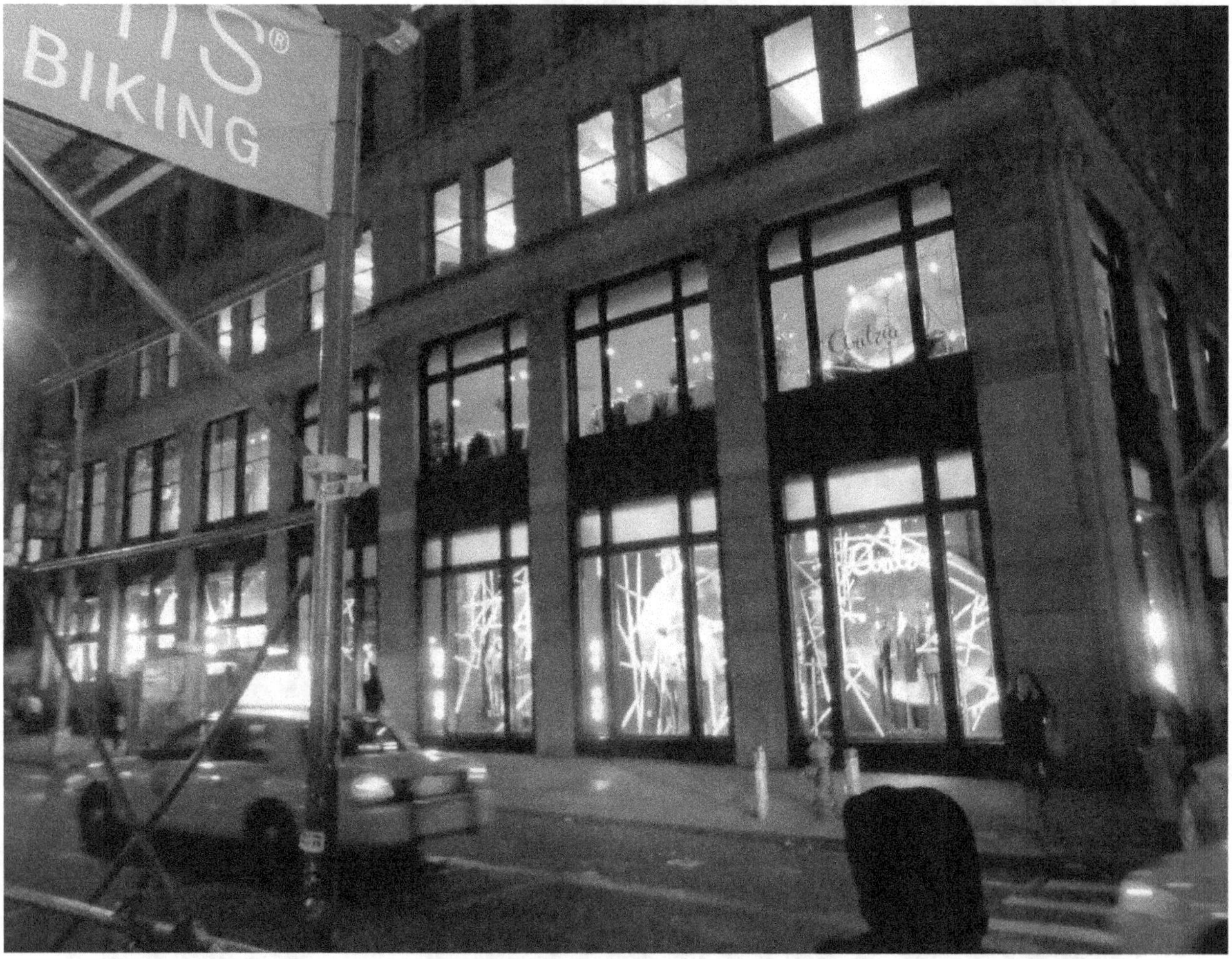

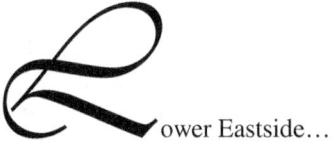

ower Eastside…

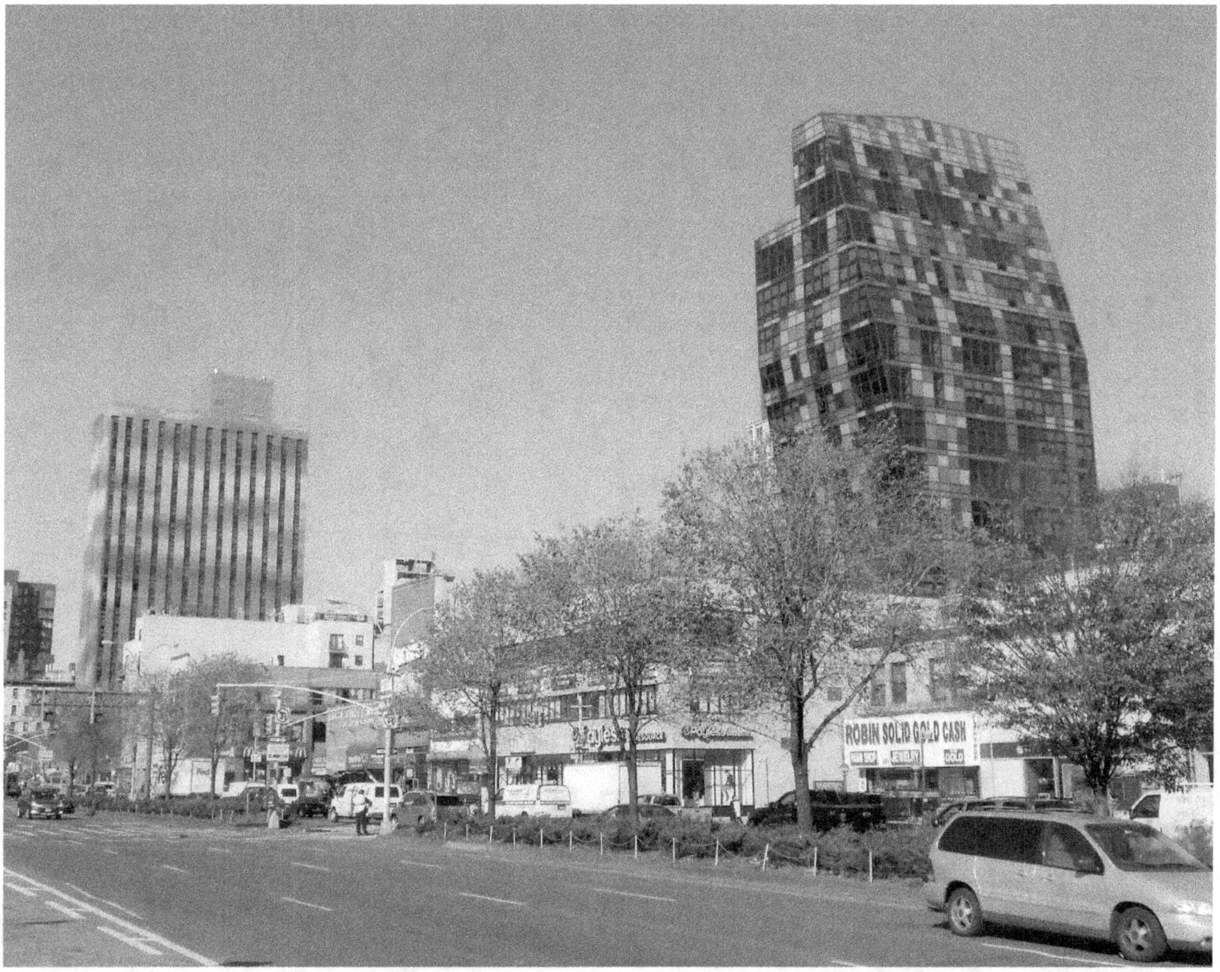

*T*he Ukrainian Museum founded in 1976 by the Ukrainian National Women's League of America

(UNWLA). It is located at 222 East 6th Street between Second Avenue and Cooper Square in the East Village of Manhattan. It is the largest American museum dedicated to the cultural heritage of people from Ukraine. Until 2005, the museum was located at 203 Second Avenue, between 11th and 12th Streets. The new building was designed by Ukrainian-American architect George Sawicki of Sawicki Tarella Architecture and Design in New York City. The executive director is Maria Shust. Museum was funded principally by the Ukrainian American community. Its collection falls into three primary groupings: folk art, fine art and items documenting the history and cultural legacy of the Ukrainian immigration to the United States, including personal correspondence, stamps and coins, photographs, posters, flyers and playbills.

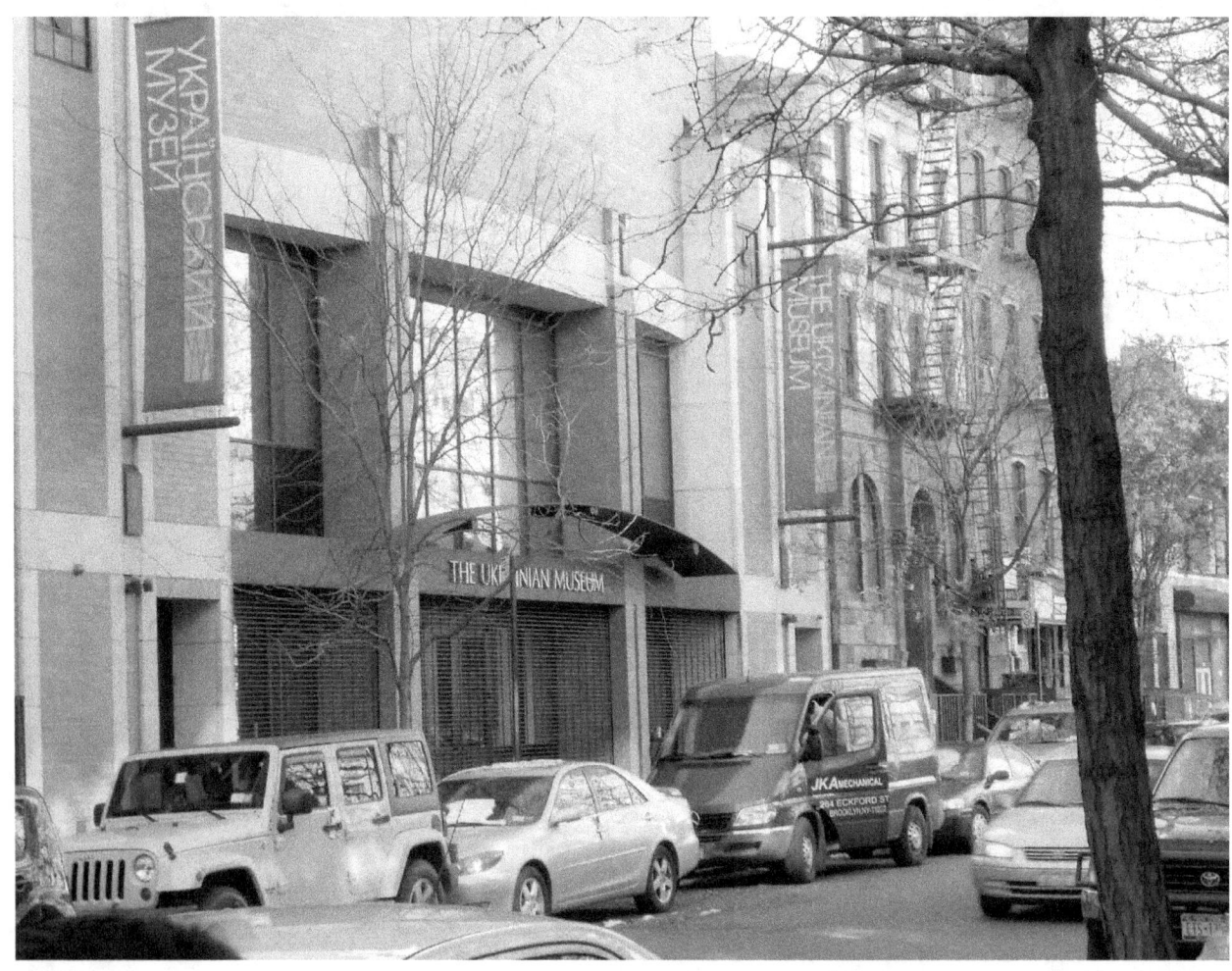

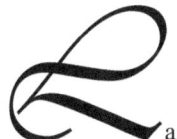a Salle Academy is a private, all boys high school in Manhattan. It is a part of the Roman Catholic Archdiocese of New York. Founded in 1848 by the Brothers of the Christian Schools, La Salle was first known as Saint Vincent's School when it first opened on Canal Street. It moved to Second Avenue in 1856 and changed its name to La Salle Academy in 1887. In 2010, La Salle relocated to 215 East 6th Street, sharing the building with the private St. George Ukrainian Roman Catholic High School. St. George Schools were founded in 1940 by the Fathers of The Order of Saint Basil the Great.

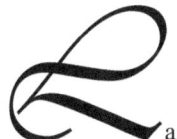

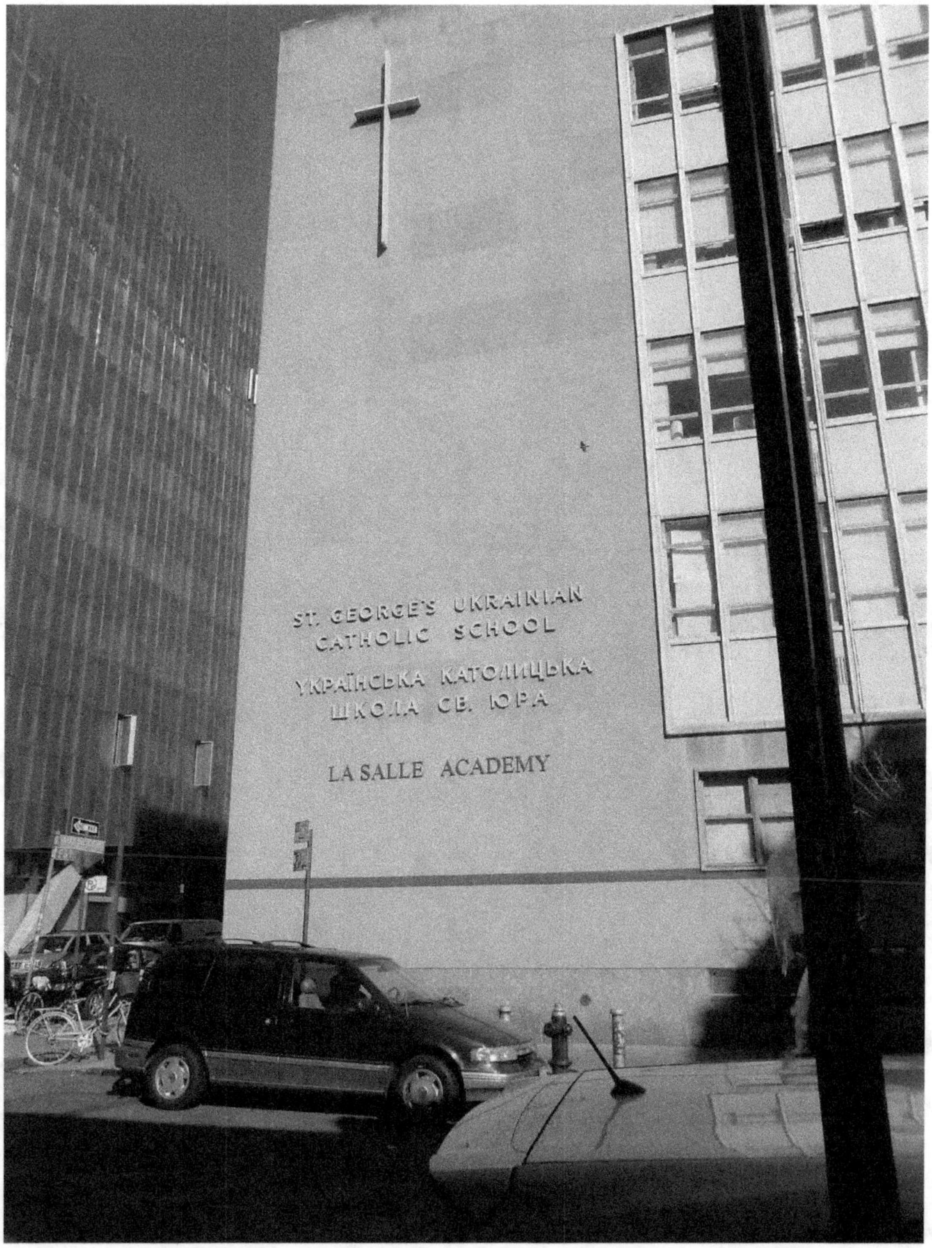

*T*aras Shevchenko Place is a street named after Taras Shevchenko, who is considered the greatest Ukrainian poet. Taras Shevchenko Place connects Sixth and Seventh Streets between Second and Third Avenues in the East Village.

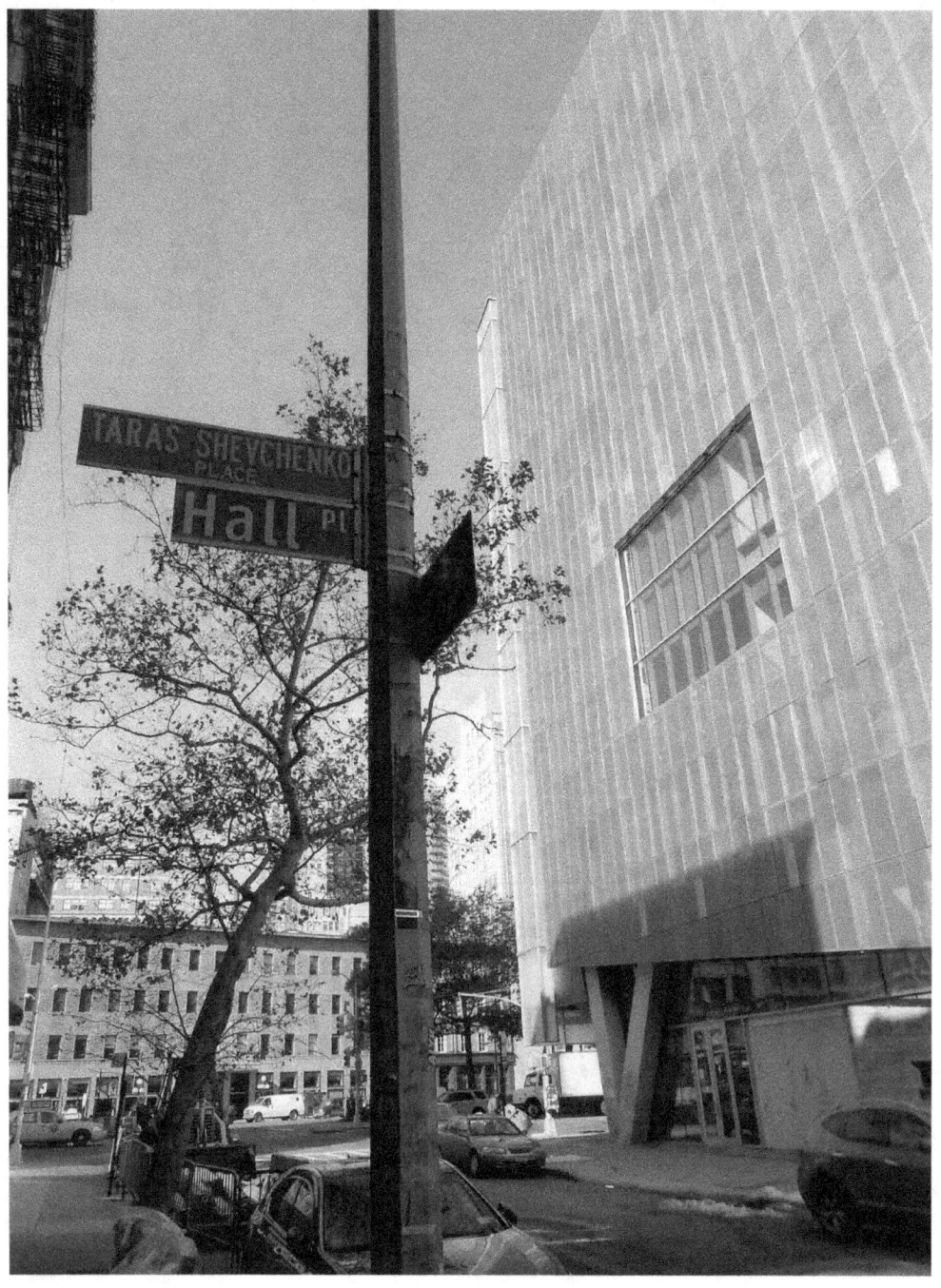

$\mathcal{T}$he Cooper Union for the Advancement of Science and Art is a privately funded college in the East

Village of Manhattan, located at Cooper Square and Astor Place. Founded in 1859, the school established a radical new model of American higher education. Its mission reflects founder Peter Cooper's fundamental belief that an education "equal to the best" should be accessible to those who qualify, independent of their race, sex, wealth, religion or social status. Education should be "free as air and water." Since 1902, according to the belief of Abraham Hewitt, Peter Cooper's son-in-law and a major figure in the early organization of the curriculum, the Cooper Union has granted each admitted student a full-tuition scholarship.

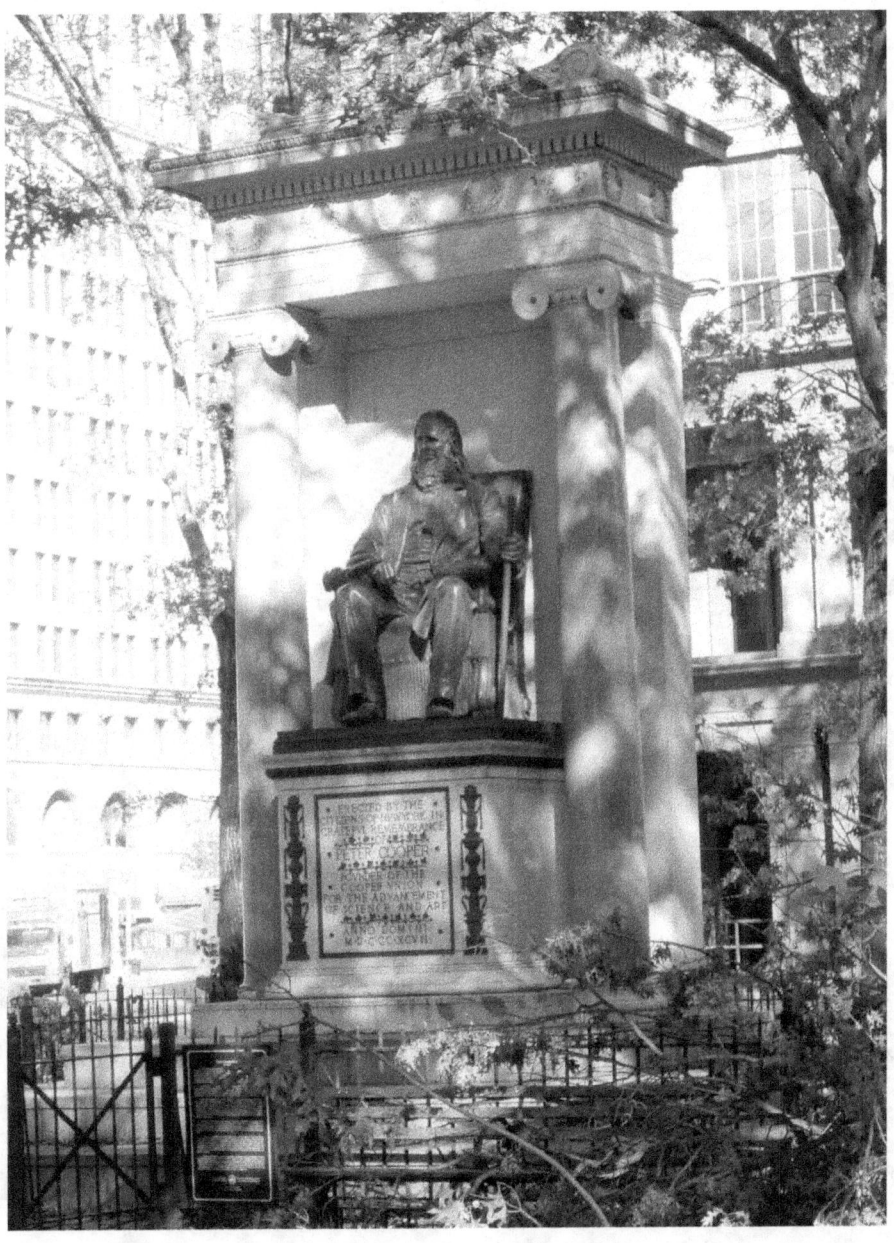

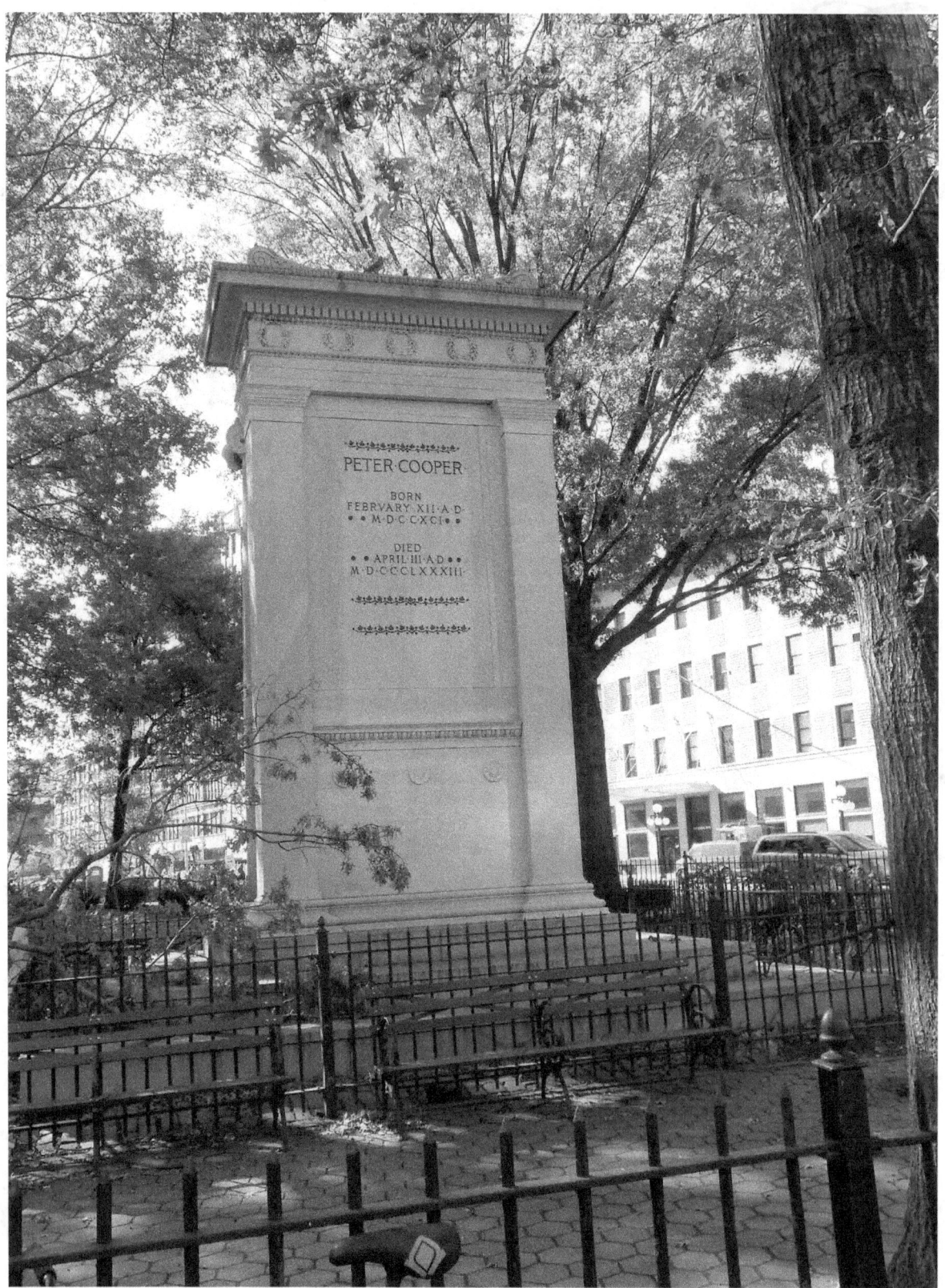

PETER·COOPER

BORN
FEBRVARY·XII·A·D·
•·M·D·C·C·X·C·I·•

DIED
•·APRIL·III·A·D·•
M·D·C·C·C·L·X·X·X·III

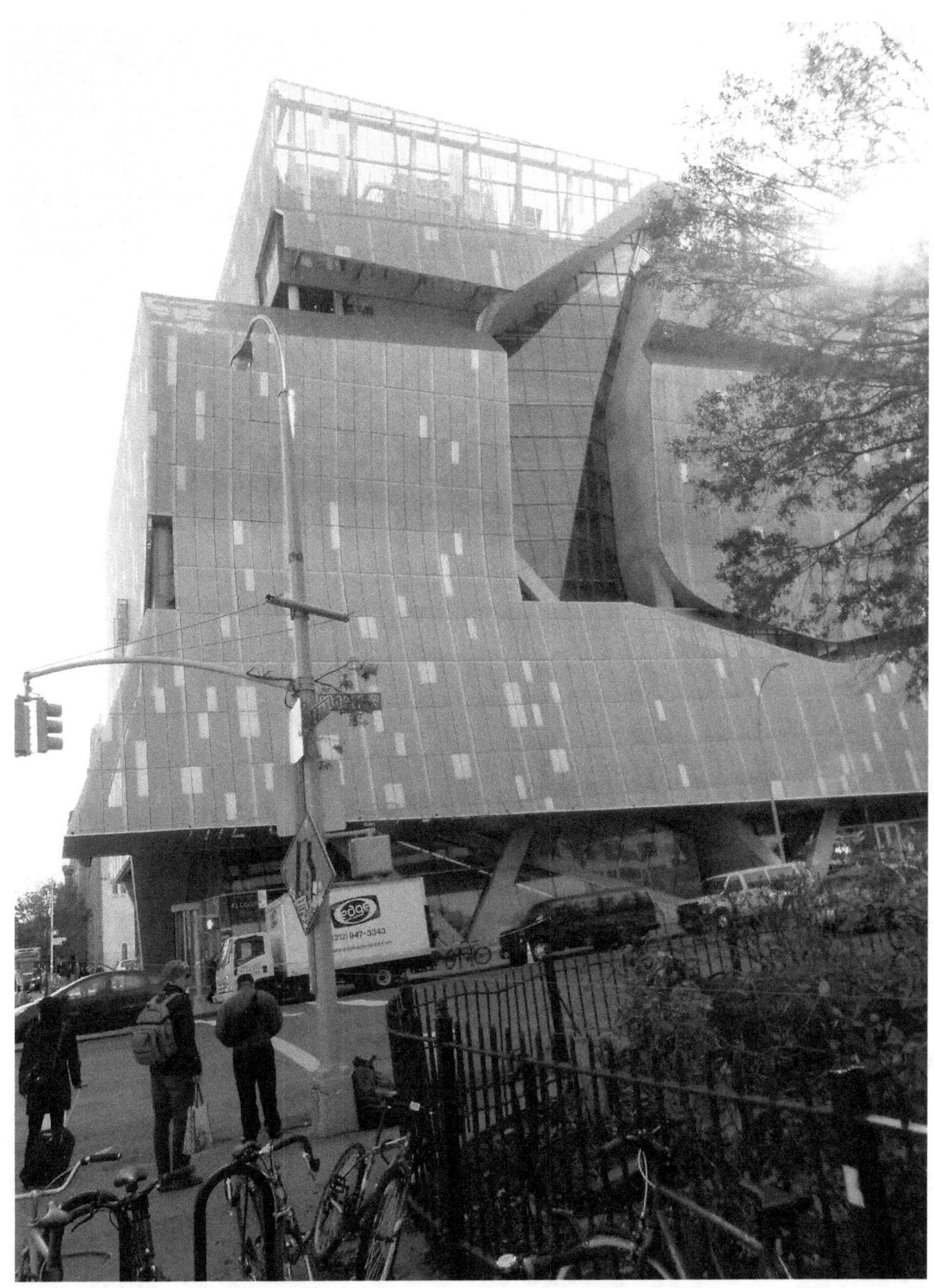

*T*he Village Voice is a free weekly newspaper that features investigative articles, analysis of current affairs and culture, arts and music coverage, and events listings for New York City. The Voice was launched by Ed Fancher, Dan Wolf, John Wilcock, and Norman Mailer on October 26, 1955 from a two-bedroom apartment in Greenwich Village, which was its initial coverage area, expanding to other parts of the city by the 60s. The offices in the 60s were located at Sheridan Square. Now, Voice's editorial is located at Cooper Square in the East Village. Newspaper has received three Pulitzer Prizes.

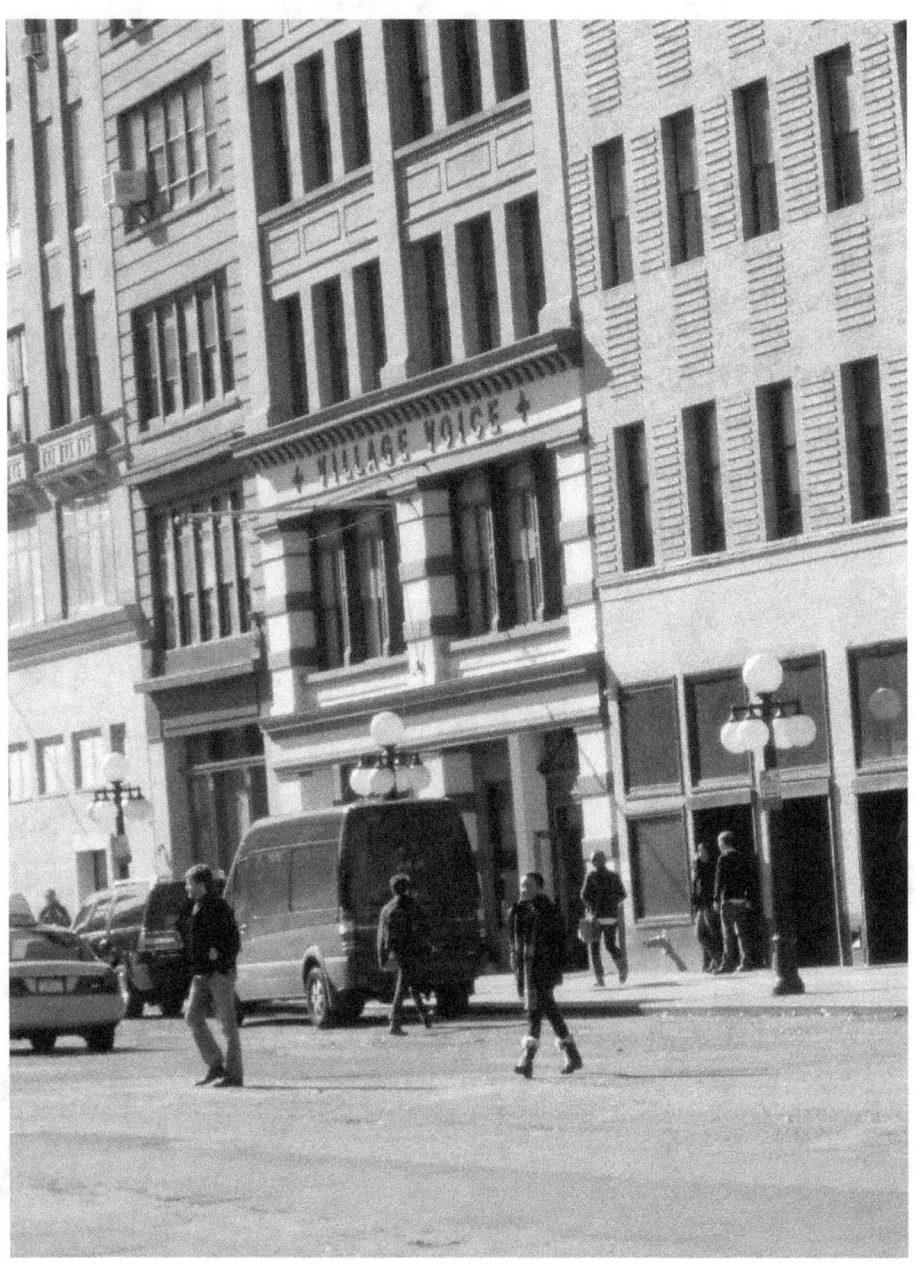

About New York City

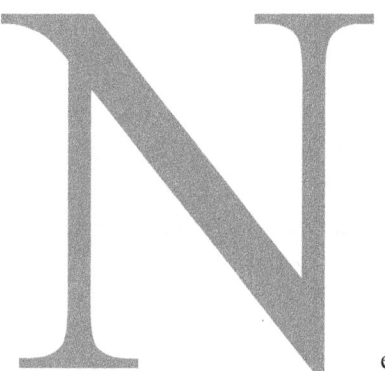

ew York is the center of the New York Metropolitan Area, one of the most populous metropolitan areas in the world. A global power city and the cultural capital of the world, New York exerts a significant impact upon finance, commerce, media, art, fashion, technology, education, research, and entertainment. New York is the home of the United Nations Headquarters and is an important center for international diplomacy. Located on one of the world's largest natural harbors, it consists of five boroughs, each of which is a state county. In 1898, the five boroughs -- the Manhattan, Brooklyn, Queens, Bronx, and Staten Island -- were consolidated into a single city. As many as 800 languages are spoken in New York, making it the most linguistically diverse city in the world. With a Census-estimated 2011 population of 8,244,910 on the land area of 302.64 square miles, New York is the most densely populated city in the U.S.. The New York City Metropolitan Area's population is the United States' largest.

New York traces its roots to its 1624 founding as a trading post by colonists of the Dutch Republic. It was named New Amsterdam in 1626. The city came under English control in 1664 and was renamed New York after King Charles II of England granted the lands to his brother, the Duke of York. New York served as the capital of the U.S. from 1785 until 1790. It has been the country's largest city since 1790.

All photograph included in this book were taken in the Manhattan, the most densely populated and smallest area of the five boroughs of the New York City. It is primarily located on the island of Manhattan at the mouth of the Hudson River. The borough is conterminous with New York County, an original county of the state of New York. The borough and county consist of Manhattan Island and several small adjacent islands: Liberty Island, Roosevelt Island, Randall's Island, Governors Island, Wards Island, part of Ellis Island, Mill Rock, and U Thant Island; as well as Marble Hill, a small area bordering the Bronx. Manhattan is the third-largest of New York's five boroughs in population. With Wall Street in Lower Manhattan, New York City functions as one of the financial centers of the world, with an estimated GDP of over $1.2 trillion. It is home of the New York Stock Exchange and NASDAQ. The major radio, television, and telecommunications companies in the U.S. are based here, as well as many news, book, magazine publishers. Manhattan has many famous landmarks, museums, universities, and tourist attractions.

The Statue of Liberty, a colossal neoclassical sculpture on Liberty Island in New York Harbor, designed by Frédéric Bartholdia, is a welcoming signal to immigrants arriving from abroad. This statue is a gift to the United States from the people of France. It is a globally recognized symbol of the United States and its democracy.

About Photographer

Nadia Russ (aka Nadejda Maloletneva, www.nadiaruss.com) is NeoPopRealism art style creator. Her work - canvases and ink drawings - was exhibited worldwide; many pieces are in the museums' permanent collections in Europe and the U.S.. She authored several art-related books.

In 2004, Nadia Russ created NeoPopRealism philosophy for happier life:

1. Be beautiful;
2. Be creative and productive; never stop studying and learning;
3. Be peace-loving, positive-minded;
4. Do not accept communist philosophy;
5. Be free-minded, do the best you can to move the world to peace and harmony;
6. Be family oriented, self-disciplined;
7. Be free spirited. Follow your dreams, if they are not destructive, but constructive;
8. Believe in god. God is one, it is harmony and striving for perfection;
9. Be supportive to those who need you, be generous;
10. Create your life as a great adventurous story.

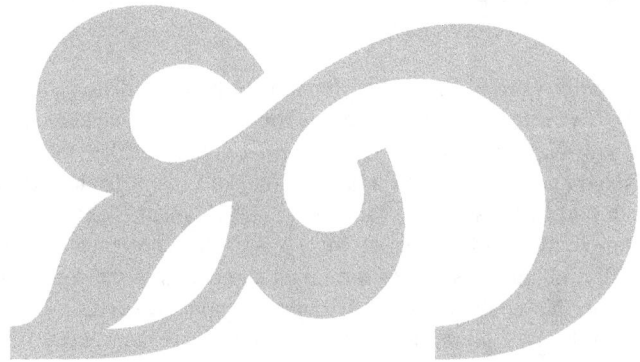

www.ingramcontent.com/pod-product-compliance
Lightning Source LLC
Chambersburg PA
CBHW080931170526
45158CB00008B/2245